THERE WAS A SOLDIER

THERE WAS A SOLDIER

First-hand accounts of the Scottish soldier
from 1707 to the present day

ANGUS KONSTAM

First published in 2009 by
HACHETTE SCOTLAND, an imprint of
HACHETTE UK

1

Cataloguing in Publication Data is available from the British Library

HB ISBN 978 0 7553 1861 2

Typeset by Ellipsis Books Limited, Glasgow

Printed and bound Clays Ltd, St Ives plc

Hachette Scotland's policy is to use papers that are natural, renewable
and recyclable products and made from wood grown in sustainable forests.
The logging and manufacturing processes are expected to conform to
the environmental regulations of the country of origin.

HACHETTE SCOTLAND
An Hachette UK Company
338 Euston Road
London NW1 3BH

www.hachettescotland.co.uk
www.hachette.co.uk

CONTENTS

ACKNOWLEDGEMENTS

This book would never have been written without the help of Brigadier Charles S. Grant (retd), a Scottish soldier himself, and a fount of information on military matters in general, and the Scottish soldier in particular. I owe him an immense debt of gratitude. I also wish to thank the staff of the various Scottish regimental museums, which – with one exception – have been extremely helpful. As the exception is now run by a local museum service rather than old soldiers, this says much for the dedication of the staff of these regimental museums. In particular I wish to thank Colonel R. L. Steele of the Royal Highland Fusiliers' Museum, his wife Mrs Joyce Steele of the Argyll and Sutherland Highlanders' Museum, Dr Alix Power-Jones of the Highlanders' Museum, Emma Halford-Macleod and Thom Smyth of the Black Watch Museum and Jenny Whitlock of the Gordon Highlanders' Museum. I would also like to thank the extremely helpful curatorial and library staff of the National War Museum at Edinburgh Castle, run by the National Museum of Scotland, as well as the staff of the National Library of Scotland, the National Archives of Scotland and the National Archives, London.

INTRODUCTION

This book is as much about education as it is about soldiering. While it contains a fascinating selection of more than 50 first-hand accounts by Scottish soldiers, covering three centuries of peace and war, it could never have been written were it not for the school dominies and headmasters, the teachers and tutors who made Scottish education something to be proud of. Whatever modern readers might think of the Scottish Reformation, its most lasting legacy was the emphasis placed on literacy. After all, the Presbyterian doctrines of the Church of Scotland emphasised the need for everyone to read the Bible, and to interpret it for themselves. As early as 1561, John Knox set out an agenda for reform, which included the provision of a schoolmaster in every Scottish parish, for 'the education and godly upbringing of the youth of this realm'. As a result, Scotland was set on the path of being a literate nation.

Scotland already had universities, and more would be founded in the centuries which followed. However, the real progress was made in local schools, where pupils learned their 'three Rs' of reading, writing and 'rithmetic. In seventeenth- and eighteenth-century Scotland, a school education wasn't free, but it was heavily subsidised by both Church and state. While the main emphasis was still on religious education, the by-product was a steady improvement in the literacy rate. By 1707 it has been estimated that the majority of the Scottish population was literate, and the proportion kept on increasing. The eighteenth century was seen as a 'golden age' of Scottish education, with 'adventure schools' providing an alternative to an educational system still dominated by the Kirk. Robert Burns attended one of these schools, as did at least two of the Scottish soldiers whose adventures are recounted in this book.

In 1872 the provision of education in Scotland was taken out of the hands of the Church and run in a secular fashion. While religious schools and private schools still flourished, education now became a right, regardless of religion or wealth. What this really means is that the educational standards in Scotland were high during the last three centuries, and were arguably the best in Britain. The Scots are rightly proud of their education system, and although national literacy rates have dropped slightly in recent years, the overall picture is one of a country with a literate, numerate and relatively articulate population, regardless of whether this education was received in Crieff, Dundee, Glasgow or Kirkwall.

The value of this Scottish education is reflected in the literate quality of the first-hand accounts contained in this book. While certainly some are provided by Scottish soldiers – usually officers – with an extensive private education, or by those who studied at a Scottish university, others are written by men whose options were more limited. During the course of reading the letters, diaries, journals and memoirs of Scottish privates and non-commissioned officers this impression of widespread literacy is reinforced. Often these are more revealing than those written by officers, as the writer has been more honest, or has concerned himself with the fascinating details of a soldier's life, rather than the bigger picture of who attacked whom and on which flank. I have marvelled at the beautiful copper-plate handwriting of Scottish soldiers from my grandfather's generation, writing in the trenches of the Great War, and I have been captivated by more hurried scrawls, words recorded by men during a halt in the action of a later, more mobile, conflict.

The important thing here is that these Scottish soldiers are speaking to us in their own voices, be it the formal tones of someone educated at Fettes Academy just before the Great War, or the less clipped manner of a soldier from Angus, who went to the Arbroath High School during the 1930s. Perhaps the most captivating first-hand accounts are those written by the men from an even earlier age – soldiers such as Corporal Balfour Kennach, born in 1781, the son of a shoemaker from Ruthven in Angus. He went to school in Forfar, and in January 1799 he enlisted into the 71st Highlanders, when a recruiting party visited Kirriemuir. He first saw action in Cape Town in 1806, and spent a year in captivity after the débâcle at Buenos Aires the following year. He went on to fight his way through Portugal and Spain, taking part in eleven full-scale battles. Just as importantly, after being discharged in 1815, he wrote about his experiences. Without a Scottish education system, and the encouragement of the dominie in Forfar, there would have been no memoir entitled *The Campaigns of Corporal Balfour Kennach, 71st Regiment, 1806–14.*

I chose 1707 as the starting-point for this selection of first-hand accounts for two reasons. First, there are relatively few suitable accounts to be found from the seventeenth century, and of these, many are written in such a stilted way as to be of little value to the modern reader. Even those I begin with – extracts from the diary of Lieutenant-Colonel Blackader of the Cameronians – are hard going, mainly because few people today are willing to wade through pages of religious exclamations in search of a few kernels of historical information. That said, several good accounts exist. For instance, that of Sir James Halkett of Dumbarton's Foot, written after his service in Tangier in 1680, is a gripping account of life alongside English regiments, in defence of a remote garrison in North Africa. However, there is potential there, and a study of first-hand accounts dating from the days of the old Scots army is long overdue.

Secondly, 1707 marks the creation of the British army, at least on paper. The year is one with especial resonance today, as after three centuries some Scots have come to question the value of the Union. At the time, the Union made little practical difference to the Scottish soldier. Like Sir James Hackett, Scottish soldiers had been serving alongside English ones for years, as both countries shared the same monarch, and since 1660 at least, military loyalty was sworn to the Crown, rather than to the state. In the decade before the Act of Union Scottish soldiers had fought alongside English regiments in Ireland, Flanders and on home ground. This said, 1707 makes a useful starting-point, as it allows us to trace the development of the Scottish soldier over three full centuries.

As for my qualifications to bring this book about, I am a military historian rather than a seasoned old veteran, and worse, my brief service career was spent at sea, rather than in the ranks. However, I'm a Scot, despite my German-Jewish surname, and like many Scots, my mother's kin include those who were proud to call themselves Scottish soldiers, and who fought alongside their fellow Scots. Above all, the historian in me relished the challenge of seeking out these often hidden voices of Scottish soldiers past and present, and a project which began as an exercise in historical research soon turned into something altogether more personal. By its end I was humbled by the experience of reading the words of those who performed so much, and honoured to be given the chance to let their voices be heard.

CHAPTER 1

THE SCOTTISH SOLDIER

Remembrance and association

If you walk up the Mound in Edinburgh you will come across an imposing bronze statue, placed on top of a war memorial. It depicts a Highland soldier, looking protectively down the Mound towards Princes Street below him, as if he is mounting guard over the former twin bastions of Scottish pride – the Bank of Scotland and the National Assembly of the Church of Scotland. Beneath him, on the granite war memorial, a list of names covers two of its sides, while its front proclaims the identity of the soldier, and the regiment of the fallen – the Black Watch. A similar statue – less imposing in terms of location but altogether grander in design – sits in the middle of the North Bridge, as if protecting Waverley Station and the old offices of *The Scotsman*. This time the statue is dedicated to the men of the King's Own Scottish Borderers, and shows a group of figures, stoically guarding the body of an injured comrade.

Passers-by might be forgiven for assuming that these statues were put up in the aftermath of the First World War. After all, almost 150,000 Scots died during those four blood-soaked years, while tens of thousands more came home bearing the scars of war. Barely a village or town in Scotland doesn't have a war memorial to these dead, a vivid testimony to the impact the war had on a generation. Similar statues dot the Scottish countryside – the Black Watch soldier who stands guard over Dundee, just beside the road north, or the similar statue on top of 'The Hill' in Kirriemuir, a memorial to the fallen of the Angus glens.

However, peer closely at the two Edinburgh statues, and the dates are wrong. Both commemorate the soldiers of these two regiments who were killed during the Second Boer War (1899–1902), which ended a dozen years before the First World War began. The Black Watch memorial bears the names of more than 120 soldiers. All those names from one regiment, and killed in a dusty corner of the empire, in a half-forgotten war from another age. If you take another look, and you've visited the memorial in Kirriemuir, you'll then notice that a lot of the names are the same. Even more poignantly, the war memorial on 'The Hill' is flanked by a smaller list, containing the names of those soldiers from Kirriemuir who died during the Second World War. Once again, the same surnames keep on appearing in all three lists. I can think of no better demonstration of the lasting association between the Scots and their soldiery, or the link between regiment and place.

It has been estimated that as many as 8,000 Scottish soldiers died in South Africa during the Second Boer War, and of course thousands more perished in other corners of the British empire – the Sudan, the North-West Frontier, Egypt, Zululand, China, Ashantiland and elsewhere. While this pales into insignificance compared with the Scottish casualties during the Great War, or the 50,000 Scottish soldiers who were killed during the Second World War, it remains a substantial figure. What is surprising is that rather than resent the sending of Scots off to fight in foreign lands, the majority of the Scottish people approved of these colonial wars, and were proud enough to build splendid memorials to the fallen.

This strange link between the Scottish people and the Scottish soldier was highlighted following the death of Major-General Sir Hector Macdonald (1853–1903), who was popularly known as 'Fighting Mac'. He participated in the First Boer War and the First Sudan Campaign, and went on to command a brigade at the Battle of Omdurman (1898), a battle fought during Britain's return to the Sudan. Even the victor General Kitchener described Macdonald as 'the real hero of Omdurman'. What is remarkable is that Macdonald was the son of a Gaelic-speaking crofter from Ross-shire, who joined the army as a private soldier. Less than three decades later he was commanding a brigade on the battlefield.

After his success in the Sudan, Macdonald took over command of the Highland Brigade, whose commander – General Wauchope – had been killed at the Battle of Magersfontein (1899), one of the opening battles of the Second Boer War. He was just as successful in South Africa as he had been in the Sudan, and by the end of the war he was probably the most famous Scottish soldier of his day. Then it all started to unravel. In 1902 he was posted to Ceylon (now Sri Lanka), and allegations of misconduct began to circulate. It was claimed that he was a pederast, and while a later investigation found no substance to the rumours, Macdonald returned to Britain, in an attempt to avoid a scandal. He was in Paris when news of the allegations were published in the *International Herald Tribune*, on 25 March 1903. On reading the paper, Macdonald returned to his room, put a revolver to his head, and shot himself.

His body was returned to Scotland for burial, but Lady Macdonald refused a state funeral, and opted for a quiet, private burial in Edinburgh's Dean Cemetery on the rainswept morning of 30 March. The people of Scotland were not to be denied the opportunity to pay their respects to a fallen hero. Many, possibly rightly, deduced the scandal had been concocted by Macdonald's many enemies, who resented the presence of a Scottish commoner among the army's elite. It was reported that by nightfall a crowd of over 30,000 people had gathered outside the cemetery, all eager to visit the grave. Over the weeks that followed, thousands more made the pilgrimage. Today the grave is all but forgotten, as is the man. However, for the people of Edwardian Scotland, Macdonald was the epitome of the Scottish soldier.

Some historians have claimed that the strong association between the Scots and the Scottish soldier was forged amid the mud and trenches of the Western Front. The national sense of loss following the death of Sir Hector Macdonald demonstrates that this special bond was formed before that. Did it develop during the 'Age of Empire', when Scottish troops like Macdonald fought in every corner of the globe, or were its origins found even earlier – possibly during the Napoleonic Wars? It might even be argued that at least on the southern side of the Highland line, Lowland Scots of the eighteenth century welcomed the presence of Scottish troops, who offered protection against the Highlanders. While historians might argue over dates, few can argue that this bond was created, and that although frayed and worn, it remains in existence today.

A matter of identity

It has often been claimed that the Scots had a unique association with the Scottish soldier, a bond forged over the generations which encompasses both pride in the past and paternalism towards the present generation of soldiers. Words like 'association', 'pride' and 'regiment' are bandied about, often by retired army officers, who speak about their 'Jocks' in a tone which is patronising as well as paternal. These spokesmen came to the fore during the recent furore over the disbanding or restructuring of the Scottish regiments, and the creation of a new 'super-regiment' – the Royal Regiment of Scotland. The trouble with old army officers – a problem that has plagued the British army since its inception in 1707 – is their frequent inability to see the 'bigger picture'. For them 'the regiment' is the cornerstone of military life, and any threat to it is an affront to their sense of martial identity. They are like the supporters of a Scottish football team, who cheer on their own team, but rarely want to address the problems facing Scottish football.

Certainly, ever since the First World War, the Scottish regiments have had a strong regional identity. The Gordons recruit in the north-east, the Queen's Own Highlanders have the run of the Highlands and Islands, the recruiting vans of the Royal Scots tour Edinburgh and the Lothians, and so on. You supported Aberdeen FC, and you joined the Gordons – a simple matter of local identity and pride. This is also one of the reasons why the names on the war memorials always sound the same. Rivalry between units – platoons, company, regiments – motivates soldiers, and encourages them to believe that their unit is better than the rest. Of course, to an outsider the differences are often minimal – one unit wears a red hackle, another wears a white one. The differences are ones which have been created by the British army, not by the Scots themselves. Consequently, leaving aside the notion of regional associations – the idea of a 'local' regiment – most Scots don't define a Scottish soldier by his regiment, but by his or her national identity.

In the last three centuries, regiments have come and gone.

The recent round of disbandment and amalgamation isn't a particularly new phenomenon – the same thing has happened at regular intervals since 1707, particularly in times of government parsimony, or after a war. In an amalgamation, regimental traditions might be lost, or the set of the kilt tartan might change, but the national identity of the men and women carrying the rifles remains constant. While most Scots bemoan the passing of the old regiments, they realise that the army needs to reinvent itself periodically, so it can adapt to new technologies, or new threats. For most Scots, the important thing is that the identity of the Scottish soldier is preserved, with all he has come to embody.

The Scots expect a lot from their soldiers. After all, they have centuries of historical baggage to carry around. Since 1707 they have fought in eight major wars and dozens of smaller ones. Of these, six of the larger conflicts were fought within the first century following the Act of Union – a true baptism of fire for the Scottish regiments. This was also a time of growing prosperity at home. The Union might have been unpopular when it came about, but the opening of new markets and opportunities proved highly beneficial to Scotland. If the price for this prosperity was the participation of her soldiers in a series of overseas wars – mostly fought against the French – then the majority saw it as a price worth paying. Of course, until 1707, these same troops, accompanied by their English colleagues, were also available to protect Lowland Scotland during the Jacobite Rebellions of 1715, 1718 and 1745–46.

Bizarrely, these Jacobite Rebellions also produced the catalyst which would transform the appearance of the Scottish soldier and strengthen his identity. Most of the Jacobite armies in these campaigns were made up of Highland clansmen, the bogeymen of Lowland Scotland. For centuries the Lowlanders had portrayed them as rapacious thieves, lacking dignity, honour and a decent pair of breeches. During the rebellions, the Scots, or at least those in the army, recognised that with the right training and leadership, the ferocity and determination of these clansmen might well be a force for good.

In one of those strange acts of historical hypocrisy, while the aftermath of the Battle of Culloden (1746) saw the steady destruction of Highland clan society, and the banning of the wearing of tartan plaid, the British army was so impressed by the fighting powers of the clansmen that they began recruiting them into the army. In truth, the process began in 1725, when the first independent companies of 'loyal Highlanders' were raised to patrol the glens. By 1739 these companies had been formed into the regiment which would become the Black Watch. However, after the Jacobite Rebellion of 1745–6, the '45, the business of recruiting Highlanders began in earnest. This recruitment would dramatically change the character and appearance of the Scottish soldier.

The influence this had on appearance was probably the most spectacular. In 1707 the Scottish soldiers of the newly formed British army looked little different from their English or Irish colleagues. This began to change after 1739 and the creation of what would become the Black Watch, and in the aftermath of the '45 Rebellion. These first Highlanders wore Highland dress, or at least a military approximation of it. By the time Britain became embroiled in the Seven Years' War (1756–63) the recruitment of new Highland regiments was seen as one solution to the manpower shortages facing the army as it fought its first truly global war. As the number of Highland regiments increased, so too did the proportion of troops in the army which wore such distinctive dress. By the end of the eighteenth century there were more Highland than Lowland Scots regiments in the British army.

These new Highland regiments performed exceptionally well during the French Revolutionary and Napoleonic Wars, and in the process the troops themselves were viewed with favour by both the military establishment and the British public. Certainly, these same troops had performed well in earlier campaigns, particularly in the Americas, where their ferocity and ability to operate in unorthodox ways worked to their advantage. A widespread mutiny during the American War of Independence was largely the fault of the army establishment, who attempted to send Highland volunteers to serve in India, rather than fight in America, which is what they had signed up to do. With that exception, the new Highland regiments had proved their mettle.

What made the difference during the Napoleonic War was that by then the press was following the exploits of the army, and the achievements of the instantly recognisable Highland regiments helped to sell newspapers. In the process the Highland soldier, if not the Scottish one, was well on his way to becoming the darling of the British public. The timing was perfect. The publication of James Macpherson's Ossian cycle of poems had done much to increase the romantic allure of the Highlands during the late eighteenth century, and by the Regency period of the early nineteenth century this romanticism had blossomed into a full-blown cultural movement.

It was Sir Walter Scott (1771–1832) who set this movement on track when he choreographed George IV's visit to Scotland in 1822, filling Edinburgh with Highlanders and tartan. In the process he made kilts fashionable again. Retired brigadiers and colonels of Scottish regiments might baulk at the notion that their uniform was largely derived from the imagination of a romantic novelist, but it is largely the truth. Perhaps the fact that Scott once served as an officer in the fashionable Royal Edinburgh Volunteer Light Dragoons might help soften the blow.

Before then, Highland regiments were recognisable by their kilts, bagpipes, broadswords and all the other paraphernalia of the Highlander in government service. After the birth of the Scottish romantic movement, even the Scottish Lowland regiments became subsumed in a wave of tartan and bagpipes. Of course, there was no historical precedent for this. While regiments like the Royal Scots or the King's Own Scottish Borderers did their best to resist this Highland frippery, elements of it still managed to creep into their uniform, and become enmeshed in their regimental customs. It all became part and parcel of the growing sense of identity of the Scottish soldier.

The Scots had already started the business of identifying with their soldiers before this. They were proud of their achievements on the battlefields of America and Europe, and were willing to see Scottish soldiers go even further afield, as long as they did so with honour. The Scottish people were the great beneficiaries of the British empire. They supplied the industry, the technical expertise and the skilled manpower which made it so successful. In the process the Scots were no longer considered junior partners in the Union, but had become fully-fledged members of an imperial elite – conspirators if you will in the establishment of Empire. In these circumstances it was natural that the Scots would identify with the soldiers who played a part in the creation of this imperial dream.

Above all, the reputation of the Scottish soldier continued to rise during the 'Age of Empire'. They fought in a succession of colonial wars, and fought well. Scottish newspapers recorded the exploits of their troops, and in the process the Scots came to adopt Scottish soldiers as their own – the kilted ambassadors of Scotland on the world stage. They revelled in stories about them being lions on the battlefield and kittens by the hearth – gentle at home and fierce in war. They took pride in their achievements, and celebrated their victories. This much-touted bond between the Scot and the Scottish soldier was not forged in the hell of the Great War – it came about during the Victorian period, when Scotland was a leading beneficiary of the fruits of empire.

The interesting thing is that after the collapse of the empire, and after two world wars, after several brutal postwar conflicts and even after the modern traumas of Afghanistan, this association between the Scottish people and the Scottish soldier is still a strong one. As for the future, the fate of Scotland and the Scottish soldier is uncertain. Once the Scots were willing partners of Union, but in recent decades the old certainties have been eroded. Margaret Thatcher had much to do with this – every time she jabbed a finger at 'You Scots' she undermined support for a once inviolate union. This helped to encourage the rise of Scottish nationalism, and made some Scots soldiers question their identity.

The Scottish soldier has always been different. An old veteran of the 51st Highland Division recalled the screening of Lawrence Olivier's *Henry V* in a Belgian cinema, during the dark winter of 1944–45. Despite it preceding the climax of the film, when the actor declared: 'Cry "God, for Harry, England and St George",' the cinema was filled with loud jeers, and many of the soldiers walked out. Scottish pride has always been prickly, and woe betide anyone – general, reporter or leading actor – who presumes that just because he swears allegiance to the Crown, the Scottish soldier is the same as an English one. The same point is made in one of our first-hand accounts – the young Scottish soldier who played 'Flower of Scotland' while driving around the deserts of Kuwait in 1991. On the surface, our unofficial anthem is a rallying cry against the English. In practice, it is a demand to be treated as a national entity.

Just as Scotland is undergoing a crisis of identity, so too is the Scottish soldier. Shortly after Margaret Thatcher came Tony Blair, who sent Scottish troops to fight in a succession of wars – some for good reasons, others for spurious ones. The Scottish people take just pride in the professionalism of their soldiers, particularly when they fight in a 'just war'. Bosnia and Kosovo was one of these – the restoring of order to a war-torn corner of Europe – whereas Iraq was not. It was an unpopular conflict, in which Scottish troops were sent into battle almost on the whim of the most unpopular American president in living memory. The jury is still out on Afghanistan.

The growing death-toll of Scottish troops has made many Scots question the need for these men and women to be involved in these conflicts. Interestingly, it hasn't eroded the support that the Scottish soldier enjoys at home. While the bond between Scot and Scottish soldier remains strong, the future is uncertain, and few Scots are willing to predict what lies ahead. The rise of Scottish nationalism raises the possibility of a break-up of the Union, and with it a dismemberment of the British army. To many this remains an unthinkable act, but in the realpolitik of modern Scotland this severing of ties is now firmly on the political agenda. One fact remains certain in this changeable climate. If such a draconian step is taken, the Scottish soldier – whatever form he takes or role he is expected to play – should still be able to count on the support of the Scottish people.

CHAPTER 2

THE AGE OF REASON

On 1 May 1707 the Act of Union came into being, and Scotland and England were effectively joined together into a single country – the United Kingdom of Great Britain and Ireland. By this time the Scottish and English armies had been serving alongside each other for decades, but the Union meant that for the first time they were united into one British army. The Scottish army of 1707 was pretty small – just seven regiments of infantry, two of cavalry and two troops of lifeguards. The army used to be much larger – as many as fourteen foot regiments at its peak in 1689, but most of these were disbanded at the end of the Jacobite Rising of that year.

Of these remaining regiments, the Scots Guards – founded in 1660 – retained their own name in 1707, and became part of the British Brigade of Guards, alongside the Grenadiers and the Coldstreams. The Royal Regiment, founded in 1633, and commanded by the Earl of Orkney became the Royal Scots, or the 1st Foot in the British army. It had actually been on the English establishment since 1662, which meant that its upkeep was paid for by the London government. In effect it was on loan for almost half a century before the Act of Union. In 1707 the Regiment of Fusiliers, founded in 1678, became the Scottish Regiment of Fusiliers, and later the 21st Foot. These regimental numbers referred to the theoretical position of the regiment in the line of battle, based on seniority. In practice, regiments were usually referred to by the name of their colonel, at least until 1751, when the numbering system was officially adopted.

Two regiments raised during the Jacobite Rising of 1689 were the Earl of Leven's Regiment and the Earl of Angus' Regiment. By 1707 Leven's (also known as 'the Edinburgh Regiment') was commanded by James Maitland, and simply transferred onto the British establishment. So too did Angus' Regiment, commanded in 1707 by Colonel Preston. It had been raised in south-western Scotland from an extreme Presbyterian sect known as the Cameronians. Even before they became the 26th Foot in 1751, they were nicknamed the Cameronians, and this eventually became the official title of the regiment. Leven's or Maitland's Regiment became the 25th Foot, a regiment which eventually developed into the King's Own Scottish Borderers. Today it forms part of the Royal Regiment of Scotland.

Two more regiments from 1707 – Sir James Moncrieff's and Lord Strathnaver's Foot – were disbanded in the years following the end of the War of the Spanish Succession (1701–13). The oldest of the two cavalry regiments, the Royal Dragoons, founded in 1681, became the Royal North British Dragoons in 1707, under the command of the Earl of Stair, and in 1713 they became the 2nd Dragoons, nicknamed 'The Scots Greys'. Today they are known as the Royal Scots Dragoon Guards. In 1707 Lord Polwarth took over command of the second Scottish dragoon regiment from Lord Jedburgh. Founded in 1690, it was disbanded after the war in 1714, but was re-formed a year later, although in its new form it was no longer considered a Scottish unit. Finally the two troops of life guards commanded by the Duke of Argyll were used for ceremonial duties in Edinburgh, and eventually became part of the Life Guards, the senior cavalry regiment in the British army.

Of course, by 1707, many of these Scots regiments had

already seen service overseas, and during the opening campaigns of the War of the Spanish Succession the Royal Scots, the Fusiliers and the 'Cameronians' all distinguished themselves at the battles of Blenheim (1704) and Ramillies (1706). The Royal Dragoons also won laurels at Ramillies, when it helped to drive the French cavalry from the field. In other words, the Union of 1707 made little real difference to the Scottish army. It simply had its blue saltires replaced by Union flags, and its pay came from London rather than Edinburgh. Apart from that it was largely business as usual. Above all, the Union came in the middle of a major war, where Britain was fighting in support of the Dutch and various other allies, against the forces of King Louis XIV of France. It was probably just as well that this transition of ownership didn't really make much difference to the troops in Flanders. The three regiments mentioned above all went on to fight in the two other major battles of the war – at Oudenarde (1708) and Malplaquet (1709), and the first of our accounts comes from this period – the first year in which the regiments fought under a British banner.

While the loyalty or enthusiasm of the Scots serving as part of a British army in Flanders was never in any real doubt, fighting closer to home raised the possibility of defection, mutiny or open rebellion. The crushing of the Jacobite Rising of 1689 did little to lessen the support of many Scots – particularly Highlanders – for the exiled King James VII of Scotland and his successors. An attempt to land French and Jacobite troops in the Firth of Forth was thwarted in 1708, and so, despite the need for troops in Flanders, a number of Scottish regiments were retained at home. When the war with France ended in 1713 more troops were shipped back, including the 'Cameronians'. The wisdom of this was shown in the summer of 1715, when the Earl of Mar raised the Highland clans in the name of James Stuart – 'The Old Pretender'.

The climax of the rebellion came in November 1715, when the Jacobites faced a small government army at Sherrifmuir. The Royal Scots Fusiliers, the '25th (Edinburgh) Regiment' and the 'Scots Greys' were all on the field that day, while the 'Cameronians' had already played their part, defeating a Jacobite force at Preston. Lieutenant-Colonel Blackader of the 'Cameronians' was in Stirling, just seven miles from the battlefield, and his account provides us with a fascinating insight into the Scottish army of the time. Like many Presbyterians, Blackader viewed the Scots as a people who – like the Israelites – had a covenant with God; they were therefore God's chosen people. Blackader's faith was sorely tested by the events he witnessed that day, but his conviction as to the righteousness of his cause remained.

One aftermath of the 1715 rebellion was the establishment of garrisons in the Highlands, at Fort George, Fort William and Fort Augustus, linked to a network of military roads and barracks. Independent companies of trustworthy Highlanders were raised, and in 1739 these were formed into a regiment, which by the 1750s had become the 42nd foot, or the Royal Highland Regiment. This was the first of several Highland regiments in the army, and the Highland clans, once seen as breeding-grounds for insurrection, were now one of the British army's prime recruiting sources.

The watershed was 1746, when the Jacobite cause was finally crushed on the battlefield of Culloden. The battle provides us with our one first-hand account from a soldier who fought against rather than for the British army. It also marked the end of the old ways in the Highlands, where loyalty was measured in the men who would follow a chief into battle. After Culloden,

Highlanders sought employment wherever they could, even if it meant donning a red coat, or serving under a new breed of Highland chieftains who were more interested in the land as a source of income than clansmen.

Two accounts written by a Highland soldier describe service in the forests of North America, where he fought the French and their native allies, and participated in a spirited battle which pitched the Royal Highlanders – 'The Black Watch' – against the North American Indians. These battles were fought during or in the immediate aftermath of the Seven Years' War (1756–63), a conflict which was fought in North America, Europe and India, and which stretched the resources of Britain to its limit. Several new Scottish regiments were raised during the conflict, including the 77th (Montgomery's), 78th (Fraser's), 87th (Keith's), 88th (Campbell's) and 89th (Gordon's) Highlanders. Even though all but the Gordon Highlanders were disbanded soon after the war ended, Highland troops were now considered part-and-parcel of the British army.

The next great wave of recruitment came in 1775, in response to the revolt of the American colonies. The war saw the creation of the 71st (Fraser's) Highlanders (disbanded when the war ended) and the 73rd (Highland) Foot, which was renumbered the 71st and eventually devolved into the Highland Light Infantry. Other units, the 74th, 76th, 77th, 78th, 80th and 81st Highlanders, were also disbanded after 1783, with the exception of the 78th, which was renumbered the 72nd, and eventually became the Seaforth Highlanders.

By the late 1780s, even though the need for troops had diminished, the army still had extensive commitments in India, the West Indies and Canada, all of which required garrisons. Scottish soldiers – whether serving in Highland or Lowland regiments – were now an integral part of the British army.

Just as importantly, they were also beginning to develop a unique identity – simultaneously part of the British army, but at the same time recognisably Scottish in character. Like holders of dual citizenship, these Scottish soldiers and their successors would balance the two halves of their identity.

━━►◆◄━━

1

BATTLE OF OUDENARDE, 1708

Lieutenant-Colonel John Blackader (Colonel Preston's Foot, later the 26th Foot 'Cameronians')

The Cameronian Regiment was raised in 1689, and in 1707 it became the 26th Foot. It first won renown at Dunkeld (1689), Steenkirke (1692), Blenheim (1704) and Ramillies (1706), but the battle of Oudenarde (1708) was its first as a fully integrated regiment of the British army. For the British, the War of the Spanish Succession (1701–13) involved a series of campaigns fought in Flanders, in support of Britain's Dutch allies. As Blackader notes in his diary, the battle was unexpected, the result of a dramatic forced march by the Duke of Marlborough's allied army, in an attempt to prevent the French from capturing the Flemish city of Oudenarde. The battle, fought on 11 July 1708, was a long, hard-fought struggle, but by nightfall Marlbourgh's men were victorious. Lieutenant-Colonel Blackader (1664–1727) was the son of the Reverend John Blackader of Dumfries, a Covenanting minister imprisoned for his religious views. From his diary it appears his son (and probably most of the Cameronians) shared these staunch Presbyterian beliefs. The colonel was also concerned about his wife, whose lodgings in Ghent lay in the path of the advancing French army. Although the information in his diary is sparse, his account remains a rare description of a Marlburian battle by a Scottish participant.

8th July (The Sabbath):
Concerned about the present posture of affairs, and somewhat anxious about my dear concern [his wife] at Ghent; but I trust her to a good God, who has been kind to us all our life.

9th July:
Marched at two in the morning – a tedious march. We camped about three hours in the evening for a feint, and then we marched all night, which was great fatigue to the army. Our mistakes and weakness give us this trouble. What a vain thing is man, the wisdom and courage of man! He who one day performs great actions, and [is] extolled as more than man, is the other guilty of great blunders, and as much decried. We have still a prospect of sudden action if the enemy defend what they have got.

10th July:
A fatiguing march, to retrieve our past mistake. Passed the Dender. In all probability it will be retrieved, and that the French will quit what they have got; and I see little else in it but a French gasconade [boast]. All is vanity!

11th July:
This day is another great Ebenezer of my life to be added to Hochstadt, Ramillies etc., never to be forgotten. We have fought the enemy, and by the great mercy of God beat them. I bless God he supplied me with everything I wanted upon such occasions. I praise him for the courage and resolution he gave me, and for a calm mind. All is his gift.

The battle began about five in the afternoon, and lasted till night put a screen of darkness betwixt us and them, and thereby saved, them, in all probability, from as great a defeat as ever they got. The battle came by surprise, for we had no thought of fighting through the day. My frame was more serene and spiritual through the day than ordinary. My thoughts ran much upon the 103rd Psalm, which I sung frequently upon the march. Our regiment was not properly engaged in attacking, but, which was worse, we were obliged to stand in cold blood, exposed to the enemy's shot, by which we had several killed and wounded, for there was heavy firing for about two hours. I was sometimes engaged in prayer, sometimes in praise, sometimes for the public, sometimes for myself.

We lay all night upon the field of battle, where the bed of honour was both hard and cold, but we past [*sic*] the night as well as the groans of dying men would allow us, being thankful for our preservation. I was mercifully supplied with the comforts of life, and wanted nothing good for me. We marched again by break of day and formed our lines, the enemy making still some appearance, but it was only their rearguard which was easily repulsed, so we returned to our camp. I went again through the field of battle, receiving a lecture on mortality from the dead.

———◆———

2
BATTLE OF SHERIFFMUIR, 1715

Lieutenant-Colonel John Blackader (Colonel Preston's Foot, later the 26th Foot 'Cameronians')

The exiled King James II of England and VII of Scotland died in France in 1701, and his son James, Prince of Wales, became the figurehead of the Jacobite cause. An attempted invasion of Scotland was thwarted in 1708, and there were fears the attempt would be repeated. In the summer of 1715 the Earl of Mar raised the Highland clans in the name of James, and by mid September his army had captured Perth. In Stirling, the Duke of Argyll gathered a small government army, and after several diversionary skirmishes the two sides met at Sheriffmuir, outside Stirling, on 13 November.

The battle which followed was a confusing one, and as Blackader suggests in his diary, a wing of the government army was routed, causing fear in Stirling that the Jacobites were poised to attack the city and castle. However, despite being heavily outnumbered, the rest of the government army held their ground, and defeated the Highlanders sent against them. In effect the battle was a bloody stalemate, and at its end Mar withdrew his force back to Perth. Eventually his army dispersed, and the rebellion failed. Blackader was a devout Presbyterian, as befitted a colonel of the Cameronians, and as his diary shows, he sought solace that the apparent victory of the 'Antichrist' was simply a test of faith.

20th June:
There was a dreadful storm, with thunder and lightning, this morning. Oh the comfort of having this God, who thunders in majesty and power, for our God and father!

9th August:
Out seeing a rendezvous, but, alas, a poor defence. Lord, give us help from trouble, for vain is the help of man. Our trust be in thee alone, for indeed we have no arm of flesh to trust to; but perhaps I despise these small things too much, having seen fine armies; but it is our sins, I fear, make us weak. I know, if God be not angry with us, He can make one of us (as we are) to chase a thousand.

23rd August:

This day was kept a fast, appointed by the commission of the General Assembly. I am sure we have good reason to keep days of humiliation. Lord, pour out a spirit of repentance, grace and supplication, that we may turn unto thee before thy wrath break out. Lord, hear the prayers which have been put up to thee today by thy people. I hope there are strong batteries raised up this day in Scotland against an anti-Christian, wicked Jacobite party, who are enemies to God and his cause.

24th August:

The alarm renewed again of an invasion. I cannot say but it always casts a damp upon my spirits when I hear of it, though it need be no surprise, for I have a melancholy view of that dismal scene of confusion, bloodshed, famine and pestilence; and all the calamities of a barbarous internecine war. God can in mercy disappoint our fears, as he has often done.

Undated:

We have got account of the death of the King of France [Louis XIV died on 1 September]. We have been long looking for it, but God's time is the best time. It is observable at this nick of time, when he had been long laying plans, and was on the point of sending a Pretender to invade us. Perhaps this may defeat their design. Follow what will, he was the main pillar and support of antichrist's kingdom. We hope it is a good omen that antichrist shall get a deadly blow, and is near his end, though he rage so much. But now, this should teach us to be humble and modest in judging. We are too apt to interpret God's providences and judgments according to our humours and passions. We thought he could never go off the world without some remarkable judgment, and now he died as a lamb, and without any horror that we hear of, but with great presence of mind and composure. God's ways are not as ours. We measure Infinite by our own little understanding.

12th November:

This morning the army marched out. I got my orders from the Duke, and received many compliments for my success in training the West Country battalion. I went out with the army a little way – sent my best wishes and prayers along with them. Oh thou Lord of hosts, go out with our armies, and thou great Judge of right, judge between them and us. I should have had less fatigue to have been out with the army, but the post which Providence allots to me is always the best. Alarmed at night by the enemy, and putting all the town in arms; I went down to the bridge with the Glasgow battalion, and I remained there all night, and it was a peaceable night. I bless God for this.

13th November (The Sabbath):

I slept two hours in the morning, and then went to church. At the dismission, we were alarmed. Upon going out, I saw one of the most melancholy sights ever I saw in my life – our army flying before their enemies. Oh Lord, what shall we say when Israel turneth their backs and fly before their enemies? We have sinned. Going down to the bridge with a heavy heart, the runners away coming fast in, and everyone giving a worse account than another, that all was lost and gone; indeed seeing is believing. All the fields were covered with our flying troops, horse and foot, all the appearance of a routed army. Oh what dismal views had we, expecting to see the rebel Highland army at their heels! Filled with such thoughts as these – Lord, thou hast turned our sword's edge, and hast not made us to stand in battle; thou hast poured shame and contempt upon us; thou goest not forth with our armies. Give us help from trouble, for vain is the help of man.

I took down all the Glasgow battalion to the bridge, and posted them in some entrenchments there; but indeed I had no great hopes of keeping them out, for thinking our army routed, I thought they would pass the River Forth at some ford, and soon become masters of Stirling. Thus, we spent all the afternoon very melancholy, till the evening, when a better prospect began to open. We got intelligence that the Duke was still on the field of battle, and afterwards that he had been victorious.

Oh what a surprising turn! We could not believe it. We were as men that dreamed; but it was confirmed to us by eye-witnesses. Oh how thou hast turned our tears and grief into joy and songs of praise! Providence has now so managed it that no flesh shall boast. Our right wing did beat their left, and their right wing beat our left; but our left was attacked before the line of battle was formed, and so every regiment, upon the long march, broke and driven back one upon another. We were also too vain and conceited, and despised our enemies too much, and reflected too much upon the arm of flesh. God humbles us, and lets us see that all flesh is grass; yet he takes care of his own cause, and lets not our enemies triumph, at the same time he humbles and mortifies our vanity.

I now see Providence was kind to me and those who remained here. We should have been posted on the left or centre, and so have been surprised and broken as the rest were, and perhaps lost both life and honour. My prayer was, If thy presence go not with me, carry me not up hence. He has heard me. Success was not to attend the left wing. I was not to be there. All is well ordered.

14th November:

This day it is expected there will be another engagement, that the Duke will attack them if they remain where they are.

We hear the rebels are retired. Lord, be praised, who puttest a bridle in their nose and hook in their jaws, and turneth them back by the way they came. Oh, what a merciful surprising turn of providence! Yesterday we were expecting a barbarous and cruel enemy at our gates by this time, and to be flying before them. God is our defence, our shield and buckler.

The army came back in the afternoon in much better condition than we expected. Lord, be blessed for this respite, and sanctify this providence, this check, to make us humble, and to depend on thee; to repent and turn to thee.

Fifteen regiments are cantoned round about us; consequently the company here is very bad – swearing, blasphemy, vile creatures, the scum of the earth. No wonder, though our carcasses be made to dung the face of the earth, God can be glorified, upon us, and work his own works without such vile instruments. Oh Lord, reform us.

3
BATTLE OF CULLODEN, 1746

James, Chevalier de Johnstone
(Aide to Lord George Murray)

With hindsight, the Jacobite Rebellion had little chance of success. Not only did Charles Edward Stuart, grandson of King James II and VII have to capture Scotland from the government, but to safeguard his foothold in Britain he also needed to march south, and attempt to overthrow the Hanoverian monarchy. He managed to secure Scotland, but then the rising began to unravel. Having marched as far south as Derby it became clear that an advance on London was all but suicidal. The Jacobites retreated to Scotland, and in January they inflicted a sharp defeat on the pursuing government forces at Falkirk. Still outnumbered, the Jacobites continued retreating northwards, until by April they were camped outside Inverness.

With battle imminent, Prince Charles attempted a night-time surprise attack on the government army at Nairn, but poor staff work led to delays, and as dawn approached the attack was called off. The Jacobites retreated to Culloden, where the government army caught up with them that morning. The 26-year-old James Johnstone, known as the Chevalier de Johnstone, served as the aide-de-camp to Lord George Murray, Prince Charles's principal commander. In his memoirs he recounts the events of that fateful day in Scottish history.

I could never comprehend why the Prince wished to attack the English army, so much superior in number to his own, with only a part of his men, in disorder, without waiting till the rest should come up, and without forming them in order of battle, to present a front of attack. A shameful repulse would have been the inevitable consequence of such an attack. A surprise ought not only to be judiciously planned, all the measures which it may naturally lead the enemy to adopt being foreseen, but it ought to be conducted and executed at the same time with wisdom, and attention to all the means necessary to ensure success. An enemy surprised, is, no doubt, half conquered; but the case is altered if he have [has] time to recover from his confusion. In that case he may not only contrive to escape, but even to destroy his opponent.

I do not mean to justify the conduct of Lord George, in retiring with the first column, contrary to the express orders of the Prince, and without informing him of it. Had he waited at the entrance into the meadow, for the arrival of the whole army, which had separated from the obscurity of the night and the badness of the roads, he might have insisted on the absolute necessity of forming in order of battle, in order to begin the attack like people in their senses, and have convinced him of the absurdity of acting otherwise. The Irishmen, whom the Prince had adopted as his only counsellors on all occasions, men of the most limited capacities, endeavoured, by all manner of clandestine reports, to cause it to be believed that, in acting as he did on this occasion, Lord George had betrayed the Prince; but, knowing this better than any other person, perhaps, I can only attribute his disobedience of the Prince's orders to the violence and impetuosity of his character.

Exhausted with hunger, and worn out with the excessive fatigue of the three last nights, as soon as we reached Culloden I turned off as fast as I could to Inverness, where eager to recruit my strength by a little sleep, I tore off my clothes, half asleep all-the-while; but when I had already one leg in the bed, and was on the point of stretching myself between the sheets, what was my surprise to hear the drum-beat to arms, and the trumpets of the piquet of Fitzjames sounding the call to boot and saddle, which struck me like a clap of thunder. I hurried on my clothes, my eyes half shut, and, mounting a horse, I instantly repaired to our army, on the eminence on which we had remained for three days, and from which we saw the English army at the distance of about two miles from us. They appeared at first disposed to encamp in the position where they then were, many of their tents being already erected; but all at once their tents disappeared, and we immediately perceived them in movement towards us.

The view of our army, making preparations for battle,

probably induced the Duke of Cumberland to change his plan; and, indeed, he must have been blind in the extreme to have delayed attacking us instantly, in the deplorable situation in which we were, worn out with hunger and fatigue; especially when he perceived, from our manoeuvre, that we were impatient to give battle, under every possible disadvantage, and well disposed to facilitate our own destruction. The Duke of Cumberland remained ignorant, till it was day, of the danger to which he had been exposed during the night; and as soon as he knew it, he broke up his camp, and followed us closely.

The Prince, on his return to Culloden, enraged against Lord George Murray, publicly declared that no one in future should command his army but himself. As soon as the English army began to appear, the Prince, who was always eager to give battle, without reflecting on the consequences, was told that, as the Highlanders were exhausted with fatigue, dispersed, and buried in deep sleep, in the neighbouring hamlets and enclosures, many could not possibly be present in the battle, from the difficulty of finding them. Besides, what could be expected from men in their situation, worn out with want of sleep and food, and quite exhausted with this night-march, a thousand times worse than any march which had been made in England? They were not possessed of supernatural strength. He was advised to fall back on the high ground, behind the plain, having his left supported by the ruins of the Castle, where he could place his cannon to advantage, as on batteries, whilst he could at the same time occupy Inverness, and allow his army to refresh themselves and obtain some sleep.

By allowing them twenty-four hours' repose, it was said, they would be quite recruited [restored], and altogether new men. In such an advantageous position, by throwing up an entrenchment to cover Inverness, there was no reason to fear

an immediate attack from the Duke of Cumberland, should
he examine our position with attention; but if the Duke
ventured to attack us notwithstanding, he could not fail to
pay dear for his temerity. We might, therefore, calculate on
remaining tranquil in this position for some days, and the
delay would give time to those who were absent on leave to
join the army. The Prince, however, would listen to no advice,
and resolved on giving battle, let the consequences be what
they might.

The ground in the hollow, between the Castle of Culloden
and an enclosure on our right, being marshy and covered
with water, which reached half way up the leg, was well
chosen to protect us from the cavalry of the enemy. The
English were drawn up in three lines, but we had much
difficulty in forming two. Our second line was composed of
the Irish piquets, with the regiments of Royal Scots,
Kilmarnock, Lord Lewis Gordon, the Duke of Perth, Lord
Ogilvie, Glenbucket, and John Roy Stuart; of which the two
last, and that of Lord Kilmarnock consisted only of from
two to three hundred men each. When the English army was
on a line with the enclosure, about six or eight hundred yards
from the eminence behind the swamp, our army descended,
with great rapidity, into the marshy ground, and charged the
enemy, sword in hand.

The Prince, who remained on the eminence with the piquet
of Fitzjames, out of reach of the musketry of the enemy,
observed them employed in throwing down the walls of the
enclosure to attack us in flank, and immediately sent repeated
orders to Lord George Murray, whilst he was at the head of
the first line, and ready to fall upon the enemy, to place some
troops in the enclosure, and prevent the manoeuvre of the
English, which could not fail to prove fatal to us. Lord George

paid no attention to this order; and the English having finished throwing down the walls of the enclosure, entered with two regiments of cavalry, and four pieces of artillery, which they fired with grape-shot on our right wing. Their fire, from the circumstance of their being quite close to our right, was so terrible, that it literally swept away, at once, whole ranks. From the inequality of this marshy ground, our right and centre came first up with the enemy, our first line advancing a little obliquely; but, overpowered by a murderous fire in front and flank, our right could not maintain its ground, and was obliged to give way, whilst our centre had already broken the enemy's first line, and attacked the second.

The left wing, where I was with Scothouse, was not twenty paces from the enemy, who gave their first fire at the moment the flight began to become general, which spread from the right to the left of our army with the rapidity of lightning. What a spectacle of horror! The same Highlanders, who had advanced to the charge like lions, with bold, determined countenances, were, in an instant, seen flying like trembling cowards, in the greatest disorder. It may be said of the attack of the Highlanders, that it bears great resemblance to that of the French; that is a flame, the violence of which is more to be dreaded than the duration. No troops, however excellent, are possessed of qualities which will render them constantly invincible. It was evident our destruction became inevitable, if the English got possession of the enclosure.

The Prince saw this from the eminence where he was posted, and sent his aide-de-camp six or seven times, ordering Lord George to take possession of it. He saw that his orders were not executed; but yet he never quitted his place on the eminence. This, however, was a critical moment, when he ought to have displayed the courage of a grenadier, by immediately advancing to put himself at the head of his army, and commanding himself those manoeuvres which he wished to be executed. He would never have experienced disobedience on the part of his subjects, who had exposed their lives and fortunes to establish him on the throne of his ancestors, and who would have shed for him the last drop of their blood.

There are occasions when a general ought to expose his person, and not remain beyond the reach of musketry; and surely there never was a more pressing occasion for disregarding a few shots than the one in question, as the gain or loss of the battle depended on it. In the desperate expedition on which he had entered, though it was proper that he should guard against danger, he ought to have done so in a manner which showed that life or death was equally indifferent to him, conducting himself with valour and prudence, according to circumstances.

But he was surrounded by Irish confidents [*sic*], whose baseness of soul corresponded to the obscurity of their birth. The natives of Ireland are generally supposed, in England, to have a great confusion of ideas; and they are, in general, very bad counsellors. But the Prince blindly adopted their opinions. Yet he combated for a crown, and was consequently more interested in our success than any man in the army; while the Scots had no other object in view than to obviate the effect of their rashness in having voluntarily exposed themselves to death on the scaffold, and confiscation of their estates.

As far as I could distinguish, at the distance of twenty paces, the English appeared to be drawn up in six ranks; the three first being on their knees. They kept up a terrible running fire on us. My unfortunate friend Scothouse was killed by my side; I was not so deeply affected at the moment of his fall, as I have been ever since. It would almost seem as if the Power that presides over the lives of men in battles, marks out the most deserving for destruction, and spares those who are more unworthy. Military men, susceptible of friendship, are much to be pitied. The melancholy fate of my friends has often cost me many a tear, and left on my heart an indelible impression of pain and regret. Mr Macdonald of Keppoch, who had been absent on leave with his clan, having made great haste to join the Prince, arrived at the moment of the charge, and in time to take his station in the first line, with his clan, where he was instantly killed. He was a gentleman of uncommon merit, and his death was universally lamented.

As the Highlanders were completely exhausted with hunger, fatigue, and the want of sleep, our defeat did not at all surprise me; I was only astonished to see them behave so well. If our right could only have maintained its grounds three minutes longer, the English army, which was very much shaken, would have been still more so by the shock of our left wing, which was yet at the distance of from fifteen to twenty paces from the enemy, when the disorder began on the right; and if our centre, which had pierced the first line, had been properly supported, it is highly probable that the English would have been soon put to flight. There were about twelve hundred men killed upon the field of battle; and, of the number, there were as many of the enemy as of the Highlanders. Thus our loss was by no means considerable.

The right wing of our army retreated towards the River Nairn, and met in their way a body of English cavalry, which appeared as much embarrassed as the Highlanders; but the English commander very wisely opened a way for them in the centre, and allowed them to pass at the distance of a pistol shot, without attempting to molest them or to take prisoners.

One officer only of this body, wishing to take a Highlander prisoner, advanced a few paces to seize him, but the Highlander brought him down with his sword, and killed him on the spot; and, not satisfied with this, he stopped long enough to take possession of his watch, and then decamped with the booty. The English commander remained a quiet spectator of the scene, renewed his orders to his men not to quit their ranks, and could not help smiling and secretly wishing the Highlander might escape, on account of his boldness, without appearing to lament the fate of the officer, who had disobeyed his orders. If this body of cavalry had not acted so prudently, they would instantly have been cut to pieces. It is extremely dangerous in a defeat to attempt to cut off the vanquished from all means of escape.

Our left, which fled towards Inverness, was less fortunate. Having been pursued by the English cavalry, the road from Culloden to that town was everywhere strewed with dead bodies. The Duke of Cumberland had the cruelty to allow our wounded to remain amongst the dead of the field of battle, stripped of their clothes, from Wednesday, the day of our unfortunate engagement, till three o'clock in the afternoon of Friday, when he sent detachments to kill all those who were still in life; and a great many, who had resisted the effects of the continual rains which fell all that time, were then dispatched. He ordered a barn, which contained many of the wounded Highlanders, to be set on fire; and, having stationed soldiers round it, they with fixed bayonets drove back the unfortunate men who attempted to save themselves into the flames, burning them alive in this horrible manner, as if they had not been fellow-creatures. This sanguinary Duke was obliged to have an act of indemnity, from the British Parliament, for these and a number of similar acts which he had committed, in violation of the laws of Great Britain. Cruelty is a proof of a base and cowardly disposition.

As soon as the Prince saw his army begin to give way, he made his escape with a few horsemen of Fitzjames's piquet.

⋯⋯

4

CAPTURED BY INDIANS, 1758

Private Robert Kirk (77th Foot – Montgomery's Highlanders)

'The French and Indian War' is often used to describe the campaigns of the Seven Years' War (1756–63), fought in North America. The term is appropriate, as the conflict often pitted British troops against Native Americans supported by their French allies. The war was essentially a struggle for supremacy between the British and the French, with control of North America as the prize. Both sides made extensive use of native auxiliaries, who had little regard for the etiquette of European warfare. In September 1758 a British army launched an expedition to attack Fort Duquesne, a French outpost guarding the Ohio valley. The assault was led by Major James Grant of Ballindalloch, who hoped to lure the enemy into a sortie from the fort, where he could then ambush them. Unknown to him the French had been reinforced by a large native contingent, who overran the British, killing or capturing over 300 British or colonial American troops in the process.

Major Grant was taken prisoner, but was paroled shortly afterwards. Private Kirk was also captured, but by the Shawnee rather than by the French. He was fortunate enough to survive his imprisonment, but his account of the fate of his comrades makes gruesome reading.

He spent eight months as a prisoner, but the following summer he escaped, and rejoined his regiment. Fort Duquesne was finally captured by the British in November 1758 and renamed Fort Pitt. Today the city of Pittsburgh, Pennsylvania, stands on the same site.

When we arrived at Bedford and had given what information we could, the greatest part of the army were ordered to march, and here was a fresh difficulty, having a road to cut for our passage as far as Ligonier, an extent of fifty miles. We built a stockade fort, and encamped a regiment of Virginians within the stockades, who were attack'd by a scouting party of three hundred men, French and Indians, but their attempt was fruitless, having only killed and scalped three or four and lost a much greater number.

In this place a council of war was held, at which Colonel Buccoad [Bouquet] of the Royal American presided, and their resolution was that Major Grant an enterprizing good soldier should go and endeavour to surprize Fort Duquesne. I had the fortune to be one of this party. When we set out, it was the latter end of August, and the fall of the leaf, so that trees and the Indians were of the same colour, and this circumstance, trifling as it may appear, ought always to be consider'd, by forces who mean to operate with success against them, as at that season they have a full view of you, but you can't have the least idea of them.

However we proceeded by a Indian path, to a place call'd the Long Meadows on the River Ohio, seven miles below Fort Duquesne; Where we rendezvous'd and refreshed ourselves, from thence to Grant's hill, a small mile from the Fort, where we lay upon our arms 'till day-break, when we were to storm. But this proved an abortive scheme, for two of the Royal Americans deserted, and informed the enemy of our strength and councils, but this unhappily did not come to our knowledge until we were routed. We began our attack, by posting three companies over against the gates of the Fort with orders to rush in as soon as they heard the main body attempt the walls. That we might the better distinguish our own people, every one had a white shirt over his coat.

Upon the information of the deserters, the French sent over the rivers Allegany [Alleghany] and Monongahela, which empty themselves into the Ohio, two large parties of Indians who were encamped on the banks, who, when they heard the report of the firearms, sailed up these two rivers in their canoes, and landed at the point which the fort is built upon. Thus, when we least expected, attacked us in the rere [rear], and the whole strength of the garrison in our front. The three companies before mentioned, stood firm a long time, and by their regular platoon firing annoyed the enemy greatly. But by their superiority and repeated attacks, this brave handful was at length broken and obliged to retreat in confusion to the main body. In this critical situation we exerted our utmost courage and kept the enemy at bay for a full hour, until we were in short almost all cut off.

It is impossible to describe the confusion and horror which ensued, when all hope of victory was gone. We were dispersed here and there, for my part I cannot inform the reader how affairs went with my fellow soldiers, for I was pursued by four Indians, who fired at me several times, and their shot went through my cloaths, one of them however made sure, and wounded me in the leg with a buckshot. I was immediately taken, but the Indian who laid hold of me would not allow the rest to scalp me, tho' they proposed to do so; in short he befriended me greatly (as you shall hereafter be informed), however I was bound hand and foot and left in his charge, in a little time some Squaws, i.e. female Indians came, and carried me into a canoe, and paddled over to the other side of the Allegany River, when they put me into one of their Wigwams i.e. Indian-houses, where one of them dress'd my wound with great care.

I cannot express the woefulness of my situation, during the night that intervened 'twixt this and the next day; which I concluded would certainly be my last. I was confirm'd in this opinion, when I saw the rest of the Indians arrive, and bring with them several other prisoners whom I did not know. They immediately stript me of my cloaths and in return gave me an old Indian blanket and britch-clout to cover my nakedness. Upon the third day after my being inward, a French officer came over and spoke to the Indians, in order to have us ransom'd; but they would not foregoe themselves the pleasure of indulging their savage natures. He enquir'd of us concerning the strength of the English, what time we thought they would lay siege to the fort, and several such questions; adding that he was sorry for us, and that it was not in the power of the French to redeem us.

Nothing but death inevitable was before us, and we remained in this painful uncertainty till the fifth day, when we were brought forth, being nine in number, amongst a great many Indians, where we were unbound, scourg'd, and tortur'd the whole day; and here I cannot help remarking [on] the inhumanity of the French, who took a great pleasure in participating in this cruel spectacle. As night approached we were carried into a council of the gravest Indians, and were by them ordered to be severally tied to posts, where there were all kinds of Pine-fir in heaps ready to be burnt. I here summoned all the fortitude I was master of, in order to enable me to resign myself to the will of providence. But I was not much longer in suspence, for the Indian who had taken me prisoner, accompanied by one of the chiefs came and told me in English, which he could speak brokenly, that I was not to be burnt; that I was for the future to be to him as a brother, his father being my father, and all his friends my friends. I was sometime before I collected myself so much as to understand him, being quite ignorant of their method of adoption, of which more hereafter.

I was carried by my adopted brother to view the war-dance, as they call it, when they burn any of their enemies; and to my unspeakable grief and terror saw five out of the nine burned in the most cruel manner. The method they follow in the perpetration of this horrid scene, is as follows, viz having purposely collected a number of the roots that grow in fir-trees, they stick these to the fleshy parts of the unhappy victims, and then set them on fire, which consumes them in a slow and lingering manner, during which time the Indians dance and skip about them, using the most insulting gesticulation; and, as if this was not enough, they frequently use the barbarity of tomahawking them, i.e. striking a tomahawk into their skulls. When they have thus finished their bloody purposes, they go to drink and festivity, throughout the whole of which, the same hellish antipathy to their unhappy enemies seems predominant, a melancholy proof of which I had like to have experienced.

Having been brought home by my adoptive mother, who celebrated my initiation by making over me for an hour or more; she then brought me some victuals, and a little French brandy, which she had saved during their debauch, which to me was a most acceptable present, nothing having cross'd my throat for two days before; it revived me greatly and I was in myself returning the Almighty thanks for my preservation, when a new danger attended, and had like to have been fatal to me.

A drunken Indian coming into our wigwam, would instantly have killed me, but was prevented by my adopted brother, who came in along with him, and resented this attempt so much as to turn him out of the hut, and turning to me presented his pipe for me to smoke, which is a certain sign of their friendship. He also gave me a better shirt, a new blanket, and britch-cloath, a pair of leggings and Indian shoes made of buck-skin. Next day he cut my hair after the Indian form, painted my face of their colour, oil'd my joints, and would have me to let him cut my ears, but he could not prevail with me to admit of this last operation; as I was apprehensive it would be painful; here we had like to quarrel, but on my begging him to be quiet, he agreed to omit it.

He then informed me that about four moons before, they were at war with a neighbouring nation called Cherokies [Cherokees], and that in an engagement they had, his brother was killed, but that the good Man, i.e. God, had sent me in his place, and that I should have all he had, and his friends should be my friends, and his enemies mine, and in token of this agreement, he gave me a gun, powder and shot, a tomahawk and scalping knife, and upon this occasion, he made an entertainment to his friends and acquaintances. I seem'd to partake of their mirth, which so delighted them, that they hugged me and called me in their broken English, Brother; they then gave me the name of him, in whose place I was adopted.

It is a custom amongst them, as I afterwards learned, when the father, brother, or other relation falls in the war, the next prisoner taken by the son or brother of the deceased is adopted in his place, and they always pay him the regard due to a father or brother. They used me with so much affection, that at first I could not help regarding them very much; but there is something in the manners and inclinations of Europeans so different from them, that is it not possible they should long agree together.

5

THE LANDING AT LOUISBOURG, 1758

Sergeant James Thompson (78th Highlanders)

The French fortress of Louisbourg in Nova Scotia protected New France (now Canada) from invasion. During the Seven Years' War (1756–63) Louisbourg prevented the British from launching an attack on Quebec – a strategic blow which would almost guarantee British victory in North America. Bypassing it wasn't an option, as it left a powerful French base astride Britain's lines of supply. General Amherst was given the task of capturing the fortress, and during the early summer of 1758 an expedition was gathered in Halifax, Nova Scotia, consisting of almost 14,000 men, 40 warships and 150 transport ships. On the morning of 8th June Amherst ordered his troops to attempt an amphibious landing. A flotilla of small flat-bottomed boats led the way, running a murderous gauntlet of French artillery fire.

As casualties mounted, Brigadier Wolfe, who commanded the landing force, gave orders for the attempt to be abandoned. However, one boat landed on a rocky inlet which was sheltered from French fire, and gained a small bridgehead. Wolfe rapidly exploited this success, and as more British troops scrambled ashore, the French retreated back within the walls of their fortress. The British laid siege to Louisbourg, and seven weeks later the garrison surrendered,

thereby opening the way to a British invasion of Canada. Sergeant
Thompson provides us with a hair-raising account of the amphibious
attack, and describes what happened immediately afterwards.

When all the troops were got into the flat-bottomed boats that
the General had provided at Halifax, and which we brought
along with us, we very soon after saw the signal from the
General's barge which was between us and the land, to push
off towards shore . . . We were so closely packed together, there
was only room for us to stand up except in the back part of
the boat, where the Officers and NCOs contrived to sit down
in the stern sheets. This left no room for rowing so we were
taken in tow by a boat from a '74' [74-gun ship-of-the-line].
During this time the French were peppering us with canister
shot from a six-gun battery on the heights, while musket balls
fired from 24-pounders came whistling about our ears. Nothing
could be like it, and as our ships of war kept up a fire upon
the batteries to cover our landing, there was a terrific hullabaloo.

One 24-pound shot did a great deal of mischief. It passed
under my hams and killed Sergeant McKenzie, who was sitting
as close to my left as he could squeeze, and it carried away
the basket of his broadsword which, along with the shot,
passed through Lieutenant Cuthbert, who was on McKenzie's
left, tore his body into slivers, and cut off both legs of one of
the two fellows that held the tiller of the boat, who lost an
astonishing quantity of blood, and died with the tiller grasped
tight in his hand! After doing all this mischief, the shot stuck
in the stern post. Although this shot did not touch me, the
thighs and calves of my legs were affected and became as black
as my hat, and for some weeks I suffered a great deal of pain.
But that was nothing – what affected me most was the loss of
my captain, Captain Charles Baillie. He was on the opposite

side of the boat to me, and he merely leaned over his head in a gentle manner upon the shoulders of the man next to him. I had no idea that he had been touched, but thought that he was trying to avoid the shot which was coming so thick up on us. So thought the other man, also, but he was struck mortally, and expired without the least struggle. Poor fellow! He was my best friend, and it was to be with him that I had volunteered to come away from Scotland.

Whilst we were in this sad predicament, I had my eye on the boat that was towing us, for I was anxious that she should get as far forward as possible, when I observed a fellow fumbling at the painter of our boat, without my knowing what he was at. At last he takes a clasp knife out of his pocket and cuts the rope, and away went the boat, leaving us a mark for the French batteries to fire at. As good luck should have it, our situation was noticed by one of our Frigates, from which two boats were sent to our relief, and into which we got. No sooner had we left our bottomed boat than she sank to the gunnel, for the men had withdrawn their plaids from out of the shot-holes into which they had thrust them whenever we were struck. The weight of the shot that stuck in her also helped a good deal to sink her. In this state she was towed alongside the Frigate, and I understand, was hoisted aboard and taken home to England as a great curiosity, for she was completely riddled with shot-holes, and nearly a bucket-full of musket balls and small shot was taken out of her. Had there been any other troops than Highlanders in our situation, they must have gone to the bottom for want of such a ready means of plugging up the shot-holes as we carried about us in our plaids.

In our fresh boats, and under the covering fire of our ships of war, we at last landed on the west side of the Town, although we were nearly swamped in the surf. We had to wait a considerable time before we could advance, until some axe men were got to cut a passage through the abattis [defence of wooden stakes] that lined the beach for about three miles, but after a great deal of difficulty we got to the top of the rock.

On our way to join the main Army, we came to the Battery that did us so such mischief. It was deserted, only one man being found, and he had his head carried away, yet he held firm hold of a lighted linstock which one of our Highlanders tried in vain to force out of his grasp. Our Fleet, as it seemed to me from the high shore, made a noble appearance, and looked as if the bowsprit of every one was made fast to the stern of the next to it – they stretched across the whole Harbour.

During the landing at Louisbourg there was a rascal of a savage on top of a high rock that kept firing at the Boats as they came within his reach, and he kill'd volunteer Fraser of our Regiment who, in order to get his one shilling instead of six pence a day, was acting, like myself, as Sergeant. He was a very genteel young man and was to have been commission'd the first vacancy. There sat next to Fraser in the boat, a silly fellow of a Highlander, but who was a good marksman for all that, and not withstanding that there was a positive order not to fire a shot during the landing, he couldn't resist this temptation of having a slap at the Savage. So the silly fellow levels his fuzee [fusil or musket] at him and in spite of the unsteadiness of the boat, for it was blowing hard at the time, 'afaith he brought him tumbling down like a sack into the water. As the matter so turned out, there was not a word said about it, but had it been otherwise he would have had his back scratch'd if not something worse.

This shot was the best I have ever seen. The Right hand man of our Company (and he was no little fellow) received a shot in his thigh which immediately swell'd up to the thickness of his body. It made him suffer exceeding great pain. The idea was that the shot was poison'd. The poor devil screamed the whole time that the boat was towing towards the Frigate, and when they were going to put him in slings to hoist him on board, his agony was so great that he expired on the gunnel of the boat!

There was one Boat load of Troops that was carried away out of her destination by the Surf that roll'd very heavily and after getting within, it pulled towards the East side of the town and the Troops in a second boat, seeing the first going in that direction thought that must be the right place to land and accordingly made after her, and these were the only Boats that landed in that quarter.

It happen'd that they had come up opposite to a high rocky precipice and no road or footpath leading up. However, with the help of one another they all got safe to the top which they found to be covered with brushwood. The next thing to be considered was how they were to join the remainder of the army. One of the officers thought he would just look about him a little and see the nature of the ground that lay between them and the army, and, going a short way, he finds himself at the edge of the brushwood, and beheld, to his great astonishment, the French army form'd in their trenches in two lines directly in a line with where he stood. He immediately returns to the party, and relates what he had just seen, and after consulting what was best – squads each to sally out in turn from the brushwood, and fire at the French, and then return to the rear to re-load in order to conceal their real numbers.

This they did only a few times when the French, supposing as it was thought that they were attacked by a numerous body of our troops, betook themselves to their seraphers, and away they ran towards the garrison which was about three miles distance from the trenches they had just quit. Some of the Highland soldiers seeing the French run away, could not resist the temptation of giving them a chase (for they were a raw, undisciplined set, just raised, and unused to restraint) and they stole away after them by two's and by three's and presently by whole companies, and there soon remain'd only the officers and non-commission'd officers of our regiment.

Upon the Quartermaster General (then Colonel Carlton) coming to the ground with the orders to 'Form Line' he was told they had already receiv'd orders to that effect, which being explain'd to the Highlanders, they said among themselves in Gaelic 'What – are we to stand and form line, and quietly look at the Enemy running away? No! No! We can't understand that they had run off after the French.' The Quartermaster General was heard to say, and I myself heard him say so, 'I thought they only wanted an opportunity and this is not more than I had expected of them.' You see most of them had serv'd in the rebellion of '45 and they were thought to be not game!

In about an hour and a half or so they all came back again to a man, after having follow'd close to the heels of the French, up to the very walls of the town and almost every man of them brought in his prisoner and some had two. Among the number, Duncan McFee of our company, a wick'd rascal as ever lived, and as bold as lion, he overtakes a French Officer in the chase, who according to etiquette drops the point of his sword in token of his submission and spoke something in French which Duncan did not understand. This wouldn't satisfy Duncan but he seizes the Officer by the 'skriff' of the Neck and snatched away the sword from out of his hand, and in this way brought him into camp and deliver'd him over to our Adjutant. This French officer was a very fine gentlemanly looking man – but devil-a-bit would he give up the sword for all the Adjutant could say – and Duncan claps the French Officer's sword in the frog of his belt, alongside his own broadsword, as a trophy of war. The French officer made great remonstrances at the treatment that he had receiv'd and stated that it was not the rule of their service that an officer, although a prisoner of War would be depriv'd of his sword; it being sufficient that he was deprived of his liberty, and he request'd earnestly that the Adjutant would see him right'd.

Upon this, the Adjutant, who knew what kind of a Fellow he had to deal with, instead of attempting to force Duncan to give up the sword, he goes up to Headquarters (this is the first time that I ever heard the term used) to Colonel Fraser, who understood how to manoeuvre him, and the Colonel's advice was to go back to Duncan, and undervalue the sword, as being a paltry looking thing compared with his own broadsword, and not worth his keeping (and indeed it was but a poor looking thing, with only a common brass hilt) but to offer him a few crowns for it, which he, the Colonel, would take care to have repaid.

The Adjutant accordingly seeks out Duncan who he finds strutting about as proud as a Peacock, much to the annoyance of the French Officer. He endeavoured, on behalf of the Colonel, to coax him out of the sword, but No! Devil-a-bit, Duncan would not part with his prize. At length, whilst endeavouring to persuade him that it was not worth a single crown, he ask'd him how many crowns he would take for it: Duncan said he did not care a straw for the money – it was the honour of the thing he most valued – but that if the Colonel would give twenty Crowns for it he might have the sword. The Adjutant said that was too much, but that he would give him ten. To this Duncan voluntarily agreed, and the sword was again put into the French officer's possession. The very next day Duncan finds his way to the Colonel's tent, and what does he see passing by him but the French officer having his sword at his side! He instantly rushes at him, and tears it away a second time, and, by my faith, it would have been no small matter to have got it back, but for our Colonel, who explained to him the Custom of War, and that it was unbecoming a brave soldier to hurt the feelings of a prisoner that might fall into his hands, and that instead of injuring him, he ought to treat him as he himself would wish to be treated if the chances of war should place him in the same situation. After having gained upon him in this way, Duncan got cool again, gave up the sword and went his way, but rather down in the mouth.

⟫•⟪

6

SKIRMISH AT BUSHY RUN, 1763

Private Robert Kirk (42nd Foot – Black Watch)

After his escape from the Shawnee, Private Kirk rejoined the 77th Foot, and participated in the campaigns around Lake George and Lake Champlain, and the capture of Ticonderoga (1759). When the war ended in 1763 his regiment was disbanded, and Kirk was transferred into the Black Watch. That summer the Indian leader. Pontiac led a tribal confederation against the British, and besieged Fort Pitt (now Pittsburgh). The 42nd formed part of an expedition sent to its relief. On 5 August the British relief column was ambushed near Bushy Run, about 25 miles short of their objective. Somehow they managed to form a defensive perimeter, and held on until dark.

Their commander, Colonel Bouquet, was an experienced Indian fighter, and he laid a trap for them. Consequently, when the Indians attacked the following morning, the 42nd launched a surprise flank attack, which drove them from the field. After the battle, Bouquet and his men went on to relieve the fort, and so help crush Pontiac's rebellion. Private Kirk took part in the battle, and describes this desperate encounter with the Indians, which included the Shawnee, who had captured him five years before. For Kirk, this was the chance for revenge.

A war breaking out with the Indians to the westward, our company being necessary in those parts, for altho' the peace between Britain, France, and Spain had been concluded some time before, yet there was no peace for us, but the horrors of a war, and one with a savage cruel enemy to encounter afresh.

The Indians had already destroyed some of the back settlements, and had entirely block'd all the avenues to Fort Pitt, in which they had also mewed up a number of traders, and that place was for want of provisions in the greatest extremity. The reason given by the Indians for this war is as follows, viz. That contrary to the treaty, by which all the land east of the Allegany mountains was consigned to the governor of Pennsylvania, and all the land to the west of said mountains was left in the possession of the Indians for their hunting ground; contrary to which, some of the English had seized upon, and built plantations, which the Indians remonstrated against without effect, in consequence of which they raised their war hatchet and vowed revenge upon all White people without distinction.

In order to force relief to the inhabitants at Fort Pitt, the remains of the 1st and 2nd battalion of Royal Highlanders, and the residue of our regiment were form'd into one corps and might consist of about 300 men. With this small army we set out for the Province of Pennsylvania, and marched with the greatest expedition, 'till we reached Carlisle 100 miles above Philadelphia, where we stayed the 19th of July 1763, and waited for an escort of 1500 pack-horses laden with flour, 500 bullocks, and a few sheep.

This convoy was destined for Fort Pitt which, as I have observed, was block'd up by the Indians, and 300 of the inhabitants, besides the garrison, in a starving condition. We were here join'd by 50 men from Virginia, and some of the Royal Americans which reinforcement made our strength some 400. We proceeded with our convoy to Bedford which the Indians had also blocked up, who retired upon our approach: we remained here just so long as was necessary to relieve their wants; and continued our march to Fort Ligonier, about 50 miles from Fort Pitt. But we had certain information, that the Indians would attack us, so took what precautions were necessary to prevent a surprize.

On the 5th of August we came within sight of the enemy's fires, and could by the fresh tracks we fell into, be certain of their approach; our commanding officer then made the following dispositions, he ordered a square to be formed, taking care to double the number of men on each of the flanks and also small parties of reserve for the angles and as a guard for the rear; we were drawn up in this manner, when our van descry'd Indians, when they were convinced that they saw them, they immediately began the attack on the front, which is contrary to their maxims in war; they being accustomed to begin an engagement in the rear.

When Col. Buccard [Bouquet] perceived their design, he ordered that part of the square which were on flank, to move forward and support the front, leaving the escort to be drove up by the rear; the front of the square was composed of the Virginians and Royal Americans and the light company of the 42nd Regiment, who withstood the enemy with a resolution which will always be remembered to their honour; they however suffered greatly, and first being almost all cut off, and only four of the Royal Americans left unhurt; the light company of Virginians had not much better fortune, for they were all kill'd or wounded.

The rear by this time had come, when the Indians perceiving they must fight a fresh party, changed their scheme, came round and attacked the rear; we faced about, and having made a kind of breastwork with the flour bags, waited their approach; when they came close up, we gave them our whole fire, and rushed out upon them with fixt bayonets; the Indians are not very well used to this way of fighting, they therefore immediately took to their heels, and left the field of battle, but they hovered in the woods about us all that day and night, which made the commanding officer not to think it expedient to leave that situation for that night.

We therefore encamped, and begun to look after our wounded, many of whom we found so faint for want of water, that they must inevitably have perished if they were not relieved; accordingly a party was sent out to look for water, of which we could find none, but what was very muddy; however we made use of it, and were glad to get it any way; we lay upon our arms all night, and at day break the Indians advanced and begun to fire upon us, as before, all the morning was spent in procuring conveniences for carrying our wounded men. About noon the firing was very hot, and the Indians become so insolent, that they told Colonel Buccard who commanded, that they would have his scalp before night, they also knew one of the men who was a cooper, and made keggs for them, they told him they would pay him for his keggs, and they were as good as their words for they shot him through both legs.

The loss we sustained broke the square entirely, so that we were in the greatest danger, when it was thought high time to make our last effort, and endeavour to free ourselves from this deplorable situation. Accordingly it was agreed, that the remaining part of the 42nd Regiment should strip to their waistcoats, and from the rear to give the Indians a warm fire, while the main body was to proceed to a clear spot of ground called Bushy Run, about a mile from the place where we engaged the day before.

This being put in force, the Indians thought we were going to break and run away, and being sure of their prey came in upon us in the greatest disorder; but they soon found their mistake, for we met them with our fire first, and then made terrible havock amongst them with our fixt bayonets and continuing to push them every where. They set to their heels and were never after able to rally again; in the meanwhile the main body proceeded to Bushy Run, and there encamped; we had a very wet night, which obliged us to make large fires in order to dry ourselves.

Next day we marched towards Fort Pitt; we were fired upon by some Indians from the top of a hill, but we soon made them run, and again encamped in a swampy ground, and staid there two days to refresh ourselves. The Indians kept whooping round us with their odious death halloo, but never appeared in our sight, being terrified with their defeat. We were now within 20 miles of Fort Pitt, & had directions if we were again attacked, and should be defeated, to make the best of our way to said Fort, but the Indians never appeared.

We at last arrived at the Fort, and relieved the Inhabitants with provisions and every other thing necessary. Our arrival gave new life to the whole, we staid but a short time here, having to escort the inhabitants down the country, and to come back with more provisions. We continued employed in this manner 'till the first of January, the snow falling deep, we were obliged to shovel it away every night to make our beds and fires; every man being provided with a hatchet to cut wood, and a shovel for the snow, we were obliged also to go in parties, and trample it before the horses, in order to prevent their being mired in it. In these excursions I think we marched 1500 miles, the Forts being stored with provisions, we settled in them until the spring of the year 1764. Provisions at last becoming scarce, we made several incursions into the fields about Fort Pitt, where we found Indian corn in great plenty, of which we brought considerable quantities to the garrison, and pounded it for broth. But upon these parties, we were frequently in great danger, for the Indians gave us many a chace [chase]. On one of these expeditions I lost my comrade, who was taken, scalped, and died the same day.

7
NEW YORK, 1776

Captain James Murray (57th Foot)

In the summer of 1776 the American War of Independence had been raging for over a year. The British had won a pyrrhic victory at Bunker Hill the previous summer, but in the spring of 1776 they were forced to abandon Boston to the rebels. Reinforcements duly arrived, and so in late June 1776 a British fleet arrived off Long Island, near New York, and on 22 August an advanced force of

15,000 men were landed, under the command of General Howe. The Americans under General Washington fortified Brooklyn Heights, in the corner of Long Island facing New York. An outer line of defences commanded by General Sullivan ran along the Heights of Guan, some three miles in front of Washington's main position, near the little hamlet of Bedford. On 26 August the British outflanked Sullivan's force, and the American position from the rear. The Americans broke and ran, and within three days Washington abandoned his fortified camp at Brooklyn, and escaped to New York. The British captured the city two weeks later. Captain Murray, a Scottish baronet, served with an English regiment during the Long Island campaign, which he described in impressive detail in a letter to his sister.

To: Mrs Smyth, Methven Castle, Perth, N. Britain

Newton Kilns, Long Island
August 31st, 1776

My dearest Betsy,

The Rebel Army appeared to be forming in line about half a mile south of the town of — [Bedford]. Our operations are now, thank heaven fairly and successfully begun, and with every prospect, in my opinion, of as fair and successful an ending. Upon the 22nd (a few days after the arrival of the Hessians) we landed upon Long Island without the smallest opposition. At a little village called Flat Bush, which unfortunately lay contiguous to a wood they made their first appearance. During three days that we halted there, they kept up a constant kind of dirty firing, in the course of which we had about 30 men killed and wounded. Upon the 26th in the evening we at last received orders to proceed. We were about three miles distant from the works which they had erected at the corner of this Island, which commanded the town of New York, and which it was absolutely necessary for us to be in possession of. Imagining that we should attempt a passage by the shortest way, they had brought 5–6,000 men to oppose us, upon a hill which overlooked the village, and in the woods adjoining to the road. The enterprise of that night certainly reflects the highest honour upon the General, and it will probably be attended with the happiest and most extensive consequences.

The Light Infantry and Grenadiers followed by upwards of ⅔ of the British army took a cross road to the right, marched several miles about, and by an unaccountable negligence on the part of the enemy, past the wood which stretches quite across the Island, and by means of which they chiefly expected to detain us, and were almost within sight of their works, in the morning before they were apprized of our arrival. Upon a signal given, the Hessians advanced in front from the village, as the rest of the British troops under General Grant had done some time before, along the sea coast up on the left; so that they were hemmed in upon every quarter. It was well that the fortune of the day repaid us for the labours of the night, which was to me at least as disagreeable a one as I remember to have passed in the course of my campaigning. I had been up three out of the five preceding nights. We dragged on at the most tedious pace from sunset till 3 o'clock in the morning, halting every minute just long enough to drop asleep, and to be disturbed again in order to proceed twenty yards in the same manner. The night was colder too than I remember to have felt it, so that by day break my stock of patience began to run very low.

We fell in with them upon the heights, which over look the village of Bedford and Brocland [Brooklyn], the latter of which was defended by their works. The situation of the country was entirely after their own heart covered with woods and hedges, from which they gave us several very heavy fires. No soldiers ever behaved with greater spirit than ours did upon this occasion. An universal ardour was diffused throughout every rank of the army. The Light Infantry, who were first engaged, dashed in as fast as foot could carry. The scoundrels were driven into the wood and out of the wood, where they had supposed that we should never venture to engage them. They then endeavoured to escape to their works a little further to the left, they were there met by the Grenadiers who behaved with the most astonishing coolness and intrepidity and effectually secured that quarter. Two companies suffered by an unfortunate mistake which might have created a good deal of confusion. They took a large body of the rebels dressed in blue for the Hessians, and received a fire from them at a very small distance, before they discovered their mistake. The two captains – Neilson and Logan were killed upon the spot.

Quite upon the left, near the seaside, there was a marsh, across which several of them, I believe, effected their escape. The two brigades under General Grant secured however the greatest part of them, tho', by all accounts, they were at one time a little staggered with the heavy fire from the woods, with which they were everywhere surrounded. Thus repulsed on every quarter, they appear to have been an easy prey to the Hessians, who took and killed and drowned great numbers of them with the loss of six men only. It requires better troops than even the Virginia riflemen who make much opposition on one side when they know that their retreat is cut off on the other. It is impossible to ascertain the loss upon their side. 12 or 1500 prisoners, and above 2,000 killed and wounded is the present calculation, and by no means exaggerated. Our loss is very trifling, considering the nature of the country, 230 or 240 killed and wounded, many of them very slightly. You will see in the newspapers a more particular account of the unfortunate few, who are destined to be the sufferers even on the happiest days. I am exceedingly sorry that poor Sir Alexander Murray should be amongst the number.

My Company was very little concerned in the first and severest brush, and was so very fortunate in all the *tiraillerie*, to which we were exposed during the rest of the day, as to escape without the loss of a single man. I had only one killed (directly in a line with me by the by) at Flat Bush. I had however fatigue and danger enough to acquire a very competent relish for a good supper and a sound sleep, which were never better bestowed than that night upon the conquerors of Bedford. I have since had a most agreeable ride about the various scenes of various actions, which, indeed, are the most beautiful in themselves, that I remember to have seen almost in any country. I forgot to tell you (by the by, but it will do very well just now) that we have killed one general and taken four, amongst whom is a *soi disant* Lord Sterling, and a certain General Sullivan, who, tho' he has been rather outwitted in this affair, wears the honourable order of the Cordon Bleu and is reckoned among the ablest of their leaders. Of 1,800 riflemen too, only 400 have escaped . . .

They are now I believe abandoning New York, we shall

follow them I hope as fast as possible, and if they ever dare to face us again, the flow of spirits and conscious superiority of our men, with the contrary feeling under which they undoubtedly labour will speedily decide the fate of the 'Western Empire' . . .

Adieu, my dearest Betsy, God bless you, and give you all the happiness that peace affords, is the sincere wish of your affectionate brother.

⬥⬥⬥

8
BATTLE OF SAVANNAH, 1778

Lieutenant-Colonel Archibald Campbell
(71st Highlanders)

By late 1778 the war in the American colonies had reached something of a stalemate. The entry of France into the war the previous year had forced the British to redeploy troops to defend other British possessions around the world. Most of the British soldiers who remained in the American colonies were tied down, defending New York and Canada. This left few troops available to strike elsewhere. One of the few offensive moves they made was the sending of a force to Florida, to support British operations there. Lieutenant-Colonel Archibald Campbell who commanded this force of 3,000 men was reluctant to waste his opportunity for independent action, so instead of merely transporting his men to St Augustine in Florida, he landed them on the coast of Georgia, a few miles south of Savannah. He knew he was stretching his orders, and only a success would justify his actions.

He was extremely lucky. Savannah was defended by a force of militia, under the command of General Howe, and on 29 December

1778, Campbell attacked the American army drawn up in front of the city, and drove it from the field. He went on to capture the city. Britain now had a foothold in the southern colonies, and Savannah remained in British hands until the end of the war. Here is Campbell's own account of the battle.

The Rebel Army appeared to be forming in line about half a mile south of the town of Savannah, and every exertion was used on our part to bring up the troops and artillery from the shore. But, although such was the case, yet from a deficiency of flat boats, and the great distance of our transports from the landing place, it was midday before the whole of the Light Infantry; the 1st Battalion 71st Regiment; the Battalion of Welworth; half the Battalion of Wissenback; the New York Volunteers and four field pieces reached the summit of Sheridoe's Bluff. A company of the 2nd Battalion 71st Regiment, and the 1st Battalion of Delancy's having just landed, they were ordered to occupy the bluff, and cover the disembarkation of the remaining troops. The corps destined for action, marched from the right by files through a narrow path towards the enemy, in the following order:

The Light Infantry under Sir James Baird having thrown off their packs formed the Advance [Guard], and were directed to extend their flankers with every precaution to the right and left of the road. The New York Volunteers, under Lieutenant-Colonel Turnbull, followed the Light Infantry; the 1st Battalion 71st Regiment, under Major McPherson, with two 6-pounders followed the New York Volunteers; the Hessian Battalion of Welworth, under Lieutenant-Colonel Porbeck, with two 3-pounders, followed the 71st, and half of the Wissenback closed the rear. Each corps was ordered to flank itself on the march.

In this order the troops proceeded one mile before they fell in with the Great Road leading from Thunder Bolt Bluff to the town of Savannah. At the junction of this road, the Wissenback companies were left to secure our rear against any attempts of a surprize from the westward, and the rest of the army marched by platoons in column towards Savannah.

A thick impenetrable wooded swamp covered the left of the troops in their progress to the opening of Sir James Wright's Plantation; and the Light Infantry with the flankers of the line effectually secured our right. About two o'clock in the afternoon, the Light Infantry got within eight hundred yards of the Rebel Army and formed along a railed fence on Sir James Wright's Plantation; their right to the rice swamps, and their left to the Savannah Road. The enemy having opened four pieces of cannon upon the Light Infantry, Sir James Baird was directed not to expose his men unnecessarily, until the ground in front and the disposition of the enemy were accurately ascertained. The other corps were also directed to halt in the winding part of the road, concealed from the enemy's artillery.

Having climbed a tree of considerable height on the left of the Light Infantry, I was enabled to discover that the Rebel Army were formed on a level piece of ground, across the Savannah road, with their front towards the west, their right to Tatnel's Houses joining a thick wood, which stretched several miles thence to the southwards, and their left was nearly extended to the Rice Swamps on the south-east quarter. The Carolina Brigade appeared to form the right wing, and the Georgia Brigade the left wing. These brigades consisted of about 1,100 men, well clothed, armed and accoutred. One field piece was planted on the right and left of the Rebel Line, and two field pieces in the centre, with a breast-work in front. The Militia and some Light Horse appeared to range in the wood upon the enemy's right, where a body of men were employed in throwing up a small work in the stile of an half-moon.

About 100 yards in front, a marshy rivulet run almost parallel with the brigades, having opposite to the centre of the line a wooden bridge across, over which the Great Road to Savannah passed. This bridge was in flames, and two small divisions of Rebel marksmen were advanced to prevent the fire from being extinguished. Some riflemen were also thrown into the houses of Tatnel's Plantation, to impede our approach.

Savannah Fort, with 8 pieces of cannon, seemed to cover the left flank of the Rebel line; and the town of Savannah, round which there was an old entrenchment, lay in their rear. A confidential slave from Sir James Wright's Plantation informed me that the Carolina Brigade was commanded by Colonel Eugee, the Georgia Brigade by Colonel Elbert, and the whole under General Robert Howe, that the former troops came lately from South Carolina, and that a large reinforcement from thence were hourly expected. That 600 militia were posted on the Ogichee road near to the New Barracks, and after many questions I found that he could lead the troops without artillery through the swamp upon the enemy's right.

From this important intelligence I determined that the Light Infantry should make an impression upon the enemy's right; while I should in person attack the Rebel line in front with the 1st Battalion 71st, and the Hessian Regiment of Welworth.

The Enemy appeared to be extending their line to the left, as if they were apprehensive of an attack upon that quarter; and to increase this idea I directed the 1st Battalion of the 71st Regiment to move up into the rear of the Light Infantry, and drew the Light Infantry along their front towards the right, as if I meant to extend my flank considerably to the right. A happy fall of ground on the right of the Light Infantry concealed the extent of this movement, and gave it the appearance of collecting a body of men in that quarter. Under cover of this rising ground, Sir James Baird was ordered to convey the Light Infantry expeditiously into the rear, and to follow the confidential slave through the wooded swamps upon the enemy's right for the purpose of attacking the Militia, and the York Volunteers were ordered to support them.

An intelligent officer (Major Skelly) was stationed in a high tree, to watch the motions of the Light Infantry, with directions to wave his hat the instant that any firing should commence to the westward of the Rebel barracks, the top of which building was visible from his situation. During the march of the Light Infantry, our artillery were formed in a field on the left of the road, concealed from the enemy by a swell of ground in their front, to which I meant to run them up, on the signal being made to engage, because they could bear advantageously on the right of the Rebel line, or take any body of troops in flank, which the Rebels might detach through the wood on their right, for the purpose of opposing the Light Infantry.

The Regiment of Welworth was formed upon the left of the artillery, under cover of the same rising ground, and the enemy continued a loose cannonade, without any return on our part, until the concerted signal from Major Skelly was made; which announced that the Light Infantry had got to their ground. On this occasion the artillery and the line were ordered to move on briskly, which was executed with great alacrity and firmness.

Our cannon directed by the very able and gallant Lieutenant Wallace of the Royal Artillery, broke the enemy's line before we had reached the marshy rivulet, which the Highlanders crossed with an alacrity peculiar to themselves. But although not a moment was lost in advancing upon the Rebels, it was scarcely possible to come up with them. Their retreat was rapid beyond conception. On the 71st having reached the height on which the fort and town of Savannah stood, a body of the Rebel militia appeared on the outside of the fort, on which the right wing of the 71st was ordered to wheel to the right and meet them. This body consisted of the inhabitants of the town of Savannah, who grounded their arms and submitted. A company of Highlanders, who took possession of the fort, gave three cheers from the parapets, as a signal to Captain Parker that the fort had fallen into our hands; and the other companies of the right wing of the 71st Regiment immediately joined in the pursuit of the Rebel Army through the town of Savannah.

The Militia of Georgia posted on the Ogichee Road near the New Barracks were at this juncture routed, with the loss of their artillery, by the infantry under Sir James Baird; and he was in full pursuit after this body when the scattered remains of the Carolina and Georgia troops passed the plain in his front. Sir James with his usual gallantry dashed the Light Infantry on their flank, which cut off the greatest part of the Rebel brigades from the Augusta Road, and hurried them towards Yawmacraw, in the hope of making their escape through the swamps on that side of the town, to which the 71st Regiment had then happily approached.

Unfortunately however for these brigades, it was flood tide; and such only who could swim effected their escape. Among these, General Robert Howe, Colonels Eugee and Elbert were successful; but they left their horses in the mud. Thirty Rebels being killed in their attempt to escape by this swamp; the rest threw down their arms and called for quarter, which was immediately granted. Among these I soon recognized the countenance of that Irishman who but a few hours before had treated the Royal Army with such opprobrious language. He was a Major of the name of More, and appeared to be as servile and crestfallen as he was but a few hours before insolent and licentious.

In the heat of this pursuit after a flying enemy through the town of Savannah, it was greatly to the honour of the 71st Regiment that although many inhabitants appeared in the streets, and with arms in their hands, none suffered, but such as were seriously in the act of opposition. Eighty-three of the Rebels were killed on the plain; 38 officers of different distinctions, and 415 non-commissioned officers and privates were made prisoners. One Stand of Colours and 9 brass field pieces were taken in the field, 39 pieces of iron ordnance, 23 coehorns and mortars, 94 barrels of gunpowder, a quantity of arms and stores; the fort and shipping; in short the Capital of Georgia fell into my hands before it was dark; and without any loss on the side of the British, exclusive of what has already been mentioned; that of Captain Peter Campbell, a gallant officer in Skinner's Light Infantry, and 2 privates killed, 1 Subaltern, 1 Sergeant and 9 privates wounded.

CHAPTER 3

THE NAPOLEONIC WARS

In the summer of 1789 France exploded in bloody revolution. After decades of royal excess, high taxation, political scandals and social unrest, the people of France had reached breaking-point. In June a National Assembly seized political power from the king and his government, and a month later the mob stormed the Bastille. While the governments of Europe had no time for these dangerous revolutionary activities, the French Revolution had many supporters in Britain, who embraced the call for liberty and equality. Prominent supporters of the Scottish Enlightenment expressed Jacobin, pro-revolutionary sympathies, and even Robert Burns, in his last years, voiced his support for the revolutionary cause. After all, what could be more egalitarian than 'A Man's a Man for a' That?'

This all changed on 21 January 1793, with the execution of the French king. All but the most radical supporters of the revolution saw this as a step too far. Another factor in the collapse of Jacobin support was the excesses of the 'Terror'. Those who criticised the revolutionary government were liable to face the guillotine, and as the death-toll mounted, popular support for the revolution beyond the French borders fell away. The crowned heads of Europe were outraged by this brutal regicide, and overnight France found herself at war with most of the military powers of the continent. Britain herself declared war against France, and once again Scottish soldiers were called upon to march into battle against the French. It now became not only unfashionable to express republican sentiments in Britain but a dangerous act of sedition. Even Highland tenants who opposed their mass eviction to make way for sheep in Ross-shire were accused of harbouring radical sentiments. Loyalty to the Crown was now expected, or else.

Recruiting parties scoured the country, and by 1794 the existing Scottish regiments had been augmented by as many as eight new ones, while many older regiments now raised a second battalion. In 1793 Lord Seaforth raised the 78th Highlanders, which became the Seaforths, while Allan Cameron of Erracht's 79th Highlanders eventually became the Cameron Highlanders. Incensed by the Revolutionaries' treatment of his late wife's coffin, Sir Thomas Graham of Balgowan raised the 90th Foot (Perthshire Volunteers) in 1794, and went on to lead a British force to victory over the French at Barossa in 1811. Another regiment raised in 1794 was the 98th Highlanders, which was renumbered the 91st four years later. They were raised by Duncan Campbell of Lochnell, on behalf of the Duke of Argyll. Further north, in Aberdeenshire, the 100th Highlanders were raised by the Duke of Gordon, who offered a fiscal bounty and a kiss from the Duchess to any likely recruit. In 1798 they were renamed the 92nd Highlanders – the Gordons. Not to be outdone, the Earl of Sutherland – the man who called his Ross-shire tenants 'republicans' – had General Wemyss raise his own regiment, the 93rd Highlanders. Eight decades later in 1881, they would amalgamate with the 91st, to create the Argyll and Sutherland Highlanders.

Membership of a Scottish Fencible or Yeomanry regiment was seen as a public duty, and even Walter Scott donned the uniform of the Royal Edinburgh Light Dragoons, raised in 1797. Fortunately for the world of literature they were never called upon to serve outside the Lothians. Back in London, the government was delighted. Scotland became a prime recruiting ground, and consequently the stock of the Scottish soldier was raised. He was now a stalwart and loyal supporter of the British crown, the nemesis of dangerous foreign revolutionaries, and a colourful addition to the army. It has been estimated that between 1794 and 1806 no fewer than 70,000 Scots joined the army, the majority of whom – but not all – served in Scottish regiments. One of the first-hand accounts in this chapter is supplied by Private Joseph Donaldson, who actually served in an Irish rather than a Scottish regiment – the 94th Foot (Connaught Rangers).

The wearing of the kilt had been banned after the 1745 Jacobite Rebellion, but this prohibition was repealed in 1782, and many colonels insisted that their Highlanders looked the part and wore their full garb. This was not always popular with the rest of the army, who would have preferred a more 'civilised' dress. In 1804 the office of the army's Adjutant-General sounded out Allan Cameron of Erracht about his views on whether his 79th Highlanders might wear tartan trews rather than kilts. Cameron's reply was to the point, claiming that any 'Highland' colonel who advocated trews was:

adverse to that free congenial circulation of that pure wholesome air which has hitherto so peculiarly benefited the Highlander for activity and all the other necessary qualities of a soldier . . . besides, the exclusive advantage, when halted, of drenching his kilt in the next brook as well as washing his limbs and drying both, as it was by constant fanning, without injury to either, but on the contrary, feeling clean and comfortable.

As for trews, he added, 'the buffoon tartan pantaloon, with its fringed frippery, sticking wet and dirty to the skin, is not very easily pulled off, and less so to get on again in case of alarm or any other hurry'. He added that trews encouraged rheumatism and fever, and caused havoc in hot or cold climes. A Highlander wearing 'pure wholesome air' under his kilt sounded much better. In 1809 the heads of the army in Horse Guards ruled that Highland regiments should 'lay aside their distinguishing dress' in favour of trousers. Thanks to men like Allan Cameron, little attention was paid to this missive.

As for the regiments themselves, a quick glance at their list of battle honours will show that both the older Scottish regiments and these new Highland ones served in just about every theatre of war, and participated in virtually every battle the British army fought. While France remained the principal opponent, these Scottish soldiers also fought the Spanish (and later fought alongside them), as well as the Dutch, the Americans, and the several smaller nations who fielded contingents to fuel Napoleon Bonaparte's war machine. In 1793 few realised that, with only one short break, the war would drag on for almost 22 years.

Technically, of course, there were two wars. The French Revolutionary War began in 1792 (Britain was a late starter), and lasted until the signing of the Peace of Amiens in 1802. For most of its duration, the British were content to rely on the Royal Navy to carry the war to the enemy, although there was a brief and dismal period of campaigning in the Low Countries. The nursery rhyme about 'The Grand Old Duke of York' was coined as a lampoon, highlighting the ineptitude of one of Britain's principal generals at the time, when the army achieved nothing apart from losing soldiers through organisational incompetence and disease. A much better opportunity to strike the French came in 1798, when Bonaparte, styling himself 'the New Alexander', led an expeditionary force to Egypt. He never really understood the principles of seapower, and when Nelson destroyed the French fleet and its transports, he was stranded. While he slipped away to France, his Army of the Orient was left to rot in the heat. Our first account stems from this period, or rather the British campaign of 1801, designed to clear the remnants of the French army from the Middle East.

British soldiers served in several theatres of war. In India the Duke of Wellesley – later the Duke of Wellington – won a dramatic victory at Assaye (1802), where the 78th Highlanders distinguished themselves. Afterwards they were granted the right to bear the image of an elephant on their regimental colours, and were given a third colour by a grateful East India Company, whose fortune had been assured by Wellesley's triumph. Others served in the West Indies or Cape Town – unpopular postings due to the high probability of a lingering death through tropical disease. In 1807 a British expedition to the Rio de la Plata (now Argentina) ended in disaster, and the 71st Highlanders were captured *en masse*. Interestingly, one of our accounts tells what happened to these Scottish prisoners in South America, while the first-hand account that follows traces what happened to the same men when they returned to Europe.

After a brief period of peace, war resumed in 1805, after Bonaparte had crowned himself as the Emperor Napoleon. The Napoleonic Wars lasted from 1805 until 1814, ending when Napoleon abdicated. They then flared up again – a hundred-day venture which ended on the blood-soaked battlefield of Waterloo (1815). In 1805 the threat of a French invasion was real, at least until the destruction of the Franco-Spanish fleet

by Nelson at the Battle of Trafalgar. The French then turned
east, campaigning against Austria, Russia and Prussia, and
winning a string of victories across Europe.

However, in 1808 Napoleon made the biggest mistake of
his career. He sent an army into Spain, ostensibly to invade
Portugual, but really to oust the Spanish royal family, and place
his brother Joseph on the Spanish throne. The Spanish rose
up in revolt, and asked the British for help. Like most of the
rest of the army, the poor 71st Highlanders – just returned
from captivity – ended up fighting the French in Portugal and
Spain in what became known as the Peninsular War. The British
could never match the size of the French army. It wasn't until
1915 that the army would be considered large enough to
intervene directly in European affairs. Instead, Spain presented
the British with an opportunity to strike at the French in an
area where the bulk of French troops were tied down protecting
supply-lines, or campaigning elsewhere in Spain or Europe.

Two British commanders rose to prominence during the
war. Sir Arthur Wellesley won a small victory at Vimeiro
(1808), and liberated Portugal, only to have the fruits of victory
snatched away by 'political generals'. A second and much larger
force arrived in Portugal the following year, led by Sir John
Moore. However, it was forced to flee from a vastly superior
French force, retreating through the snows to the coast at
Corunna. Scottish soldiers were present in both campaigns,
and first-hand accounts from them have been included in this
collection.

The campaign really started in earnest later in 1809, when
Wellesley returned to Portugal, and led a British army to
victory at Talavera, despite the incompetence of his Spanish
allies. Other victories followed, at Bussaco (1810), Fuentes de
Orono (1811) and at the sieges of Ciudad Rodrigo and Badajoz

(1812). Our selection includes a detailed first-hand account from Talavera, and a grim recounting of the storming of Badajoz. After that the Spanish frontier lay open, and the victories continued – Salamanca (1812), Vittoria (1813) and Toulouse (1814). In effect the British and their allies had driven the French from Spain, and were marching northwards through the French rural heartland.

Napoleon abdicated, and was exiled to the island of Elba. Unfortunately he refused simply to fade away, and in March 1815 he returned to France, and reclaimed his throne. The Allies were forced to march against him again, and so in mid June 1815 Napoleon and the Duke of Wellington finally had the opportunity to fight each other on the battlefield of Waterloo. Our final first-hand account in this chapter is (appropriately enough) supplied by a soldier from the long-suffering 71st Highlanders – a tale of more suffering, of bloodshed and, ultimately, of triumph. After Waterloo the stock of the Scottish soldier had never been higher. The Scots were seen – rightly or not – as elite troops, the people to call upon when you really needed them. In the decades which followed they would be needed in every corner of the globe.

———⋙◆⋘———

1

BATTLE OF ALEXANDRIA, 1801

Lieutenant George Sutherland (92nd Highlanders)

One of the strangest episodes of the period was the French decision to invade Egypt. It flew in the face of military logic, and its political and cultural objectives were poorly defined and wildly ambitious.

Bonaparte's Egyptian expedition of 1798–1801 began in a blaze of publicity and good intent, and fizzled out in ignominious defeat. After Nelson's victory over the French fleet at the Battle of the Nile (1798), Bonaparte's Army of the Orient was stranded in Egypt. Although he went on to conquer the country, defeating the Mameluke Turks, further success in Palestine was thwarted by the British, who defiantly held the port of Acre, blocking the French advance into Syria. As casualties mounted and disease began taking its toll, Bonaparte was forced to retreat back to Cairo. The General returned to France by frigate in August 1798, leaving his stranded army to fend for itself. Then, in early 1801, a British army led by General Sir Ralph Abercrombie landed in Egypt and brought General Menou's French army to battle, first at Mandora on 13 March, and then at Alexandria just over a week later, on 21 March. Although Abercrombie was mortally wounded, he won a spectacular victory, forcing Menou to surrender his army, in return for a passage home. Lieutenant Sutherland's diary recorded the events which led up to this climactic battle.

13 March 1801

The army got under arms at 4 o'clock this morning, without knapsacks, which are left behind, and marched exactly at 5 [a.m.] in two lines, moving from the left and right to the natural order of battle, which was

First Line: General Coote (centre) and General Craddock (left).

Second Line: Brig. Gen. Doyles (right) and the dismounted part of the 12th Dragoons, General Stewart (centre) and Lord Cavan (left).

The 90th Regiment formed the Advance Guard of the First Line, and the 92nd [Highlanders], that of the Second Line. Two howitzers from General Coote joined General Craddock, and two guns from General Stewart's Brigade joined Lord Cavan. The rest of the artillery marched with its respective brigades. The mounted part of General Finch's brigade marched between the two lines, following the Advanced Guards, and each regiment composing the Advanced Guard had an officer of cavalry and 30 men attached to it.

As soon as General Craddock perceived he had advanced so far as to have gained the enemy's right flank, he formed, and commenced the attack. Lord Cavan formed at the same time, and supported him, and the rest of the army formed in succession as it came up.

On the march we were joined by a body of 500 marines under Colonel Smith. General Craddock attacked the enemy's right with great spirit, who, instead of waiting for him on their heights, descended to the plain with their cavalry, and charged the 90th Regiment, which was the advance, but were repulsed with loss. Our brigade, having formed line, advanced to his support, and received a warm and galling fire of shot and shells before we could get within musquetry of them. A heavy musquetry and a terrible carronade from the whole line, intermixed with loud 'Huzzas' took place.

About 100 yards [on] we discovered the French infantry which the smoke of the fire from General Craddock's Brigade had hitherto concealed from our view, regularly drawn up, and maintaining a constant discharge from firearms and artillery upon us. We advanced rapidly on them. The firing was now most heavy and tremendous, and numbers were dropping on all sides. I was here wounded, and obliged to quit the line. The ball passed through my thigh, and lodged in the back of it. I was supported to a small bush, under which with many others I lay, to protect me from the scattered shot of the enemy, which was flying in all directions. I understood that the enemy had abandoned his ground, and put himself under cover of the heights which defend Alexandria.

The loss of our army was 1,500 killed, wounded and missing. The enemy's was about 600. We had 3 officers wounded, 6 men killed and 56 wounded, many of whom died shortly after of their wounds. From the immense quantity of cannon shot fired, more of the wounded men were shockingly mutilated. One unfortunate circumstance attended our advancing – our guns never could keep up with the line, but fell in the rear, having no horses to drag them. Their occasional fire as they came up only seemed to draw on us a powerful and constant discharge from the enemy.

On the 18th March Aboukir Castle surrendered by capitulation, after a cannonade of two days. 145 prisoners were taken in it. One of our batteries shot away its flagstaff, which killed 7 men as it fell.

On the 19th [March] a party of cavalry approached our outposts, and the field officer on duty ordered a detachment of our dragoons without a proper support to attack them. Their cavalry retired hastily, and ours pursued them to a small height, when a concealed support of infantry attacked our people, killed or took near 30, and wounded a great many. The Commander-in-Chief in orders found much fault with the officer who ordered our cavalry out, without having them properly supported, or acquainting headquarters of the circumstance.

A Colonel of the Guards – Bryce – [was] killed going the rounds. He had mistaken his way. A Turkish Admiral with 11 sail, with troops arrived. The army camp equipage landed, and employed throwing up works to defend its position.

On the morning of the 21st, before daylight, the enemy attacked with all their force. Of this attack we had received some information by deserters, and therefore we prepared for it. Their advanced party got close to our left before they were discovered, and took possession of a redoubt in which we had a party at work. There they only made a feint, and attacked the right with their collected force, and the greater rigour. General Lanuse led the attack there. Our troops had been under arms half an hour before and after a long, severe struggle in which horse and foot were mixed together among the tents. The French were drove from the posts they had gained, while our musquetry and cannon in their retreat strewed the sands with their dead and wounded. This defeat was signal and complete. 1,100 lay dead on the right, near some old ruins, and their loss in all did not come under 4,000. The loss of the British was also great – nearly 1,000. Among the wounded, our Commander-in-Chief Sir Ralph, to the regret of the army stands first, and General Moore, Sir Philip Smith and General Oakes.

Lieutenant Sutherland soon recovered from the wound he received at Mandora, and after the surrender of the French at Rosetta in late April he took part in a voyage up the River Nile. Before we leave him, it is worth hearing what the young Scottish gentleman had to say about Rosetta, and the strange people and customs he encountered:

On entering this famous river I felt the pride of being in a place of which our travellers talk with so much enthusiasm but excepting this idea, the river has nothing very superior in its appearance to any in our own country. [I] passed some villages delightfully situated, and surrounded with wood; but the instant they are entered all their beauty disappears, and little else than wretched ruins, filth and a set of miserable inhabitants are seen.

The city of Rosetta, which I walked a good deal in, partakes entirely of this description. It has a fine and elegant appearance, is built upon the river, has good gardens and rivers built on the Turkish stile around it, but in itself it is dirty and ruinous. The narrow streets are full of sand and stench, and involved in a cloud of smoke and tobacco, threatening the stranger both in his sight and breathing, and making him rejoice to get out of the air of it.

Here I saw the funeral of a Turkish soldier who had just been drowned. The body was carefully washed with soap and water, a custom which is in this country as old as the days of Homer, and carried to burial, much in the Maltese fashion, tho' without its monks and friars, the attendants making a loud lamentation over him.

What we felt a pride in regarding as beautiful objects were innumerable boats and jerms plying in the Nile, having the British colours flying triumphantly on them.

The women we saw at Rosetta are ragged and filthy to a degree of absolute abhorrence. They, however, had their faces carefully covered with a dirty veil, leaving the eyes only visible, and seemed to have less concern at our seeing other parts which the generality of the fair sex are most careful to conceal.

<hr />

2
BUENOS AIRES, 1806

Corporal Balfour Kennach (71st Highlanders)

In October 1804 Spain allied herself with France and declared war against Great Britain. Exactly a year later Lord Nelson defeated the joint Franco-Spanish fleet at the Battle of Trafalgar. Having gained mastery of the seas, Britain looked for ways to exploit the advantage of seapower. One obvious stratagem was to attack Spain's isolated colonies of South America. In June 1806 a force of 1,600 British soldiers landed on the coast of Rio de la Plata (now Argentina), and seized Buenos Aires, the heavily fortified capital of the Spanish colony. The 71st Highlanders formed part of this expedition. The rich South American city was plundered, and the loot sent back to Britain. However, in August the Spanish counterattacked, and soon recaptured the city. Corporal Kennach therefore found himself the prisoner of the Spanish colonists. His account of his treatment at their hands is astonishing, particularly his account of Spanish attempts to convert him to the Roman Catholic faith. As the 27-year-old Kennach was a staunch Presbyterian from Ruthven near Forfar, the Spanish priest had his work cut out.

The capture of Buenos Ayres was an easy affair; the defence by the British before redelivering it was a different thing. We sustained considerable loss, and the conduct of the Spaniards towards the dead was truly barbarous. Not content with stripping the dead naked, with fiendish delight they cut their throats, mangled their bodies in every form, cut the ears from their heads and wore them in their hats as trophies.

Two days previous to our surrendering the place we were ordered to lodge our knapsacks in the Castle, in order to lighten us as well as for their better security. Some days after the surrender of the place our packs were delivered to us, plundered of their contents by the enemy, no useful article of any description being left. After remaining in prison two or three weeks we were ordered to be distributed in small parties through the different towns in the Province of La Plata. It fell to the lot of the party I belonged to, to go to Saint Juan, a town on the frontier of La Plata, situated at the foot of the

Andes and distant from Buenos Ayres [by] one thousand miles.

On this long and painful march I felt nothing but misery. My life was a burden to me. Having nothing to subsist on but beef, our living was wretched in the extreme. We had no cooking utensils, no knives, no salt; our walking staff served as a spit, and on the pampas plains, where neither wood nor water can be found, the dried excrements of the animals served for fuel; there were neither towns nor villages, not a single house. We had nothing to shelter us from the inclemency of the weather but the canopy of heaven. How disagreeable the word 'prison' sounds in the ear of a soldier. Captivity in a palace is but misery when compared with sweet liberty.

How often did I think of my native country on those trying occasions, and would cheerfully have given the gold mines of Mexico to be free. Although our course of living was filthy, we were perfectly healthy, none having died, nor any sick. When a person is exposed to misery such as I have described, it is easy to conceive the state the body must be in. We had nothing to wear and were only midway upon our journey, still five hundred miles to travel, and having not once changed our body clothes they were almost worn out. My shoes had long fallen to pieces, and what remained of my red coat was turned parson grey; nothing of the trousers remained but the waistband; of the shirt nothing but the seams; and the plumed bonnet, the Highlander's pride, with all its gaudy ornaments totally disappeared on the barren plains of La Plata.

After a period of twenty-eight days' travel we arrived at Saint Juan, the place of our destination, and were once more committed to prison. Our situation for some time was truly miserable, nothing but the bare walls of a ruined convent, damp floors without bedding or any other comfort. Seven weeks had now elapsed since I was a prisoner, during which time I had not shaved; and with some prospect of being permitted to rest, at least for a time, I pulled up courage, the spirits rose, and I commenced cleaning. It absolutely became necessary to extirpate a certain bosom enemy. I accordingly commenced shaving, washing and scrubbing, and in a short time I got rid of my troublesome neighbours.

About this time the Governor of the place granted permission to any of the inhabitants, who had a mind, to select one or two of the prisoners if they were agreeable, to reside with them. The gentleman, an old Spaniard, and his lady, a Creole, selected me – for what cause I knew not – but the effect proved good. They carried me along with them to their hospitable home, for so it proved to me. They had no family and were both very delicate, and, as far as I could learn, had few relatives. Their establishment consisted of three slaves – one man and two women who were very kindly treated.

I had now changed from a prison to a comfortable home, but before being permitted to sit at table it became necessary to instruct me in the principles of Christianity. Accordingly a Padre, their confessor, attended the house daily for some time. He commenced with telling me that the British were fine-looking people, good soldiers and seamen, but withal they were a nation of heretics, and enemies of Christianity. He then pointed out the beauties of the Roman Catholic religion, and after enumerating a host of saints, concluded by telling me that none would be eternally saved but Roman Catholics.

I was now instructed to say the Lord's Prayer, Creed, Av [Ave] Maria, and also to make the sign of the Cross. I thought there was no harm in learning the Lord's Prayer and Creed in the Spanish language. After I learned these different Articles which I soon did, I was declared fit to be baptised and enrolled amongst Spanish Christians. I had by this time by study and practice learned a considerable part of their language. I was now to be baptised, take an oath of allegiance, become a Catholic, and a subject of Spain. I told them I had taken the oath of allegiance to the King of Great Britain, that I was bound to maintain his laws and nothing would induce me to betray my country. I had now lived six months with this excellent family, and had everything the heart could wish, and had acquired some knowledge of the customs and manners of the people.

By this time the Governor of the place had received intelligence of the defeat of the British in an attempt to retake Buenos Ayres, and, at the same time, agreeably to the articles of capitulation, to send home the British prisoners as soon as possible. This brought matters to the point. The domestic circle was formed, the old Padre sat President. I was told the attempt to retake Buenos Ayres by the British had failed, how their General and his army were made prisoners, and how foolish it was for me to attempt to run the chance of a long and dangerous passage to Britain when I had it in my power to live in peace and comfort.

I thanked them kindly, and told them I had sworn allegiance to our sovereign, and that it was out of my power to betray my country. I now parted with my kind benefactor, Don Pedro Bertaren and his amiable lady Maria Garcia, whom I sincerely loved; now after a lapse of 42 years I still remember them with a grateful heart. We were assembled, and commenced our long and dreary march across Lapampa, nothing extra occurring, and after a march of 28 days safely arrived in Buenos Ayres, dropped down La Plata in lighters, and went aboard British transports in Mote Vido [Montevideo] Harbour, set sail for Old England, the land of liberty, and after a quick and agreeable passage cast anchor in the Cove of Cork.

We landed just in time to gather fresh laurels in the Peninsula.

※

3

BATTLE OF VIMEIRO, 1808

Ensign William Gavin (71st Highlanders)

After being released from captivity in South America, the 71st Highlanders were shipped to Ireland, where they were re-equipped, allowed to let their hair down, and then sent back to war. They formed part of Sir Arthur Wellesley's force sent to drive the French from Portugal. At the end of July Wellesley landed his troop at Mondego Bay, then defeated a small French advanced guard at Roliça on 17 August. The 71st played no real part in the battle, but four days later the British encountered the rest of the French army at Vimeiro, a force of 14,000 men commanded by the experienced General Junot. Not only did the 71st perform well, but the regiment created the first hero of the Peninsular War – Piper Clarke, who was wounded, but kept playing the regimental march on his bagpipes. Here, the diary of Ensign Gavin of the 71st Highlanders tells us what happened when the regiment returned from South America, and recounts the events before and after the first real battle of the Peninsular War.

We were put on board the *Nelly*, our headquarter ship, commanded by Lieutenant-Colonel Campbell. The evening that we escaped from the *Princessa* we saw her go to the bottom at about four miles off, so that if providence had not been pleased to abate the wind, nearly 300 souls would have met a watery grave. Nothing particular happened on the passage, but the death of Lieutenant Thomas Murray, who was suffocated in his berth by leaving his leather stock [his neck protector] on. He was a brave soldier and a worthy young man.

We saw no land during the passage, and arrived at the Cove of Cork on the 27th December, after a passage of nearly 17 weeks. In the latter part of it we suffered greatly for want of fresh water. The officers were on the allowance of a pint a day, and the men were obliged to suck this quantity through the touch hole of a musquet barrel from the scuttle butt.

When we landed we marched to Middleton Barracks, where the men received a year's pay, reserving sufficient to purchase necessaries, etc. But, such a scene of drunkenness for eight days was never seen in the British or any other army. The barrack gates were closed only when drays from Cork were admitted with barrels of porter and hogsheads of whisky, and in some rooms they were actually ankle-deep in liquor.

After some time we marched to the new barracks of Cork, and were completely re-equipped with arms and accoutrements, clothing, etc., which was sent from London by Colonel Pack, who joined us here. We were also presented with a new pair of colours [the previous colours having been captured by the Spanish at Buenos Aires] by Sir John Floyd.

June 27th 1808:

Embarked at the Cove of Cork on an expedition under the command of Sir Arthur Wellesley, consisting of nine regiments of infantry. We were brigaded under the command of Major-General Ferguson – the 40th, 36th and 71st. We remained at anchor until the 12th July, and arrived off Mondego Bay on the 29th July, where we cast anchor.

The writer was sent by Colonel Pack on shore to purchase mules. He embarked in a country boat with three Portuguese. The surf is so great in this bay that the natives can, [only] with difficulty, weather it. Wave succeeded wave, mountains high, and when it approaches the boat the crew abandon their oars and threw themselves flat in the bottom of the boat, invoking the Blessed Virgin and all the Saints in the calendar. After a complete ducking and a terrible fright, we got on shore, but found all [the] horses and mules taken off by the French army.

The army disembarked from 1st August to 5th. We received four days' rations of beef and biscuits, and marched over a very sandy country. Several of our men died of thirst, and were buried where they fell.

August 14th:
Bivouacked at the village of Acobaça.

15th:
Attacked the enemy at the village of Brilos, and repulsed them.

17th:
The French, under the command of General Laborde [Delaborde] was attacked at the village of Roleia [Rolica], and were routed by the British army.

18th:
Marched to Lourinha and to Vimeira [Vimeiro].

On the 19th [we] halted, and were joined by Brigadier General Anstruther's brigade of 2,400 men, landed at Maceira on the 19th. The writer was sent by Colonel Pack to receive camp equipage at Maceira on the 20th. On this night Sir

Harry Burrard arrived and took command of the army, but approving of Sir Arthur Wellesley's arrangement, did not assume it till after the battle next day.

21st: Under arms at daylight, and at about 8 o'clock advanced towards the enemy, who were posted on the heights opposite us. Our brigade was attacked by the French cavalry, which we charged and repulsed, taking six pieces of cannon. They made an effort to retake their artillery, but were routed by the 71st, supported by the 82nd, taking the French General [Brenier] prisoner, by Corporal John McKay, 71st Regiment. When sent to the rear he offered McKay his gold watch, which he refused, and escorted him safely to the rear.

Next day the General, at an interview with Sir Arthur Wellesley, reported the high spirit of the corporal. His Excellency was pleased in that night's orders to appoint him Assistant Provost Marshal. He afterwards got a commission in a West India Regiment, where he died, and a gold medal from the Highland Society was given to him.

The conduct of our Pipe Major [George Clarke] was worthy of the name of a Highlandman. In the charge where General Brenier was taken, he received a musquet ball in the leg. Being unable to advance, he sat down on a rock and played the charge on the pipes, to encourage his brave companions. He also got a gold medal from the Highland Society, and was held in high esteem in London, after being discharged from the 71st Regiment.

Officers killed, wounded and missing of the 71st Regiment at the Battle of Vimiera [Vimeiro] on the 21st August 1808: Captain Jones, slightly; Lieutenant J.D. Pratt, severely; Lieutenant William Hartley, severely; Lieutenant Ralph Dudgeon, severely; Lieutenant A.S. McIntyre, slightly; Ensign William Campbell, slightly; Acting Adjutant McAlpin, severely.

Mr McAlpin was not wounded by the enemy, but fell from a rock on which he was standing.

22nd:
Advanced to Torres Vedras, where a line of demarcation was drawn, and the town was to be neutral ground during the negotiations carrying on at Cintra.

September 2nd:
Marched towards Lisbon.

⋙——◆——⋘

4

RETREAT TO CORUNNA, 1809

Private John Maclerlan (91st Highlanders)

In late October 1809, a small British army led by General Sir John Moore marched across the Portuguese border into Spain, to campaign alongside his Spanish allies. Unfortunately, by mid December, when he reached Sahagun, some 350 miles from Lisbon, he learned that the Spanish army had been defeated, and their troops scattered. Worse, the Emperor Napoleon was approaching with a vastly superior force, which included the corps of Marshals Soult and Ney. After a cavalry skirmish with Soult's advance guard on Christmas Day, General Moore decided to retreat to the coast. Lisbon was too far, so he opted for the port of Corunna (La Coruña) in the north-west corner of Galicia. The retreat that followed became a grim march through the snow-covered mountains, a ten-day ordeal where discipline was lost, and stragglers were left in the snow, to die or be captured. On reaching Corunna the army turned and defeated the French, but General Moore died at the moment of victory. However, his triumph was that the army escaped, to fight again.

Private Maclerlan had a worse ordeal than most, as he was captured during the retreat. Although his diary was damaged and parts lost, his account conveys the horror of those ten days.

Being the rear brigade to cover the retreat, we remained in Stargo [Astorga] till the rest of the army marched off. Our brigade was commissioned to move [on] the 31st, and that evening halted at a small village 4 or 5 leagues from Stargo. About 11 o'clock at night we received a few biscuits and a glass of rum, and at 1 o'clock in the morning [1st January 1809] we moved on towards Benbriley [Bembibre], where we arrived about 10 o'clock in the morning. Where we staid that day and night, and next morning marched off, the enemy being then within a league of us. We arrived at Kirhavilla [Cacehelos] in the evening, where we took up our quarters for the night, and next morning a Brigade drumhead [improvised] Court Martial was ordered to assemble on the Alarm Guard, where the brigade was formed.

Several were found guilty of pilfering from the Spaniards. Two that was more unfortunate was sentenced to death by a General Court Martial. General Lord Paget, who commanded the Rear Division, ordered them to be brought out, which accordingly was done. With ropes about their necks and brought to a tree that was within the circle of our Brigade, who had two triangles at the same time at work [other culprits were being flogged]. The sentence of those two men were read, and in the middle of this hurly-burly we was in, word was brought the General by one of his Aide Camps that the enemy was approaching. In a few minutes we could discern them coming in two large columns, at the distance of about a league.

The General had answer that he was determined to put the law in force upon these two men, if they [the enemy] were within 500 yards. However, he cryed out to the whole Brigade if they would come surety for their behaviour in future, that they would be forgiven. The whole Brigade as one man answered that they would, upon which they were liberated. At the same time another soldier was shot at Villafranca, about a league further on, for making free with a piece of bacon and some wine that he found in some of the Spaniards' houses.

The enemy advancing close to Kirhavilla in the evening, our Brigade with the 95th Rifle Regiment skirmishing in front, was drawn up to stop their progress as much as possible, in order to give time to the rest of the army and baggage, to move forward. But they soon dislodged us from the position we had taken, after killing a few of the 95th, and taking some prisoners. We was ordered to move on to Villafranca which we passed about 8 o'clock in the evening. The weather being so cold and the frost and snow so great in these mountains of Galica [Galicia], and us being without any provision for some days, that we was ready to drop down with real fatigue and hunger.

After we had passed Villafranca, five or six men of a company was ordered to turn back to Villafranca for some pork and flour, which they were to receive from the General Stores, where there was plenty, altho we stood so much in need of it. We hardly entered the town, when we found Villafranca swarming with Frenchmen, who already had several hundreds of men prisoners. But thro' the darkness of the night we got out of town unobserved, after we had filled our haversacks. We had not travelled very far that night before we overtook some hundreds of the army who lagged behind with real fatigue, the severity of the weather and hunger together. Some [were] laying down here and here on the roadside, a great number of which never rose again.

Our party then began to disperse, every man shifting for himself the best way he could, and of course the strongest and healthiest man had the better chance. I travelled on with some others till about four o'clock in the morning, always expecting we would overtake the Brigade. We came to a small village and went in, expecting to get a fire to warm ourselves, but was disappointed. During this days march, we was overtaken by plenty of the army, and at the same time, as many, if not more, was lagging behind. We passed several Waggons which was broken down and put across in the road to see and prevent their cavalry moving on so fast. Our Army kept all day shooting horses belonging to the Dragoons who was not able to keep up.

Some horses and oxen was in three or four carts which was loaded with money, Spanish Dollars and Doubloons, packed up in Casks. They could not get on with them, so that they were under the necessity of breaking them up and throwing them over the roadside; down a steep hill amongst some would [wood]. Whilst this was transacting an officer stood with a pistol loaded in each hand to shoot any soldier that should attempt putting forth his hand to take any of it. However before they got them all destroyed the enemy came in for a share of the booty.

At this point Private Maclerlan's diary was torn, and the text becomes disjointed. The section evidently recounted how he and his remaining companions were overtaken and captured by the French.

They made us all break our firelocks [muskets] and throw away our ammunition. They collected about three or four hundred of us together, turned us out of all houses, into a field that was adjoining the village, where they planted sentinels over us. I had a good greatcoat on me, and one of the soldiers who thought he had a better right to it than me took it from me. However, I was content with this having a good new blanket in my pack. We lay in this miserable state in the cold snow all night, and next morning marched for Villa Franca, and we could hardly get going forward, with cavalry and infantry, and with all sorts of artillery coming on the road.

The Horse Soldiers is very well, but when we meet the infantry they began to plunder the knapsacks and everything else the unfortunate prisoners had, even the very shoes on their feet. After I had gone about a league a soldier demanded my pack, which he opened, and took from thence a case of razors, after which he returned me my pack, but shortly afterwards it was taken from me, a shirt and a pair of shoes taken out of it, upon which I moved on, leaving my knapsack behind me, so that I would be no more stopped on its account.

But however I had not gone far before a barefooted soldier desired to look at the shoes I had on my feet, but he found they were too small for him and left me, but another came up to me and found that they would answer him, upon which he desired me to strip them off. This I refused, but found an expedient for that, having knocked me down with the butt-end of his firelock, and I was glad to get quit of them for fear he would blow out my brains. Thus I was left in a dreadful situation, barefoot, amongst frosts and snows without any covering but my blanket, which I expected every moment would also be taken from me.

Passing a park of artillery, one of the gunners came after me and cryed to me to stop. I thought he was going to give me something, but instead of that he cast his eye upon my blanket which I had wrapped round me, pulled it off my back. I resisted as much as I could, but all in vain. I was now left, destitute indeed, an old reid coat, a pair of linen trousers, an old waistcoat and a rag of a shirt that I was afraid to wash for fear it should tumble to pieces was all I had left me. What made my case worse [were] the thoughts of a long march before me. I arrived at the convent and found Miller and the rest. In the convent lay a great number of Spaniards and English who had died, and it was very lucky for us that it was the winter season, otherwise all these corpses must have been in a putrefied state, which might have proved fatal to the whole of us.

⫸◆⫷

5

BATTLE OF TALAVERA, 1809

Corporal Daniel Nicol (92nd Highlanders)

In April 1809 Sir Arthur Wellesley landed near Lisbon at the head of 23,000 British troops. He defeated Marshal Soult's army on the Douro River near Oporto, then turned south to face Marshal Victor, who retreated towards Madrid. After joining forces with General Cuesta's Spanish army, Wellesley marched in pursuit, following the line of the River Tagus until he encountered Victor's French army near Talavera, some 70 miles west of the Spanish capital. By this time Victor had been reinforced, and the Emperor Napoleon's brother, King Joseph, commanded the combined French army. The Battle of Talavera, on 28 July 1809, was a singularly hard-fought engagement. Wellesley's Spanish allies proved virtually useless, and it was left to the British infantry to halt the French, who launched repeated attacks on the British position, the first of which was the surprise night-time assault on the Medellin hill, described by Corporal Nicol. He was a good observer, and as the 92nd spent much of the engagement on high ground, Nicol was able to chart the course of the battle – a singular achievement for a staff officer, let alone a man in the ranks of a regiment.

On the 27th the Spaniards began to arrive. They took up the ground on our right, in two lines, and entrenched themselves, and made batteries on the high road leading from the town to the bridge over the Alberche, and planted their heavy cannon in front of a chapel on our right. We expected a general attack, and our line was drawn between the river and the hill, a distance of about two or three miles. General Sherbrooke was called in from Casalogas, and General MacKenzie was stationed with a strong advanced post at some houses in a wood. I was sent with a working party to raise a battery on some rising ground among the olive trees.

About 2 o'clock the French arrived at the side of the Alberche, and opened fire on our advanced guard, fording the river at the same moment. We kept them in check; but from where I was I could see that our people were suffering much, and retiring to take up their position in the line. The working parties were ordered to stand to their arms, as the shot from the French was coming thick amongst us. We were then ordered to join our regiments as quickly as possible, and we joined our battalion on the side of the hill, to the left of the line.

A dreadful cannonade commenced on the British right, and the enemy attacked the Spaniards with their cavalry, thinking to break their lines and get into the town; But the Dons repulsed them manfully. The firing ceased on the right after dark, when the French had made a charge of infantry, without success. From the place where we stood we could see every movement on the plain.

At this time our brigade got a biscuit each man served out, when a cry was heard – 'The hill! The hill!' General Stewart called out for the detachments to make for the top of the hill, for he was certain that no regiment could be there so soon as we. Off we ran in the dark, and very dark it was; But the French got onto the top of the hill before us, and some of them ran through the battalion, calling out 'Espanioles! Espanioles!', and others calling 'Allemands'. Our officers cried out 'Don't fire on the Spaniards!' I and many others jumped to the side to let them pass down the hill, where they were either killed or taken prisoners in our rear.

I saw those on the top of the hill by the flashes of their pieces. Then we knew who they were, but I and many more of our company were actually in rear of the French for a few moments, and did not know it until they seized some of our men by the collar, and were dragging them away as prisoners. This opened our eyes, and bayonets and the butts of our firelocks were used with great dexterity – a dreadful mêlée.

The 29th Regiment came to our assistance, charged, and kept possession of the top of the hill. This regiment lost a number of men on the highest point of the hill, where the French had a momentary possession, and affairs hung in the balance ere it was decided who should have this key of the position. The enemy tried it a second time, coming round the side of the hill; But, as we now knew who they were, to our cost, a well-directed running fire, with a charge, sent them into the valley below, their drums beating a retreat.

General Hill's division arrived, with two guns, after the affair was over, and, I was told, got credit for this hard contest, though really they were dragging their guns about the foot of the hill, and did not fire a shot here until next morning. The firing ceased by 11 o'clock. All was silent on the plain long before. Our brigade got into formation as well as it could, with our left to the top joining General Hill. A deep ravine or hollow was to our front. Some other regiments came on the side of the hill, and formed a second line, and some guns were posted to the right of our brigade. I believe it was only after nightfall that our Generals found the importance of this post.

We got ammunition served out, and had time to count our loss, which was very great. Vedettes were placed a few yards in front, and we sat down in the ranks and watched every movement of the enemy. About one in the morning we could hear and see the French moving their artillery on the other side of the hollow, about 200 yards from us. Some firing commenced. It ran from the left to the right, for we could see every flash in the plain below us. Order was restored, and a deathlike silence reigned among us. The French kindled great fires in rear of their lines. I had a sound sleep for a short time, being one of those who can sleep half an hour or 20 minutes, and feel myself much refreshed.

When daylight appeared each army gazed on the other, and viewed the operations of the last night. Round the top of the hill many a red coat lay dead. About 30 yards on the other side the red and blue lay mixed, and a few yards further, and down to the valley below, they were all blue. The French fired one gun from the centre as a signal for all their line to commence action. Their guns began to pour grapeshot and shell into our lines, and three columns came bearing for the hill.

We were ordered to lie close to the ground, but when the enemy were about 50 yards from us we started to our feet, and poured in a volley. We then charged with the bayonet, and ran them down into the valley, cheering and firing upon them, for they proved better runners than we. They retreated across the valley to our left, leaving many killed and wounded behind them. We took some ammunition wagons, from one of which I took 3 pound loaves of bread. This was a noble prize where there were so many hungry men.

We were ordered to pursue no further than the rising ground at the foot of the left side of the hill. They crossed the valley and formed on some rocks on the other side, and threatened to turn [to] our left. Two Spanish battalions were sent over to them, which kept them in check, and they kept up a popping fire at each other most of the day. Our guns on the top and side of the hill kept blazing away upon the French guns and columns within reach.

After the march was over here, we heard some heavy firing down in the plain, among the olive grounds, but from where we now were we could not see what was going on. The 48th Regiment and some others were withdrawn from the hill to the plain. About 11 o'clock the enemy, being baffled in all its attacks upon our lines, withdrew his troops a little. As we did not move to follow them they deliberately piled arms and set about kindling fires, and cooking their victuals. A brook ran through the plain. To it both armies went for water as if truce was between us, looking at each other, drinking, and wiping the sweat from their brows, laughing and nodding heads to each other. All thoughts of fighting for the time were forgotten. Water was in great demand by our brigade, and parties were sent off for it. Others were sent to bury the dead that lay thick about us, and to assist the wounded to the rear.

Our brigade took up the ground it had quitted in the morning, and the 48th and 66th Regiments took up our ground, for we expected the enemy to make another rush for the top of the hill, and in this we were not deceived. About 1 o'clock the French army was in motion again, and three divisions were on their way to the hill, one on each side, the other to the front. Our guns on the hill opened upon them, but did little execution to what we expected. It was said, 'They are German Legion artillery.' The enemy's right division got under shelter of a large house in the valley, where they stood in close column, and sent forward their sharpshooters to within a few yards of us.

At this time the British cavalry entered the valley to check the French right. The 23rd and German hussars formed across the valley, and, supported by the heavy dragoons, charged the right division of the enemy. This charge, though nobly executed, had not the effect intended. The French opened up a steady fire upon them, killed and wounded and took many of the 23rd Light Dragoons prisoners, and forced the remainder back on General Anson's heavy brigade, which kept this division of the enemy from advancing any further.

We stood looking at the fray for a few moments, until General Stewart's brigade was ordered to advance to the top of the hollow, when all the others were ordered to lie close to the ground. The French had taken up a position with their heads above the rise, and were doing much mischief. We sustained a heavy fire from the enemy's guns on the other side of the hollow. They were making lanes through us, and their musketry attacked us from our front and right, but they remained [on] the heights on the other side. As we were lower than they, they punished us severely. All the other troops were brought into action, and the battle raged along the lines from right to left, and nothing could be heard but the long roll of musketry, and the thunder of the artillery intermixed. Captain MacPherson of the 35th Regiment, who commanded our company this day, was shot down, and my right file was taken off by a cannon-shot. William Bowie and John Shewan were killed on my left, and Adam Much lay in the rear, wounded.

About 4 o'clock I was struck by a musket ball, which grazed my left knee and passed through my right leg about 2" below the cap of the knee. I finished my loading, and fired my last shot at the man who wounded me, for I could plainly see him on the height, a few yards to my front. I think I should have known him if he had come in my way afterwards. I called out to Sergeant John Gordon that I was wounded. He was the only non-commissioned officer belonging to the regiment I saw at his post. I made along the side of the hill as well as I could, using my firelock as a crutch.

I now looked back at the brigade, and saw it was much cut up. I passed Colonel Alexander Gordon, formerly Captain in our regiment – killed, and Brigade-Major Gardener, who had been an active officer in our brigade all morning – he and his horse lay dead together. Major Ross, 38th, and Captain Bradley, 28th Light Company (I knew him in the Light Battalion in Dublin) – badly wounded. I stepped over many men lying on the ground here, to rise no more. The shot was tearing up the ground on my left and right, as the French cannon were doing great execution at this time, and their shells had set the cornfields on fire in the plain, and brushwood and long grass were blazing on the sides of the hill. Many wounded men, unable to get away, were burned to death.

If I had sat down, no doubt the same lot would have been mine, so I kept hopping along until I came to a large white house, where many wounded men were waiting to be dressed. Here I found the surgeon of the Gordons, Dr Beattie, who came at once to me, and dressed my leg, and put a bandage on it. He then gave me a drink of water, and told me I had got it [wounded] at last. I, smiling, replied 'Long run the fox, but he is sure to be caught at last.' This made many smile, whose bones were sore enough.

I had now time to look about me, and I saw that we were going on in the plain little to our advantage. Some of our guns were drawn to the rear to take up a fresh alignment. Feeling very weak, I took a mouthful of water and a slice of the loaf that I got in the morning, when I found a musket ball in it, which had pierced my haversack and lodged in the loaf. I sincerely returned thanks to God for preserving me in the dangers to which I had been exposed, and gave myself a great credit for all I had done. Thus pleased with myself, I got up and hopped along for the town of Talavera.

━━◈◈━━

6

STORMING OF BADAJOZ, 1812

Private Robert Eadie (79th Highlanders)

By the start of 1812 the Duke of Wellington had cleared the French from Portugal and turned the country into a secure base from which to launch a campaign to liberate Spain. However, before advancing eastwards, he first had to capture the Spanish towns of Ciudad Rodrigo and Badajoz, which guarded the frontier. Both were defended by formidable fortifications and strong French garrisons. Of the two, Badajoz was the strongest of these fortresses, and the French regarded the town to be all but impregnable.

In January 1812 Wellington's men captured Ciudad Rodrigo by storm, after a ten-day siege. The Anglo-Portuguese army then marched south to Badajoz, and in mid March they laid siege to the city. By 5 April two breaches were made in the walls, and on the night of 6 April Wellington ordered his men to assault the town. The breaches became killing grounds, where over 2,000 British troops lost their lives. Wellington was on the verge of calling off the attack when the men of General Picton's 3rd Division gained a foothold on the walls. The British stormed into the city and captured it. What followed was one of the most disgraceful events in British military history. The British and Portuguese troops ran riot through the streets, murdering, raping and looting for the best part of three days, before Wellington's officers could restore order. Private Eadie recounts the horrors of the fight for the breach, but seems to have played a relatively minor part in the orgy of looting and violence which followed.

Our division, under the command of General Graham, in conjunction with two brigades of cavalry, crossed the River Guadina, and moved forward to Lherena, with the design of cutting off all communication betwixt Badajoz and that quarter. Meantime, the rest of the troops having invested Badajoz, the usual operations were begun with the greatest alacrity. No obstacle could retard the exertions of the troops, though drenched with the rains that continued to pour down incessantly upon them. The result of such activity was that in a few days the completion of six batteries, in the first parallel, opposite to an outwork called Picuvina [a fortification outside the main fortress walls].

Immediately the menacing thunders of the cannon commenced. They had made the walls of Cuidad Rodrigo tumble to the ground, and they were also about to be no less destructive to the defences of Badajoz. The night of the same day on which the batteries opened fire, it was resolved to storm

Picuvina. A detachment of 500 men, belonging to the Third Division, was destined for this attack. Under the cloud of night, they moved forward, and after vanquishing various difficulties, they found their enterprise successful.

This outwork was defended by 250 men, all of whom were either killed, or falling into the River Guadiana, were washed away by its swelling waters. On the capture of this, 25 pieces of cannon were planted nearer the body of the place. The fire from these was terrible and destructive. The places against which they were levelled exhibited breaches that in a short time were pronounced practicable. In consequence of this, the storming of the town was determined on.

The disposition for the attack was as follows: Lieutenant-General Pack, who commanded the Third Division was to assail the castle by scaling it with ladders. The ravelin of St Roque upon the left of the castle, was to be attacked by a detachment of the Fourth Division, under the direction of Major Wilson, belonging to the 48th Regiment. The remainder of the division was led on by Major-General Colville, to attack the bastions of Santa Maria, and La Trinidad. The false attack was to be made upon one of the outworks, by Lieutenant-General Leith. The different divisions being thus arranged for such an arduous and momentous undertaking set out amidst the deepening gloom of night to the respective places which they were to assail.

No noise disturbed the awful silence that then reigned, except the hollow murmuring waves of the Guadiana, as it hastened forward to pour its tribute into the ocean. Alas! How many were never more to see the morning dawn; but, mingling with the dust of their ancestors, would then sleep for ages on the banks of a foreign river – their names may be forgotten, but their achievements, enrolled in the annals of history, shall continue, like an unfading flower, to captivate with its perfume, succeeding generations.

At the entrance of the breaches, through which our troops were to force a passage, were planted numerous pieces of cannon, charged with round and grape shot, which commenced their destructive work as soon as our troops arrived in front of the bastions. The scene was appalling – though rank after rank, as they advanced, were mowed down by these dreadful implements of death, yet they continued pressing forward to the very mouths of the cannon.

The enemy, at such a terrible conjuncture, fought with the most determined bravery, and repulsed their assailants. Death, clothed in all the horrors, did not, however, intimidate our brave troops. Forward they again rushed, with all the fury of enraged combatants, and possessed themselves of the breaches. Behind these breaches were large ditches, in which pikes and old swords were so thickly planted that those who fearlessly leaped into them, met speedily their awful fate. They were again compelled to give way before the enemy's artillery, which still continued to sweep the passage with their terrific thunders:

> Again unto the breach, dear friends, once more,
> And close the wall up with our English dead!

A third time it was attempted. But it was yet ineffectual. What a dreadful scene of mortality was exhibited when the following morning was ushered in. Though success did not attend their arduous labours in this quarter, yet it failed not to accompany Lieutenant-General Pack in his important enterprise. In the face of the most vigorous opposition, he, with his intrepid followers, succeeded in escalading the castle. In little more than an hour and a quarter, he was in possession of a place, the importance of which was as great as the undertaking was arduous.

The Governor, General Philepon, upon seeing the castle (the most commanding place of the whole time) in the power of the besiegers, found that resistance was useless, and therefore fled with all his troops into St Cristobal, where he remained until the following day, when he voluntarily surrendered. In the memorable siege, our loss amounted to 3,860 British and 1,000 Portuguese, killed and wounded – a great part of which were officers. The enemies' loss, in killed and wounded, during the whole siege, was 1,200 men, besides 4,000 that surrendered themselves [as] prisoners of war.

Our commander received orders to march his division to Badajoz – now a conquered city. When we arrived there, the town presented one scene of festivity. In every street soldiers were to be seen sitting on casks of wine, rum and brandy, and imbibing exhilarating draughts of these genial liquors. Others, bestriding the most valuable French steeds, were actively engaged in vending them to their officers. Money was wanting to none; dollars and doubloons replenished the purse of every one who had activity enough to look out for them.

After partaking somewhat freely of the joys of Bacchus, as may well be conjectured, I repaired to a house, with the intention of being as dextrous as possible, in turning to my account whatever kind of fortune might throw in my way. On entering, I found that it had already been visited; but I resolved to have a search. Shortly after I had commenced the work of searching, I lighted upon 80 dollars, deposited in a recondite corner. I was overjoyed at my success, and calculated on the advantage that should result from it, little thinking how soon I was to be deprived of them.

Being much fatigued, I laid myself down, and was not long in this reclining position when Morpheus gently stole upon me. How long I remained in this state I cannot say, but as soon as I awoke, I found to my great mortification that my valuable haversack – valuable on account of the treasure lately found, and which it contained – was cut from my shoulders. Musing a while on this unlucky incident, I consoled myself with the old adage, 'The thing that comes light, gangs light!'

⋙◆⋘

7

THE FIELD HOSPITAL, 1812

Private Joseph Donaldson (94th Foot)

Private (later Sergeant) Donaldson was a Scotsman, attached to an Irish formation, the 2nd Battalion of the Connaught Rangers. As part of General Picton's 'Fighting Third' Division his regiment participated in the Siege of Badajoz (April–May 1812), and Donaldson played his part in the bloody storming of the French-held fortress city on 6 April, when over 3,000 men were killed in a single night. He was disgusted by the drunkenness and lack of discipline which followed the fall of the city, but he could do little to prevent the excesses of his fellow soldiers. When the army finally quit Badajoz and marched into Spain in pursuit of the French, due to illness Donaldson was unable to march with them. Instead he spent more than a month in a field hospital – an experience he was lucky to survive.

A few days after the town [of Badajoz] was taken, I took the fever and ague, with which I was so extremely ill that when we marched, which we did immediately after, I was unable to keep up with my regiment, and was left with four others, about five leagues from Castello Branco [in Portugal], in charge of a sergeant who was to endeavour to bring us on; but being unable to proceed, he was obliged to put us into a house in the small village in which we were left. It was occupied by a poor widow, who had two children; there was only one apartment in the house, in which there was a loom; and having crept under it, I lay there for four days without bed or covering, with the exception of an old great coat, my necessaries, which I was unable to carry, having gone forward with the regiment.

The poor Portuguese widow had little to give except commiseration, and seemed to feel much for me in particular, as the others could move about a little. I have often heard her, when she thought I was asleep, soliloquizing on the grief it would give my parents, were they to know my situation; and in her orisons [prayers] which she was in the habit of repeating aloud, she did not neglect a petition for the *povre rapaz Englese* ('poor English boy'). She often brought me warm milk, and pressed me to take a little of it; I felt very grateful for her sympathy and kindness, but I was too sick to taste it.

As we were here without any means of support, the sergeant managed to press five asses to carry us to Castello Branco, where there was a general hospital forming; on one of these I was mounted, and supported by the man who drove it. I took leave of the tender-hearted widow, while the tears stood in her eyes. Such disinterested feeling I was at that time little accustomed to, and it was precious. We proceeded on our journey, but never did I endure such torture as I did all that day, and I often begged of them to allow me to lie down and die.

On the second day we reached our destination, and remained

waiting in the street for two hours before the general doctor would look at us. When he did come, his countenance foreboded no good. 'What's the matter with you, Sir?' said he to me, in a scowling tone of voice; 'You ought to have been with your regiment; a parcel of lazy skulking fellows – there's nothing the matter with any of you!' I said nothing, but I looked in his face, with a look which asked him if he really believed what he said, or if he did not read a different story in my pale face and sunken cheek. He seemed to feel the appeal, and softening his countenance he passed on to another.

We were then placed along with others in the passage of a convent, which was converted into a hospital; here I lay that day on the floor, without mattress or covering. No light came, and a burning fever raged through my veins; I called for drink, but there was no one to give it me. In the course of the night I became delirious; the last thing I remember was strange fantastic shapes flitting around me, which now and then catched me up, and flew with me like lightning through every obstacle – then they would hold me over a precipice, and letting me fall, I would continue sinking, with a horrid consciousness of my situation, until my mind was lost in some wild vagary of a different nature.

For some days I was unconscious of what was passing, and then I recovered my senses. I found myself in a small apartment with others who had bad fevers, but I was now provided with a mattress and bed-clothes. A poor fellow, a musician of the 43rd (Monmouthshire) Regiment, next berth to me, [was] sitting up in his bed in a fit of delirium, addressing himself to some young females, whom he supposed to be spinning under the superintendence of an old woman, in a corner of the ceiling; he kept a constant conversation with his supposed neighbours, whom he seemed to think were much in awe of the old dame, and he frequently rose out of his bed to throw up his handkerchief as a signal. When he recovered, the impression was so strong, that he remembered every particular.

There was a great want of proper attendants in the hospital, and many a time I have heard the sick crying for drink and assistance during the whole night, without receiving it. There seemed also to be a scarcity of medical officers during the Peninsular War. I have known wounded men often to be three days after an engagement before it came to their turn to be dressed, and it may be safely calculated that one-half of those men were thus lost to the service. Those medical men we had were not always ornaments of the profession. They were chiefly, I believe, composed of apothecaries' boys, who, having studied a session or two, were thrust into the army as a huge dissecting room, where they might mangle with impunity, until they were drilled into an ordinary knowledge of their business; and as they began at the wrong end, they generally did much mischief before that was attained.

The extent of their medical practice in most disorders was to 'blister, bleed and purge' – what then? Why, 'blister, bleed and purge again'. This method of cure with poor wretches who were any thing but over-fed, and whose greatest complaint often was fatigue and a want of proper sustenance, was quite à-la Hornbrook, and the sufferers were quickly laid to rest. In the field they did more mischief, being but partially acquainted with anatomy; there was enough of what medical men call *bold practice*. In cutting down upon a ball for the purpose of extracting it, ten chances to one but they severed an artery they knew not how to stem; but this gave no concern to these enterprising fellows, for clapping a piece of lint and a bandage, or a piece of adhesive plaster on the wound, they would walk off very composedly to mangle some other poor wretch, leaving the former to his fate.

Here I may be accused of speaking at random, on a subject I do not understand; but there is no man who served in the

Peninsular War, but can bear witness to the truth of what I have stated. I, however, do not pretend to say there were not many exceptions to this character; and in justice to the whole, it must be admitted, that the duties of a surgeon on the Peninsula were fatiguing and arduous in the extreme. The medical department of the French army was much superior to ours at that time in every respect; this can only be accounted for by the superior opportunity they had of studying anatomy, which in Britain is now almost prohibited – more the pity! Those who have witnessed the evils resulting to the army in particular, from imperfectly educated surgeons, must regret that government does not afford greater facilities to the study.

The ague fits having returned when the severe fever left me, I recovered very slowly; the medicine I received, which was given very irregularly, having done me no good. While in this state, General Sir John Hope, who lately commanded the forces in Scotland, happened to pay a visit to the hospital, and going round the sick with the staff-surgeon, he inquired 'What was the prevailing disease?' the reply was, 'Fever and ague.' Sir John, whose kind and humane disposition is well known, mentioned that he had heard of a cure for that disease among the old women in Scotland, which was considered infallible. The staff-surgeon smiled, and begged to hear what it was. 'It is,' said the good old general, 'simply a large pill formed of spider's web, to be swallowed when the fit is coming on. I cannot pledge myself for its efficacy, but I have heard it much talked of.' The staff-doctor gave a shrug, as much to say it was all nonsense, looked very wise, as all doctors endeavour to do, and the conversation dropped.

I had been listening eagerly to the conversation, and no sooner was the general gone, than I set out in quest of the specific. I did not need to travel far, and returned to my room prepared for the next fit; when I felt it coming on, I swallowed the dose with the greatest confidence in its virtues, and however strange it may appear, or hard to be accounted for, I never had a fit of the ague after, but got well rapidly, and was soon fit to march for the purpose of joining my regiment, which I overtook at Pollos. They had been quartered for some weeks in a village on the frontiers, from whence they advanced, and having passed Salamanca, were now in this place, which was situated on a rising ground on the bank of the River Douro, our army occupying the one side, and the French the other.

━━◆◆═━

8

BATTLE OF SALAMANCA, 1812

Private James Anton (42nd Highlanders)

By the spring of 1812 the Duke of Wellington's Anglo-Portuguese army had marched deep into Spain, in an attempt to bring Marshal Marmont's French army to battle. However, when Marmont was reinforced, Wellington decided to avoid seeking a battle, unless it could be fought on his terms, and on ground of his choosing. The two armies spent weeks marching and counter-marching, but on 22 July (Private Anton gets the date wrong), Wellington noticed that the French were badly strung out. He decided to fight his battle. Marmont made the first move. Thinking he was facing a small British rearguard, he launched a pinning attack, then moved the rest of the army forward to cut the British off.

In fact Wellington had hidden the rest of his own army, and when the moment came he launched them in a vigorous counterattack. It was the turn of the French to be isolated and defeated in detail, and by late afternoon the remnants of Marmont's army were in full retreat. As part of General Campbell's 1st Division, the 42nd didn't play a particularly active part in the battle, and only advanced into action during the closing stages of the fighting. Private Anton lays the blame for this at the feet of his divisional commander. However, the following day, the 42nd took part in the small rearguard action at Garcia Hernandez, where Private Anton witnessed the bloody aftermath of the breaking of a French square by Wellington's cavalry. His version of events also provides us with a rare insight into the aftermath of battle, and the opportunities this presented to the pursuing troops.

We got under arms before day. This was the 28th of July. The sound of musketry announced an engagement: but the firing at this time was occasioned by the different divisions taking up their ground in position; and the piquets alone were engaged.

Our division marched from its nocturnal position and formed in rear of a small village to support the centre of the army. We were the reserve division, and were marched from one place to another till about two o'clock. Then we were marched to the left of the army, and took up a strong position on a range of small hills in front of the right of the enemy. At this time there was assembled on our positions an immense artillery, which kept up a tremendous and well-directed fire against the French. The infantry and cavalry were at the back of the heights I allude to.

The ground on the left of the 42nd was greatly exposed to the fire of the enemy's artillery, on account of a large slope that was between two of the small hills. Belonged to the 8th company at this time. We moved and formed in rear of one of the hills before any loss was sustained. There was a regiment of German riflemen marched across the slopes, at the time we had passed it, in column of companies, going to support the right of the army. The French attempted, as each company passed, to make their shot tell; but there was only one company struck; the ball hit an officer that commanded the company and passed on to the right; they were marching left in front. I saw eight men levelled with the dust by that one shoot – the like of it I never witnessed.

At this time the battle was raging with great fury; and there was no one could tell which army was to be the conqueror, for both fought with obstinate valour. For about two hours, the roar of the cannon and musketry was tremendous; and though we were not in the brunt of the action, we lost a few men, in killed and wounded. The right of the army suffered most; for there the action was hottest.

It was said that the general who commanded our division, that was Major-General Campbell, received orders from Wellington to bring the division into action at the time the battle was raging with such fury. We were to have dashed forward, they said, and formed in some large fields of wheat, in front of those heights, the enemy having a very strong line at the farther side of them.

The light companies of our brigade were sent out to skirmish on our new position; but it was long ere we were marched from the high ground. I think General Campbell took his own time to form the division on this new position, knowing that there would be a great deal of bloodshed, had he obeyed the orders sent to him by Wellington. That is what was said at the time in the division; and I report what I saw and what I heard from those who looked farther than I did perhaps. The truth is, General Campbell saw the victory was ours without this movement and sacrifice; it was then complete in his eyes; but it would have been a perfect annihilation of the enemy if our division had been pressed forward at the moment Wellington commanded us to move. We should then have had the brunt of the battle in its close, and the French would have been overthrown inevitably. At last, our brigade marched, and formed line in the wheatfields, but did not advance, as the enemy's line had fallen back.

By this time the French army was all in confusion, making the best of its way from the field of battle; and now it was almost sunset. But our division having received orders to pursue the retreating foe, we were marched off the wheatfield; yet it was not marching, it was rather running. The day had been very hot; we were greatly fatigued. We could get no water to drink; we had little or nothing to eat. About dusk we got into a wood, and we were still on the trot. We continued in this manner, till a little before daylight next morning, when we had halted, expecting, as the day dawned on us, to behold a great many of the enemy surrounded by our division; but, to our great surprise, we were a long way out of our course. General Campbell had a guide, but I could never learn whether he or the guide was in fault. The general in a few days more quitted the division, and went home to England, they said. This was what the world called the battle of Salamanca.

The enemy retreated in two columns, one making for Madrid, the other for Burgos. We halted a few hours from sunrise, then started again, taking a direction to our right, having gone altogether to our left during the night. In the course of two hours we came up with a regiment of German heavy cavalry that had just been engaged with the French, and had taken about 500 prisoners. They broke into a square that the enemy had formed to allow a safe retreat to the rest of their army. The slaughter had been great which the Germans made; for as we traversed the ground on which this affair had been achieved, the dead and the wounded were beyond belief. In the course of an hour we got within sight of the French army; they were formed in line of battle, as if to make a stand, not thinking on the drubbing they had received the day before, and a fresh division going to attack them.

When we came within reach of shot, General Campbell began to form his line, and our six pieces of cannon were set to work. They had not fired two rounds when the enemy wheeled back into columns of companies, and made off at double-quick time. We continued our march after them till it was near sunset, when we halted, at a small village, where we bivouacked that night, being in great want of rest and refreshments. We were certain of sleeping unmolested, as the enemy reckoned themselves fortunate to escape from us. They left everything they had in the field of battle and near it, on their precipitate retreat. Their baggage, I suppose, was one day's march in rear of their army.

On this day there were horses, mules, asses, bullocks, sheep and goats, all wandering the fields in great numbers. All these the enemy had abandoned on their retreat; so our women, who were not provided with beasts to carry their lumber, were furnished now, if they had address enough to catch the horses and mules. My mess caught a sheep and killed it, and cooked it that night, being in great want of both meat and drink.

⋙◆⋘

9

BATTLE OF WATERLOO, 1815

Private Thomas Howell (71st Highlanders)

The 71st Highlanders were veterans of the Spanish Peninsular campaign, having fought their way through Spain and into France. When the war ended in April 1814 they were shipped to Ireland,

and many of the older soldiers hoped to be discharged. The Emperor Napolean was exiled to the island of Elba, the French monarchy was restored, and Europe enjoyed the benefits of a hard-won peace. However, in March 1815 Napoleon escaped from Elba and rallied France behind him. While the French Emperor mobilised his army, the Duke of Wellington was placed in charge of a hastily assembled coalition of British and Dutch–Belgian troops, stationed near Brussels. The 71st were sent to join Wellington's army, and were stationed at Leuze, 40 miles south-west of Brussels. On 16 June the order came to march to intercept the approaching French army.

We immediately marched off towards the French frontier. We had a very severe march of sixteen miles, expecting to halt and be quartered in every town through which we passed. We knew not where we were marching. About one o'clock in the morning we were halted in a village. A brigade of Brunswickers marching out, we took their quarters, hungry and weary. Next morning, the 17th, we got our allowance of liquor and moved on until the heat of the day when we encamped, and our baggage was ordered to take the high road to Brussels. We sent out fatigue parties for water, and set a-cooking. Our fires were not well kindled when we got orders to fall in and move on along the high road towards Waterloo.

The whole length of the road was very much crowded by artillery and ammunition carts, all advancing towards Waterloo. The troops were much embarrassed in marching, the roads were so crowded. As soon as we arrived on the ground, we formed in column. The rain began to pour. The firing had never ceased all yesterday and today at a distance. We encamped and began to cook, when the enemy came in sight and again spoiled our cooking. We advanced towards them. When we reached the height they retired, which caused the whole army to get under arms and move to their positions. Night coming on, we stood under arms for some time. The army then retired to their own rear and lay down under arms, leaving the 71st in advance. During the whole night the rain never ceased.

Two hours after daybreak General Hill came down, taking away the left sub-division of the 10th Company to cover his recognisance. Shortly afterwards we got half an allowance of liquor, which was the most welcome thing I ever received. I was so stiff and sore from the rain I could not move with freedom for some time. A little afterwards; the weather clearing up, we began to clean our arms and prepare for action. The whole of the opposite heights were covered by the enemy.

A young lad who had joined but a short time before said to me, while we were cleaning: 'Tom, you are an old soldier, and have escaped often, and have every chance to escape this time also. I am sure I am to fall.' 'Nonsense, be not gloomy.' 'I am certain,' he said. 'All I ask is that you will tell my parents when you get home, that I ask God's pardon for the evil I have done and the grief I have given them. Be sure to tell I died praying for their blessing and pardon.' I grew dull myself, but gave him all the heart I could. He only shook his head. I could say nothing to alter his belief.

The artillery had been tearing away since daybreak in different parts of the line. About twelve o'clock we received orders to fall in for attack. We then marched up to our position, where we lay on the face of a brae, covering a brigade of guns. We were so overcome by the fatigue of the two days' march that, scarce had we lain down, until many of us fell asleep. I slept sound for some time while the cannonballs plunging in amongst us, killed a great many. I was suddenly awakened. A ball struck the ground a little below me, turned me heels-over-head, broke my musket in pieces and killed a lad at my side. I was stunned and confused and knew not whether I was wounded or not. I felt a numbness in my arm for some time.

We lay thus, about an hour and a half, under a dreadful fire, which cost us about 60 men, while we had never fired a shot. The balls were falling thick amongst us. The young man I lately spoke of lost his legs by a shot at this time. They were cut very close; he soon bled to death. 'Tom,' he said, 'remember your charge: my mother wept sore when my brother died in her arms. Do not tell her all how I died; if she saw me thus, it would break her heart. Farewell, God bless my parents!' He said no more, his lips quivered and he ceased to breathe.

About two o'clock a squadron of lancers came down, hurraying, to charge the brigade of guns. They knew not what was in the rear. General Barnes gave the word, 'Form square'. In a moment the whole brigade were on their feet, ready to receive the enemy. The General said, 'Seventy-first, I have often heard of your bravery, I hope it will not be worse than it has been today.' Down they came upon our square. We soon put them to the right-about.

Shortly after, we received orders to move to the heights. Onwards we marched and stood for a short time in square, receiving cavalry every now and then. The noise and smoke were dreadful. At this time I could see but a very little way from me, but all around the wounded and slain lay very thick. We then moved on in column for a considerable way and formed line, gave three cheers, fired a few volleys, charged the enemy and drove them back.

At this moment a squadron of cavalry rode furiously down

upon our line. Scarce had we time to form. The square was only complete in front when they were upon the points of our bayonets. Many of our men were out of place. There was a good deal of jostling, for a minute or two, and a good deal of laughing. Our quartermaster lost his bonnet in riding into the square; got it up, put it on, back foremost, and wore it thus all day. Not a moment had we to regard our dress. A French general lay dead in the square; he had a number of ornaments upon his breast. Our men fell to plucking them off, pushing each other as they passed, and snatching at them.

We stood in square for some time, whilst the 13th Dragoons and a squadron of French dragoons were engaged. The 13th Dragoons retiring to the rear of our column, we gave the French a volley, which put them to the right-about; then the 13th [made] at them again. They did this for some time; we cheering the 13th, and feeling every blow they received. When a Frenchman fell we shouted, and when one of the 13th, we groaned. We wished to join them but were forced to stand in square.

The whole army retired to the heights in the rear; the French closely pursuing to our formation, where we stood, four deep, for a considerable time. As we fell back, a shot cut the straps of the knapsack of one near me; it fell and was rolling away. He snatched it up, saying, 'I am not to lose you that way; you are all I have in the world', tied it on the best manner he could and marched on.

Lord Wellington came riding up. We formed square, with him in our centre, to receive cavalry. Shortly the whole army received orders to advance. We moved forwards in two columns, four deep, the French retiring at the same time. We were charged several times in our advance. This was our last effort; nothing could impede us. The whole of the enemy retired, leaving their guns and ammunition and every other thing behind. We moved on towards a village and charged right through, killing great numbers, the village was so crowded. We then formed on the other side of it and lay down under the canopy of heaven, hungry and wearied to death. We had been oppressed all day by the weight of our blankets and greatcoats which were drenched with rain and lay upon our shoulders like logs of wood. Scarce was my body stretched upon the ground when sleep closed my eyes.

Next morning when I awoke I was quite stupid. The whole night my mind had been harassed by dreams. I was fighting and charging, re-acting the scenes of the day, which were strangely jumbled with the scenes I had been in before. I rose up and looked around, and began to recollect. The events of the 18th came before me, one by one; still they were confused, the whole appearing as an unpleasant dream. My comrades began to awake and talk of it; then the events were embodied as realities. Many an action had I been in wherein the individual exertions of our regiment had been much greater and our fighting more severe; but never had I been where the firing was so dreadful and the noise so great.

When I looked over the field of battle it was covered and heaped in many places, figures moving up and down upon it. The wounded crawling along the rows of the dead was a horrible spectacle; yet I looked on with less concern, I must say, at the moment, than I have felt at an accident, when in quarters. I have been sad at the burial of a comrade who died of sickness in the hospital and followed him almost in tears; yet have I seen, after a battle, fifty men put into the same trench, and comrades amongst them, almost with indifference. I looked over the field of Waterloo as a matter of course, a matter of small concern. In the morning we got half an allowance of liquor and remained here until midday, under arms; then received orders to cook. When cooking was over, we marched on towards France.

CHAPTER 4

THE WARS OF EMPIRE

Before and even during the Napoleonic Wars, if the British soldier was viewed with distaste by the British public, then the Scottish soldier was seen in an even worse light. To most civilians who lived south of Berwick he was often little better than a barbarian – someone to threaten young children with, in order to keep them quiet. By the end of the Crimean War, three decades later, all this changed. The Scottish soldier had become the darling of the British empire, and a stalwart of the military establishment. Naturally, this is a gross oversimplification, but it demonstrates how attitudes were changing towards soldiers in general, and the Scottish soldier in particular.

Attitudes were changing in Scotland too. The army had been greatly reduced in strength after the defeat of the French, and by 1820 it numbered less than 100,000 men – a quarter of its wartime strength. Roughly half the army served overseas, and we have included one first-hand account from a Scottish soldier stationed in India during this period, by way of light relief. The rest of the Scottish battalions were kept in Britain as garrison troops, primarily to aid the civil powers in the event of unrest. There was certainly plenty of that, although the Scottish Yeomanry tended to be given the job of policing the industrial centres of lowland Scotland, which largely meant protecting the interests of the mill-, factory- and pit-owners. While soldiers were no longer despised and barred from the centre of towns, their duties in aid of the civil powers did little to improve their image within their own communities. As a result, recruitment suffered, and by the mid 1840s most Scottish regiments had to recruit outside the borders of Scotland. In some Scottish regiments as many as a third of the soldiers in the ranks weren't actually Scottish at all.

The problem was particularly severe in the Highlands, where the old order was breaking down. For a start, the clan chiefs and landowners who had once offered their tenants to the crown as soldiers were no longer willing or able to bear the cost of these patriotic gestures.

By that time many of the old Highland tenantry were being evicted from their land, to make way for sheep, and while this might have increased the number of recruits who signed up in order to feed their families, few joined the army because their clan chiefs told them to. As an example, when the Duke of Sutherland tried to raise a regiment from his tenantry during the Crimean War (1854–56), he was bluntly told that his tenants no longer owed him allegiance, and certainly wouldn't join his regiment.

The Crimean War represented something of a watershed – the end of a period of military stagnation in Britain. Certainly, the army which was transported to the Crimea was little different from the one that fought at Waterloo. Its uniforms were largely the same, as were the tactics the soldiers employed. While the weapons might have improved slightly with the general introduction of the rifled musket, soldiers were still expected to form into lines, stand their ground and shoot the enemy at point-blank range. This chapter includes two first-hand accounts written by Scottish soldiers during this war – one recounting an assault at the Battle of Alma, and the other a defensive battle, fought as part of the Battle of Balaclava. While this last battle might have been dominated by the Charge of the

Light Brigade, Sir Colin Campbell's 'thin red line' also became a symbol of Scottish military prowess. Both battles showed the Scottish soldier at his best – modest, brave and virtuous – the very model of the Victorian military ideal.

The war began amid a furore of popular support for the army, but the incompetence of its commanders and the appalling lack of organisation led to more soldiers dying from disease or poor conditions than ever succumbed to Russian shot and shell. The result was a public outcry, which did much to improve conditions for the common soldier, and ensured that in future campaigns he was given the clothing and equipment he needed to do his job. The war also served to raise the profile of the Scottish soldier, as these exploits came at a time when all things Scottish had come into vogue.

Sir Walter Scott had a lot to do with creating a romantic view of Scotland, but it was Queen Victoria who really changed public attitudes. When she fell in love with all things Highland, the British establishment scrambled to follow her example. This romantic view of Scotland and the Highlands was reflected in the public perception of the Scottish soldier. The deeds of the Scottish regiments in the Crimea helped instil the view that Scottish soldiers were some kind of romantic heroes, bravely serving the colours and performing deeds of derring-do. The exploits of the Highland regiments during the Indian Mutiny (1857–59) did much to reinforce this image. Nobody had really wanted to hear in 1815 that Sergeant Mitchell of the 93rd was starving, and his comrades were blown up beside him. However, in the 1850s, they cared that the besieged garrison of Lucknow heard the pipes of the 78th Highlanders in the distance, and therefore knew that help was on its way.

For the next half century the Scottish soldier could do no wrong. Scottish regiments were sent to every corner of the

British empire, and beyond. They were engaged in almost every major engagement of the era, and won acclaim for their exploits, almost as if the soldiers themselves were living up to their public reputation. Between the end of the Crimean War and the start of the First World War, Scottish soldiers garnered no fewer than 55 Victoria Crosses. Of these, 32 were won during the Indian Mutiny, the campaign that confirmed the view of the Scottish soldier as a hero of the Victorian age. Eleven more were awarded for services during the Boer War (1899–1900), a campaign where for once the British were outfought and outgunned by their wily Afrikaner opponents. The remaining dozen medals reflected Scottish service throughout the empire – in the Ashanti kingdom of West Africa (1874 and 1900), Zululand (1879), Afghanistan (1879–82), Egypt (1882), the Sudan (1882–84 and 1898), and the North-West Frontier of India (1897).

All these small wars of empire presented the Scottish soldier with fresh challenges. For instance, campaigning in Afghanistan or the North-West Frontier involved fighting against an unseen enemy, who hid amid the rocks and mountainsides and relied on his *jizhail* (musket).

In a way this was similar to the situation in which the British found themselves during the Boer War, where their opponents fought at long range, using cover to their advantage. The Zulus and the warrior peoples of the Sudan preferred to fight at close quarters. There the aim was to stop them before they reached the thin red or khaki line, as once the British soldier came within range of their stabbing spears he was at a disadvantage. In Egypt – as another first-hand account demonstrates – the Scots were fighting an altogether more organised enemy – an Egyptian army which had been trained by the British themselves.

In all these situations, what mattered was that the Scottish soldiers would remain firm and disciplined under fire, and were willing to close and engage the enemy at bayonet-point when they had to. This was an age when personal heroism was much admired, and while Rudyard Kipling might have lamented the lot of the British soldier in his poem 'Tommy Atkins', he made the clear point that the Victorians loved a dashing hero, and preferably one wearing a kilt. At home, or even on campaign but off the battlefield, the Scottish soldier – as ever – was known for his penchant for drink, and what might politely be called 'letting off steam'. On the battlefield, this same wild spirit was expected to result in ferocious charges, displays of conspicuous gallantry, or defences against impossible odds.

The other great advantage the Scots enjoyed – at least in most colonial campaigns – was firepower. Breech-loading rifles were introduced into the British army in 1866, and five years later Scottish soldiers were issued with the Martini-Henry – a powerful weapon in the hands of a well-drilled soldier. By the 1870s the first Gatling machine guns appeared on campaign, and when they worked they proved to be battle-winning weapons. Within two decades these early breech-loading rifles and hand-operated machine guns had been replaced with even more lethal weapons – bolt-action rifles and the Maxim machine gun. As the old rhyme had it: 'Whatever happens we have got, the Maxim gun, and they have not.' Unfortunately, even though most of the time these Scottish soldiers were facing natives armed with more primitive weapons than their own, tactics never kept pace with firepower.

That was also why the Boer War came as such a shock. For the first time, British soldiers were going into battle against opponents who were armed with weapons every bit as good as their own, but, while the Boers sneakily hid behind rocks, the British tended to advance in extended lines, in the open. The result was inevitable, and another two first-hand accounts from the conflict neatly demonstrate exactly what happened. Interestingly enough, the letter from Lord Lovat shows that the Boers could be vulnerable – they were easy to locate, and therefore a combination of firepower and manoeuvre could be used to wrest them from their positions. This emphasis on firepower and marksmanship was the one great military legacy of the Boer War. The British army learned its lesson, and so by the time the First World War began, fourteen years later, the British regular soldier had become a proficient marksman – a skill which would stand him in good stead in August 1914.

Today it is easy to dismiss this period – the Age of Empire – as a strange, misguided bygone age. However, the Scots themselves were willing players in the imperialist game. After all, the majority of the world's steamships were built on the River Clyde, the import of jute from India made Dundee one of the most prosperous textile-manufacturing cities in Britain, and the financiers of Edinburgh held a stake in companies from Vancouver to Ceylon. The Scots did well out of the empire, and so it made perfect sense to fight to preserve it.

⋙◆⋘

1

GARRISON DUTY, GOA, 1824

Private John Williamson (78th Highlanders)

Like many Scottish regiments, the 78th Highlanders (Ross-shire Buffs) were reduced in strength at the end of the Napoleonic Wars, losing one of its two battalions. The regiment had spent most of the war in South Africa, India and the East Indies, only returning home in 1816. Two years later it was dispatched to India once again, this time serving as a European garrison regiment in Goa, where its main job was the suppression of illegal trade and local piracy. It was hardly the most glamorous posting, but as this account shows, these Scottish soldiers tried to make the most of it. The account also demonstrates that two things haven't really changed – the touchy pride of regimental pipers, and the penchant of Scottish soldiers for any form of alcohol. Despite this and other similar adventures, John Williamson eventually became a sergeant, and was pensioned out of service in the 1830s. An account of his experiences, containing this letter, was published in 1838.

My dear friend,

A party of us, consisting of five privates and Donald McLeod, one of the pipers, procured leave of absence from our commanding officer to go to Agoade to take leave of some acquaintances we had in the 86th, previous to their departure on an expedition to the Isle of France; and for this purpose we engaged a double canoe.

We arrived safe at our friends' quarters, where we were very kindly received and spent a pleasant day amongst them. As the evening approached we began to make preparations for our return, and a little before dark we took leave of our acquaintances, and again took to the canoe. We had got about halfway from the mainland, towards the Island of Goa, when a squall overtook us, which we tried to bear up against, and had it not been for the conduct of one of the natives who was working the canoe we would have been reached; but the fellow had taken too much arrack, and through his carelessness in losing his paddle, we were left to drift at the mercy of the wind and waves, and ran a great risk of being all lost.

It was dark by this time, [so] that any attempt to recover the paddle was useless; so with the remaining one we kept working as we best could to make the island, which we accomplished near midnight, much exhausted, as the canoe kept shipping water all the time, and every one had to exert himself in bailing, otherwise we should have perished. Not having any proper utensil with us for the purpose of bailing, we were under the necessity of putting our hats and shoes into requisition, which proved to be very poor substitutes.

At one period the water was gaining on us so rapidly that it seemed impossible that our frail bark could continue long afloat, and one of the party, seeing the danger of our situation, began to resign himself to our sad fate. He knelt down to pray, but McLeod, who was rather a strange sort of fellow, told him that if he did not keep bailing along with the rest, he would pitch him overboard, asking him if he could not both bail and say his prayers at the same time. The poor fellow immediately got up, and again set to work, acting upon the suggestion of the piper, whose determined perseverance and example helped much to carry us through.

We effected a landing at Panjum, about six miles from our quarters, and after dragging the canoe safe on to the beach, set off in quest of lodgings for the night, as we felt so fatigued that we could not proceed further until we got refreshed. The only place that would receive us was one of the lowest arrack shops in the outskirts of the town, where we got some supper, along with a supply of arrack; after which some mats were laid on the floor for us to sleep on.

In a short time we lay down to procure some rest, with the intention of starting very early next morning for Cabo; but our repose was soon interrupted by the annoyance of mosquitoes, along with the croaking of frogs that inhabited a large tank of stagnant water in the neighbourhood of the house, which put sleep out of the question; and we were discussing the propriety of an immediate start for our barracks when McLeod, unknown to any of us, adjusted his pipes, and commenced one of his favourite tunes.

It was of no use to attempt to stop him, he being as stubborn as a rock, and his noisy instrument had aroused every soul in the house, most of them in a dreadful state of alarm at being awoke at such an unusual hour, and with such a hideous noise as the pipes produced. Many of them rushed out of the house in a state of nudity, and ran into the street, screaming. Donald, in the meantime, played away with all his might.

The landlord, a Portuguese, having procured a light, made along with a party of men, an attack on our apartment; but we beat them off, and shutting the door, two of us sat down behind it, to keep them from making a second entrance. Several ineffectual attempts were made to force open the door, but at last a tremendous shove brought it completely off its hinges, and in came our assailants by the dozen. A general engagement took place, during which Donald kept blowing his pipes to encourage us, till at last the lights were put out in the scuffle, and we were captured one by one and dragged out of the house, which put a stop to the sweet sound of the pipes.

The whole party were marched off to the guardhouse and kept locked up till morning, when we were carried before the Viceroy, who, after pointing out the impropriety of our conduct, told us that he would report it to our Colonel. At first he seemed much enraged by us, and in broken English declared that we were a disgrace to the army. After his first burst of passion was over, Donald applied to him to have the pipes returned, saying they were the King's property, and he could not return to Cabo without them. They were given up to

Donald, who no sooner got hold of them, than he began to argue in favour of the elegance of their music, and offered to give his honour a specimen; which the gentleman declined.

Donald still persisted, and told him that it was out of compliment that he made the offer. The Viceroy smiled; which Donald interpreting into the grant of his request, struck up, and having given him fair proof of his powers, and of that of his instrument, asked him, if it were not an 'infernal shame for a man to be pelted and imprisoned for playing such beautiful music'. The viceroy took a hearty laugh at Donald's earnest remark, and told him that the untimely hour and unearthly sounds of his music were the cause of his misfortune. Donald held out his hand, which the Viceroy accepted. 'God bless you for that,' said Donald; 'there is no such other music in this wide world, and your honour will find, when you get to heaven that this is quite correct.' The Viceroy was convulsed with laughter.

Having got fairly out of the scrape, we returned to Cabo, somewhat sceptical of Donald's opinion as to the sound of his instrument, seeing what evil it had brought upon us.

2
BATTLE OF THE ALMA, CRIMEA, 1854

Private Alexander Robb (42nd Highlanders)

In October 1853, growing tension between Russia and Turkey led to the declaration of war. Alarmed by Russian success on land and sea, Great Britain and France allied themselves with the Turks and declared war on Russia in March 1854. Six months later an army was sent to the Black Sea, with orders to strike a blow against the Russians. When the Black Watch landed in the Crimea in September 1854, they formed part of Sir Colin Campbell's Highland Brigade. The plan was that the allied army would march on the Russian port of Sevastopol, and lay siege to it. First though, they had to deal with the Russian army. They found them beyond the small River Alma, deployed in a strong defensive position along a ridge, protected by numerous well-sited and entrenched artillery batteries. On 20 September Lord Raglan ordered his army to launch a frontal attack. While the French assaulted the right of the Russian position, close to the coast, the Highland Brigade was ordered to march straight across the river and up towards the waiting Russians. Decades later, Alexander Robb recalled his baptism of fire at the Alma.

I can only write of what I saw myself, and what I understood. I was only seven months a soldier at that time.

Now the order came that we were to advance. We came on to the village and through the bushes that I speak of, which formed a vineyard hung with nice ripe grapes. I fain would have plucked some had I got the chance. We were all broken up, and we came on a river, and where I was I saw Sir Colin [Campbell] in the midst of the bushes. I heard him calling out – 'Come away, men; you have to come through.' While going through this vineyard the musketry was falling around us very thick, and when in the river it put me in mind of a shower of rain. We had some loss both in killed and wounded. As an old 42nd man, I am proud to write that the two young officers who were carrying the colours had got across, and were standing with them, and that the regiment formed on them the same as before we were put out of order by the village, vineyard and river, the men forming up as cool as though on a field exercise day, with our commanding officer and the other officers at their places, and covering sergeants, and all this under a very heavy fire. When we advanced it was no easy matter to do so, for it was up a steep hill, with our heavy knapsacks and sixty rounds of ammunition, and some of us were dropping down. I heard Sir Colin give the orders that we were not to fire a shot till the bugle would sound, and if any of us were wounded we were to lie still till the bandsmen would come to us.

We were close on the Light Division, and when we came to the 77th they formed four deep and we did the same. I heard the words come from some of them as we marched through their line, 'Let them through; they are mad.' I may here state that the Duke of Cambridge came riding through the heavy fire, and asked Sir Colin something, and rode back to his other brigade. I am not well pleased with Mr Kinglake for the way he speaks of the Duke. I have heard it said because he was a Prince he liked to pick a hole in his coat, but if Mr Kinglake had been in the same position there might have been a bigger hole made in his.

As we got near the top, and still under a heavy fire, a few of my own company dropped a sergeant and Corporal William Forester, a Dundee man, and John McNeish. 'Oh, what is this?' I felt as I thought a blow on my left side; I fell, and when I gained my breath I saw I was minus my water keg. I was by this time some distance below my regiment, and the musket balls were falling very thick around me, so I got up as hard as I could to my company, who were on the top of the heights, and were advancing, now keeping up a brisk fire. As I was going up to it I went through plenty of killed and wounded Russians. I joined in the fire, and could see a large column in front of us, and they were firing, while another large column was marching on our left flank. As the roll of musketry increased, that column stopped all at once. The cause of this was that the gallant 93rd had come up, and was giving them what they did not expect. Some distance from this column, and further to the left, was another large column, and it was coming briskly upon the line, keeping up a fire, and it also got a damper, for the 79th Camerons had got on the heights, and bade them good day in the same fashion.

Now, that was the three regiments of the Highland Brigade engaged on the heights of Alma, and keeping up a brisk fire, but not so very long, for the three columns of the Russians wavered under it and retired. Our bugles then sounded the 'cease fire'. But still at this time musket shots were coming now and again from the Russians. At this I heard Sir Colin call out 'Move about, mounted officers, by God, move about.' Then up got a cheer, but as I turned round and looked to the rear, I could see some of our men lying, some killed and some wounded. During this time the Russians were moving as if meditating another attack on us.

We were startled to hear a field piece go off at our right, and then another. This was the work of a brave artillery officer and those under him, who made out to get up two field pieces, and splendid work they did make. Every shell they threw landed in the centre of the Russian columns, and the havoc could be seen by us. Some distance in front and to the right there appeared to be rising ground, and about in line with the Russians; a line or column was seen coming down on the enemy. This was the French, who poured in a heavy fire of musketry that fairly routed them. The Russians retreated, leaving behind them bag and baggage. The Brigade of Guards had also done good work. I saw the left of them engaged with my own eyes the time I was getting over my stun, and while going up to my place. This was the best thing that I could do, for the bullets were falling very thick around me, as the Russians fired high, being deceived by the feather bonnets. So this ends, as far as I can give an account of it, the battle of the Alma.

When the French and Turks landed and marched the same time as we did they marched by the sea side, but as we marched we inclined in landwards. There must, however, have been communication kept up between the two Generals. I heard it said that the Russians were under the belief that their position could never be taken, and their plan was to drive us, French and all, before them into the sea. But here were the British and French on the heights of Alma cheering, and the Russians retiring from them with a heavy loss. It was said they lost ten times our number. It was also said that the swells were out from Sebastopol with their carriages to see us driven into the sea. There must have been something of the kind, for I saw carriages and harness all smashed when we marched, and all this in the inside of three or four hours.

I will tell you now about myself. Sergeant Lockart came to me and seized my hand and said, 'Is that you, townie?' He was married to a Dundee woman. 'I thought it was all up with you; I saw you fall.' I said I was only stunned, showing him my waistbelt, that had the mark of the ball that struck me and carried away my water keg. 'Well done,' he said, and called to the officer in command of the company, 'The boy is back, Sir; he was only hit with a spent ball.' The Captain said to me, 'Bravo!'

Just about this time up got another cheer. It was the Commander-in-Chief and his Staff, and joined by the Duke of Cambridge. Lord Raglan lifted his hat to us as he rode past the regiment. Sir Colin, who was riding along the line, and happened to be about the centre of our regiment, went up to his Lordship, and as the cheering had ceased, he was heard in a loud voice to ask permission to wear a feather bonnet. The words that Lord Raglan said were: 'That is granted. Sir Colin.' This is a fact. There are four other men still alive in Dundee who were in the same company with me that can tell the same. As the Commander-in-Chief rode along, the cheers of the 93rd and the 79th were as enthusiastic as those of the 42nd. When the Staff had ridden past the line we got 'Pile arms', and took off our knapsacks and fell out of the ranks.

Now was the time for shaking hands and congratulating each other on the narrow escapes – and no mistake there were some very narrow shaves. There was a Huntly shoemaker of the name of Crookshanks, who is still alive. After this he was nicknamed 'Crookie', for it was nearly a 'crook' with him. A ball went along his neck at that part below the chin that is called the 'apple', leaving a sore mark. Bonnets and kilts showed marks of balls going through them, and there were also some new holes in our colours which I had the pleasure of seeing in Dunkeld Cathedral some years ago. Tom Shaw was struck in the side of his knapsack and folded greatcoat, the force nearly knocking him over. The ball was got in the knapsack.

We were served out with an allowance of biscuit and a ration of rum; and as it was getting towards evening we were ordered to fall in; and we marched to the front, leaving the battlefield, and when on clear ground halted, piled arms, and a watering party had to go for water, each man taking as many water kegs with him as he could carry. I was one of them, and was under Lieutenant Webber. As it was getting dark we had to go through among the killed and wounded. I could hear the groans of them. When we got up to the line again it was quite dark, but there was plenty of firewood now, for the Russians had plenty of boxes, etc. that they left behind them,

and my comrade had a nice tin of coffee waiting [for] me;
and as the night advanced we unrolled our blankets and lay
down on the ground to dream over our day's sport.

3

BATTLE OF BALACLAVA, 1854

Private Donald Cameron (93rd Highlanders)

The Allies laid siege to the Crimean port of Sevastopol, but it was
clear the Russians would try to drive the allied army back into the
sea. A battle was inevitable, and as the Allies tried to improve their
own defences, the Russian army prepared to launch their attack –
an engagement now known as the Battle of Balaclava. Perhaps the
most famous single incident of the whole Crimean War was the ill-
fated 'Charge of the Light Brigade', which took place during the
battle. Few now remember the more successful 'Charge of the Heavy
Brigade' during the same engagement, when the Royal Scots
Dragoon Guards routed their Russian counterparts. A little
better remembered is the stand made by the 93rd (Sutherland)
Highlanders, an incident which is better known as 'the Thin Red
Line'. On 25 October the regiment was deployed to protect the small
port of Balaclava, where supplies were being landed. When the battle
began they formed into line, and waited for the onslaught of the
Russian cavalry which was forming up in front of them. The Highlanders
were all that stood between the Russians and the army's only depot.

We turned off the road into a smooth valley in which we
marched, and some of the men were letting go the meal, for
[they were] . . . seen on the grass as we were going along, till

we came to some water and then turned up a hill to our left and halted, and then another forage for fuel and water. It is my turn again for water, so back to the stream that we passed a little time before. Got my kegs filled and up the hill again, and my comrade having a fire ready, we soon had our supper, and we then thought we would bake the meal and got some stones placed round the fire. I took one of the kegs and placed it firm on the ground and, meal and water beside me, commenced baking on the keg, and my comrade setting up the cakes up against the stones round about the fire. So we had oatcakes for a few days afterwards, my comrade and I – but there is worse on before.

On the move again till we reached the plains of Kadikoi, with hills in front of us, and coming in sight of the harbour of Balaclava, we halted, and off with our blankets and coats, and left them there and advanced to the foot of the hill next the harbour. A fort being on the top of the hill, it was necessary for to take it. Parties went up both sides of the harbour and fired a few shots and it surrendered, and we came back to where we left our blankets, gathered some grass for a bed and went to rest, my comrade and I. Having no tents since we left Eupatoria, we were getting used to lying in the open air, the weather being favourable – but there is worse on before.

Kadikoi was a nice place at this time with its vineyards and clean-looking cottages, and a church amongst them, and surrounding hills, and the harbour of Balaclava about two miles from it. The people seemed to be making their living by the vineyards' fruit. It was said that they were driven away by the Cossacks before we arrived, for the houses were furnished and none occupying them. We got in position for to guard the harbour and the way to the front. The 93rd had a heavy gun battery beside them.

One day a man on horseback was seen leaving the 79th's camp and was watched from the battery. When he passed the lines a shell was let after him. When it bursted, he could not be seen till the smoke cleared. He was then seen going into a house on the plain, but soon left it. Another shell was sent after him, and when the smoke cleared he was still galloping on till he was out of range, and some Russian cavalry came to meet him. They went out of sight together. He turned out to be a Russian spy, and being dressed as a British officer, he was not suspected while in the camp.

The 42nd and 79th is up to the front, and the 93rd the only British regiment left on the plain. Some were sent out to Number One Redoubt, and a company of the 93rd sent to the heights of Balaclava, along with a battery of Royal Marine Artillery, where we could have a good view of the place, past Number One Redoubt, where the Turks were, and parading every morning about daybreak, and when all was right we dismissed.

On the morning of 25th October, we turned out as usual to parade, when our officers with their spying glasses made out some Russian cannon at the front of Number One Redoubt, covered with bushes. We were dismissed with orders to dress. I got dressed and a fire kindled, and my canteen on with water for my coffee, and the beef beside me, when I was ordered to fall in. I slung my haversack on my shoulder, which happened to be well supplied with biscuits at the time, and left the canteen on the fire and the beef not far from it.

I fell in with a company and we lined with the Marine Artillery. The Russians commenced cannonading Number One Redoubt, where the Turks were, and a Russian column of infantry came round and lay on the south side of it. The Marine Artillery beside us fired, trying to dislodge them, but could not reach them. Another Russian column came along and when it came near the first, both started up the Redoubt, and the Turks being so much outnumbered, what was left of them, retired towards the plain.

We got orders to join the main body and take our store of ammunition with us. We went down from the heights and joined the Regiment on the plains of Kadicoi, which was in line two deep with some convalescent men from different regiments and the Turks on our right with a battery of big guns, and a battery of artillery on our left with cavalry, and Sir Colin Campbell a few paces in front of us on horseback, the same as if he was to give a Royal Salute on a review day in the Queen's Park at Edinburgh, and the Russian cavalry coming pouring over the hill in front of us, and no word of forming square to receive them, but opened fire on them in line two deep as we were, and Sir Colin still in front till he noticed that he was in the way of some of our firing, and then wheeled round and came to our rear. Now is the time to try our courage and steadiness with a mass of cavalry coming on us, but there we stood like a rock, determined to stand or fall together.

Being in the front rank, and giving a look along the line, it seemed like a wall of fire in front of the muzzles of our rifles. The Russians turned off to their right until they were opposite our cavalry, which charged into their centre. We ceased firing and cheered our cavalry, being all we could do while they were engaged in such a close struggle. The Russians coming again towards us, we opened fire on them the second time and turned them. They seemed to be going away. We ceased firing and cheered. They wheeled about and made a dash at us again. We opened fire on them the third time. They came to a stand, wheeled about and off at a canter. We ceased firing and cheered. Our heavy guns fired after them. They were soon back over the hill the way they came. Our light cavalry charge was at the back of the same hill. In the afternoon the trees between us and the Russians were cut about three feet off the ground and holes dug among them, and everything we thought necessary for our defence.

⋙◆⋘

4

LUCKNOW, THE INDIAN MUTINY, 1857

Sergeant William Forbes Mitchell (93rd Highlanders)

The Sutherland Highlanders had only just returned to Britain from the Crimea when they were sent overseas again, this time to India. The native Bengal army had mutinied against their British officers, and the northern provinces were in a state of violent revolt. In October the regiment formed part of Sir Colin Campbell's expedition to relieve the besieged garrisons of Cawnpore and Lucknow. While they arrived too late to prevent a massacre at Cawnpore, the expedition relieved Lucknow in mid November, the 93rd fighting their way from house to house through the city, until they reached the besieged residency. The rescued garrison was withdrawn, and the army retired back to Cawnpore.

The following spring the British returned, and this time their objective was not rescue but revenge. The British force stormed the city, and the 93rd fought their way into the Dilkusha Palace, a mutineers' stronghold, followed two days later by two more strongpoints, the Martinière College and the Begum's Palace. Sergeant Mitchell recounts what happened during these assaults, and in their immediate aftermath.

Early on the 7th of March General Outram's division crossed

the Goomtee by the bridge of boats, and we returned to our tents at the Dilkooshi [*sic*]. About midday we could see Outram's Division, of which the Seventy-Ninth Cameron Highlanders formed one of the infantry corps, driving the enemy before them in beautiful style. We saw also the Queen's Bays, in their bright scarlet uniform and brass helmets, make a splendid charge, scattering the enemy like sheep, somewhere about the place where the buildings of the Upper India Paper Mills now stand. In this charge Major Percy Smith and several men galloped right through the enemy's lines, and were surrounded and killed. Spies reported that Major Smith's head was cut off, and, with his helmet, plume and uniform, paraded through the streets of Lucknow as the head of the Commander-in-Chief. But the triumph of the enemy was short. On the 8th, General Outram was firmly established on the north bank of the Goomtee, with a siege-train of twenty-two heavy guns, with which he completely turned and enfiladed the enemy's strong position.

On the 9th of March we were ordered to take our dinners at twelve o'clock, and shortly after that hour our division, consisting of the Thirty-Eighth, Forty-Second, Fifty-Third, Ninetieth, Ninety-Third, and Fourth Punjab Infantry, was under arms, screened by the Dilkooshi palace and the garden walls round it, and Peel's Blue jackets were pouring shot and shell, with now and again a rocket, into the Martinière as fast as ever they could load. About two o'clock the order was given for the advance the Forty-Second to lead and the Ninety-Third to support; but we no sooner emerged from the shelter of the palace and garden-walls than the orderly advance became a rushing torrent. Both regiments dashed down the slope abreast, and the earthworks, trenches and rifle-pits in front of the Martinière were cleared, the enemy flying before us as fast as their legs could carry them. We pursued them right through the gardens, capturing their first line of works along the canal in front of Banks's bungalow and the Begum's palace.

There we halted for the night, our heavy guns and mortar-batteries being advanced from the Dilkooshi, and I, with some men from my company, was sent on piquet to a line of unroofed huts in front of one of our mortar-batteries, for fear the enemy from the Begum's palace might make a rush on the mortars. This piquet was not relieved till the morning of the 11th, when I learned that my company had been sent back as camp guards, the captains of companies having drawn lots for this service, as all were equally anxious to take part in the assault on the Begum's palace, and it was known the Ninety-Third were to form the storming-party. As soon as the walls should be breached, I and the men who were with me on the advance-piquet were to be sent to join Captain McDonald's company, instead of going back to our own in camp.

After being relieved from piquet, our little party set about preparing some food. Our own company having gone back to camp, no rations had been drawn for us, and our haversacks were almost empty; so I will here relate a mild case of cannibalism. Of the men of my own company who were with me on this piquet one was Andrew McOnvill (Handy Andy as he was called in the regiment) a good-hearted, jolly fellow, and as full of fun and practical jokes as his namesake, Lever's hero, a thorough Paddy from Armagh, soldier as true as the steel of a Damascus blade or a Scotch Andrea Ferrara. When last I heard of him, I may add, he was Sergeant-Major of a New Zealand militia regiment. Others were Sandy Proctor, soldier-servant to Dr Munro, and George Patterson, the son of the carrier [local delivery man] of Ballater in Aberdeenshire. I forget who the rest were, but we were joined by John McLeod, the pipe-major, and one or two more.

We got into an empty hut, well sheltered from the bullets of the enemy, and Handy Andy sallied out on a foraging expedition for something in the way of food. He had a friend in the Fifty-Third who was connected in some way with the quarter-master's department, and always well supplied with extra provender. The Fifty-Third were on our right, and there Handy Andy found his friend, and returned with a good big steak, cut from an artillery gun-bullock which had been killed by a round-shot; also some sheep's liver and a haversack full of biscuits, with plenty of pumpkin to make a good stew. There was no lack of cooking pots in the huts around, and plenty of wood for fuel, so we kindled a fire, and very soon had an excellent stew in preparation. But the enemy pitched some shells into our position, and one burst close to a man named Tim Drury, a big stout fellow, killing him on the spot. I forget now which company he belonged to, but his body lay where he fell, just outside our hut, with one thigh nearly torn away.

My readers must not for a moment think that such a picture in the foreground took away our appetites in the least. There is nothing like a campaign for making one callous and selfish, and developing the qualities of the wild beast in one's nature; and the thought which rises uppermost is Well, it is his turn now, and it may be mine next, and there is no use in being down-hearted! Our steak had been broiled to a turn, and our stew almost cooked, when we noticed tiffin and breakfast combined arrive for the European officers of the Fourth Punjab Regiment, and some others who were waiting sheltered by the walls of a roofless hut near where we were. Among them was a young fellow, Lieutenant Fitzgerald Cologan, attached to some native regiment, a great favourite with the Ninety-Third for his pluck. John McLeod at once proposed that Handy Andy should go and offer him half of our broiled steak, and ask him for a couple of bottles of beer for our dinner, as it might be the last time we should have the chance of drinking his health. He and the other officers with him accepted the steak with thanks, and Andy returned, to our no small joy, with two quart bottles of Bass's beer.

But, unfortunately he had attracted the attention of Charley F., the greatest glutton in the Ninety-Third, who was so well known for his greediness that no one would chum with him. Charley was a long-legged, humpbacked, cadaverous-faced, bald-headed fellow, who had joined the regiment as a volunteer from the Seventy-Second before we left Dover in the spring of 1857, and on account of his long legs and humpback, combined with the inordinate capacity of his stomach and an incurable habit of grumbling, he had been re-christened the 'Camel', before we had proceeded many marches with that useful animal in India. Our mutual congratulations were barely over on the acquisition of the two bottles of beer, when, to our consternation, we saw the Camel dodging from cover to cover, as the enemy were keeping up a heavy fire on our position, and if anyone exposed himself in the least, a shower of bullets was sent whistling round him.

However, the Camel, with a due regard to the wholeness of his skin, steadily made way towards our hut. We all knew that if he were admitted to a share of our stew, very little would be left for ourselves. John McLeod and I suggested that we should, at the risk of quarrelling with him, refuse to allow him any share, but Handy Andy said, 'Leave him to me, and if a bullet doesn't knock him over as he comes round the next corner, I'll put him off asking for a share of the stew.' By that time we had finished our beer. Well, the Camel took good care to dodge the bullets of Jack Pandy, and he no sooner reached a sheltered place in front of the hut, than Andy called out: 'Come along, Charley, you are just in time; we got a slice of a nice steak from an artillery-bullock this morning, and because it was too small alone for a dinner for the four of us, we have just stewed it with a slice from Tim Drury, and begad – it's first-rate! Tim tastes for all the world like fresh pork'; and with that Andy picked out a piece of the sheep's liver on the prongs of his fork, and offered it to Charley as part of Tim Drury, at the same time requesting him not to mention the circumstance to anyone.

This was too much for the Camel's stomach. He plainly believed Andy, and turned away, as if he would be sick. However, he recovered himself, and replied: 'No, thank you; hungry as I am, it shall never be in the power of anyone to tell my auld mither in the Grass Market o' Edinboro' that her Charley had become a cannibal! But if you can spare me a drop of the beer I'll be thankful for it, for the sight of your stew has made me feel unco' queer.' We expressed our sorrow that the beer was all drunk before we had seen Charley performing his oblique advance, and Andy again pressed him to partake of a little of the stew; but Charley refused to join, and sitting down in a sheltered spot in the corner of our roofless mud-hut, made wry faces at the relish evinced by the rest of us over our savoury stew. The Camel eventually discovered that he had been made a fool of, and he never forgave us for cheating him out of a share of the savoury mess.

—⊳◆⊲—

5

THE EGYPTIAN CAMPAIGN, 1882

Lieutenant H.H.L. Malcolm
(79th Queen's Own Cameron Highlanders)

The opening of the Suez Canal in 1869 suddenly made Egypt a country of strategic importance. It guarded the route between Britain and India, and consequently it was vital that it be governed by a friendly power. In 1875 the Khedive of Egypt sold his country's share of the canal to the British government, and many Egyptians feared a British takeover would follow. While the Egyptian Khedive was willing to acquiesce to the British in return for gold, the army was less flexible. In June 1882 the Egyptian army rebelled against the new Khedive, and took control of much of the country. A British expedition was sent, and the Royal Navy bombarded Alexandria, securing a bridgehead for the army. The expedition included several Scottish regiments, including the Scots Guards, the Highland Light Infantry, the Black Watch, the Seaforth Highlanders and Lieutenant Malcolm's own regiment, the Cameron Highlanders. His diary provides a detailed account of the brief campaign that followed, which reached its climax on 13 September, with the Battle of Tel-el-Kebir.

Note by Lieutenant Malcolm: (My diary was not used when the records of the Regiment were written, as these records were completed by Capt. Baynes before I rejoined the Regiment after being wounded. This diary was written each day, except the portion from 9th to 15th Sept., which was written up on 15th Sept. These explanatory remarks in brackets are added now, February 1933, over 50 years later. Additions in brackets were made in 1882 and 1883, as more information became available.)

7th August 1882:
Sailed from Gibraltar in the *Orontes* after having been held in readiness for exactly one month. Half a battalion of the 95th Rifles was also on board; three battalions of Guards with the Duke of Connaught were in front of us; the Life Guards with Sir Garnet Wolseley behind us. Very comfortable on board; shared the ladies' cabin and bathroom with Murray-Grant, two Davidsons, Scott-Elliot and Ewart.

14th:

Reached Alexandria; landed in evening; most of the European and finest part of the town had been burnt by the natives.

15th:

Landed in drill order; inspected on the quay by Sir John Adye and Sir Archibald Alison, and marched for 2 hours all over the town; cheered by 49th (Berkshires) and natives in Square; passed the Duke of Connaught and Sir Evelyn Wood.

16th:

Visited Forts Ras-el-Tin, Pharos and Kum-el-Dik, which had been much pounded by the naval bombardment; 6 or 7 shots had hit the tower of the lighthouse, one from the *Inflexible* had passed right through it. All the Armstrong guns had been split by Fisher of the *Inflexible*.

17th:

Went to Ramleh (Arabic for sandy place); visited the 46th (D.C.L.I.) Mess and Gun Hill; saw enemy's vedettes, entrenchments and camp at Kafr Dowar in the distance.

18th:

The Brigade of Guards and the 46th embarked for a secret destination (Ismailia), and we waited all day to disembark to take their places.

19th:

We disembarked early and went to Ramleh by train. In the afternoon the 38th (S. Staffords) skirmished along the canal towards the enemy's lines. I saw it splendidly from the top of the Red House. They received some shells and had 2 men wounded. 75th (Gordons) came in, the night before.

20th:

We turned out about 4 p.m. with the 75th and some regiments of the 2nd Division and advanced in ½ battalion echelon to about 1500 yards from Arabi's position without firing a shot, preceded by a few skirmishes; we then retired by alternate battalions under Arabi's fire; we replied with a few shells from Gun Hill. We received about 15 shells altogether, but nobody was hit. (These reconnaissances were made to draw the enemy's attention from Wolseley's landing at Ismailia.) 42nd and 74th (H.L.I.) both arrived during afternoon and completed the Highland Brigade.

21st:

The 42nd and some other troops went out to be shot at.

22nd:

Another reconnaissance.

23rd:

On picquet at Red House. Some Bedouins came in to loot houses about 1000 yards distant; I did not fire. Later captured several stragglers. In the evening went out to the left outpost instead of a Sergeant and patrolled to the sea every 2 hours. Heard afterwards that one of our posts was occupied by 200 Bedouins a few minutes after we had left it.

24th:

Wauchope of the 42nd, when on Red House picquet, put his head into a window and as he withdrew it a shot-gun was discharged at him. His Colour Sergeant shot the man through the head. (I had been in Captain Wauchope's Company when in 42nd. Wauchope was killed when commanding the Highland Brigade at Magersfontein in 1899.)

30th:
To Alexandria by train; transport by road; embarked on *Lusitania*, a capital ship.

31st:
Sailed at 3 p.m.; were cheered by *Inconstant, Sultan* and other men-of-war, who dressed ships and played lively tunes, which we returned. Hamley on our ship, followed by three other transports with rest of Highland Brigade.

1st September:
Reached Port Said early; went through Suez Canal all day; reached Ismailia about 7. Lake Timsah (means crocodile) full of transports and men-of-war, both British and foreign.

2nd:
Hear that there is 24 hours' armistice; Arabi Pasha had asked for 21 days. Very pleasant on board. The lake is about a mile wide. Hear that railway stock brought from England is wrong gauge and useless.

3rd:
Very hot nights; flies very bad. Salt bath is like a Turkish bath. 72nd (1st Seaforths) with Indian contingent is 6 miles from here. Sir Garnet [Wolseley] at Kassasine, 22 miles. Arabi's position at Tel-el-Kebir (means 'big hill'), 35 miles from here – all on Sweet-Water Canal. Tel-el-Kebir a very strong position

(it was the practice ground of the Egyptian Artillery). The lines of Tel-el-Kebir extend to 5 miles in width, with other lines at Salahiyah, beyond to north.

4th:

Malabar came in with a draft for us, dressed in trews and line serges. Very hot day. Sailed round the harbour.

5th:

Went ashore. Khedive's Palace turned into a hospital, 350 beds; about 70 invalids come down daily from front with dysentery, colic and sunstroke. One of our men fell down on the deck with sunstroke.

6th:

Reports that Arabi has evacuated Tel-el-Kebir. Sir Garnet will not advance till he has 14 days' supplies up. 400 men land, each day on fatigue.

7th:

Arabi has withdrawn all but 4000 men from Kafr-Dowar and is concentrating at Tel-el-Kebir.

8th:

We are to land tomorrow. Was on fatigue, taking valises and blankets to station.

9th:

(Today's diary and up to 15th written in hospital on 15th.) Left the *Lusitania* amid much cheering about 1 p.m. Never was in a more comfortable ship. We marched out about two miles, where the Brigade was assembled. After about an hour we went on and marched too much to our right, nearly losing our way; got into El Magfar, supposed to be about seven miles, at about 9 p.m. Tea was waiting for us, and we had a good night, but when we woke we found ourselves saturated with dew. Arabi attacked the outposts of our force at Kassassine with about 10,000 men; was driven back right into his entrenchments. We had [a] loss of about 70 killed and wounded. Graham blamed for not going further in pursuit.

10th:

Marched 2½ miles to commissariat stores at Tel-el-Mahuta, where we lay in the sun all day, and it was stifling hot. I rigged up a shelter of bullrushes. Got some soup, very badly cooked, for dinner. Marched at 3 p.m. One of the 75th died of the sun. The Indian contingent had passed us during the night; now we passed their camp. The 72nd came out with their band and water, and played us past amid much cheering. Halt about 8.30 p.m. at Mahsameh, where an Egyptian camp had been. The stink was excessive, and we were very done up with the heat. 200 men fell out in the Brigade, principally from the 75th. I was on picquet all night with half of 'F' Company.

11th:

Up before daybreak and marched at 5.30 without any breakfasts for about three miles to Kassassine. Our tents came up about an hour after. The heat was terrific; too hot to get much rest or sleep. The canal water was very foul, the Egyptians having thrown dead camels into it. Hear that the grand attack was postponed a day.

(The Regimental records are wrong. They say we reached Kassassine on 12th, the day we started our night march, which is decidedly wrong. According to my diary, we rested there nearly 36 hours, and had a Battalion parade at 6.30 a.m. on 12th: a very valuable rest before our night march and battle.)

12th:

The cavalry marched last night to cut off Arabi's left. At 5.30 we got orders to strike tents and parade at 6.30 p.m. with 100 rounds and water bottles only. We were to attack with fixed bayonets only amid perfect silence. No man to load or fire a shot. All enemy on the ground to be bayoneted. No man on any account to fall out to help the wounded. Great excitement and expectation.

The Brigade marched off about 8 p.m. for 'Nine Gun Hill', distant about 3 miles. Very nice cool marching over firm ground. Felt very fresh. Our supplies had come from Ismailia just before parading. Halted on near side of 'Nine Gun Hill'; looking back there was a splendid scene of masses of troops in the dusk and cavalry in front, with camp fires all along the railway, which were kept up large to deceive the enemy.

Went on about a mile, formed up about 10.30 and lay down to sleep. About midnight Sir Garnet's Staff moving round startled someone sleeping and caused a sudden stand-to all along the line. Everyone jumped up, thinking that the enemy were attacking, and bayonets were fixed amid considerable confusion. We settled down again, and an hour later rum was issued, and we formed our attack formation-column of ½ battalions in double companies at deploying interval, leading line being at one pace interval, 2nd line at double company distance.

Our right, ½ battalion had 'A' and 'B' Companies in front

line, supported by 'C' and 'D'; our left ½ battalion had 'E' and 'F' in front line, with 'G' and 'H' in support in 2nd line. I was leading the left half of 'F' Company on the left of our front line, next to the 74th; Blackburn, who commanded 'F' Company, took the right, our directing flank. Our Brigade had the 42nd on the right, then the 75th, then ourselves, with the 74th on our left.

Graham's Brigade, 18th, 84th, 87th and Marines, was on the right of ours. The Naval contingent was next [to] the canal. The Indian contingent were on the south side of the canal. The Guards Brigade was in reserve, with the 46th and 60th; the 46th and part of the 60th were afterwards moved up on the left, and part of the 60th on right, to fill gaps. Nominal distance to Arabi's position was 7 miles. We really marched about 9 or 10 miles.

13th:
Marched till 3 a.m. north-west (I could read my compass and watch nearly all night), then changed front to left; after half an hour's delay started again south-west. Halted several times and changed direction with frequent delays. About 4 a.m. I saw some mounted men indistinctly in front, and just after we got the order to 'Form Groups', they turned out to be Bedouins, who retired at once. (The Bedouins always move at night in summer, so are excellent for night work; there is no doubt they warned the enemy, hence the sheet of fire which greeted us 50 minutes later.)

About 4.30 it began to lighten a little, and every minute it got lighter; I was afraid we were too late, and were let in for a daylight attack; no sound was heard and we were marching on still, when suddenly about 4.50 a shot was fired just in front, followed by several more, and the order to 'fix bayonets'

Incident in the Rebellion of 1745 by David Morier

Culloden, 1746: According to the Chevalier de Johnstone, the only real chance the Highlanders had of breaking the government line was on the Jacobite's far right – at the spot chosen by Morier in his depiction of the battle.

The Battle of Waterloo: Curiassiers Charging Highlanders in Square by Felix Philippoteaux

Waterloo, 1815: Several Scottish regiments took part in the Battle of Waterloo, but for most their greatest test came when they faced a charge by the massed ranks of Napoleon's French cavalry.

(Opposite, top) The Battle of Bushy Run by Don Troiani

Bushy Run, 1763: By the time the French & Indian War ended the Black Watch were highly trained in the loose formation tactics needed to counter the fighting methods of Pontiac's Indians.

(Opposite, bottom) The Battle of Alexandria, based on an original painting by Philip de Loutherbourg

Alexandria, 1801: The group comforting the dying General Abercrombie includes a soldier from the 92nd Highlanders, who points towards the battlefield, as if to demonstrate the scale of the Scottish-born general's victory over the French.

The Thin Red Line: 93rd Highlanders at Balaclava by Robert Gibb

Balaclava, 1854: An iconic moment in Scottish military history, the stand of 'the thin red line' at Balaclava was actually an easy victory – the Russian cavalry were unable to counter the firepower of the 93rd Highlanders.

Alma: Forward the 42nd by Robert Gibb

Alma, 1854: Private Robb, who took part in the assault of the Highland Brigade against the heights at Alma recalled how Sir Colin Campbell was an inspiring figure, leading his Highlanders into the attack.

Tel-el-Kebir by A. De Neuville

Tel-el-Kebir, 1882: Lieutenant Malcolm recounted how the Highland Brigade were surprised to discover a wide ditch in front of the main Egyptian positions. The Highlanders struggled over it, to capture the enemy's earthworks which lay behind.

Loos, 1915: During the attack at Loos the British used poison gas for the first time – a hazard to friend and foe alike. Lance-Corporal Forman was particularly ill-prepared for this new threat.

(Opposite, top) The Planning of the Attack by Officers of the 51st Highland Division by Ian Eadie

El Alamein, 1943: The assault of the 51st Highland Division at El Alamein recounted by Captain Green was a meticulously planned operation, where each unit was given well-defined objectives – most of which were given Scottish placenames.

The Platform Canteen, Victoria Station by Bernard Meninsky

Off to War, 1916: As Private Lyon recounts, the mass of volunteers who joined the ranks of the Scottish regiments were given only the bare rudiments of training before they were sent off to war.

Labels visible on the map in the image: START LINE, VICTORIA, 24 AUS.DIV., MONTROSE, ARBROATH, FORFAR, CRIEDEN, ELGIN, LEVEN, FRISE, COQUE, DOLLAR, TURRIFF, INSCH, KILLIN, CRIEF

Korea, 1953: For much of the Korean War, Scottish soldiers like these Argyll and Sutherland Highlanders defended hilltop positions, waiting for a massed Chinese assault like the one Corporal Halley experienced in 1953.

Warrenpoint, 1979: Hours after Lord Louis Mountbatten was killed by the IRA, a double booby-trap caused the death of eighteen soldiers, including two Queen's Own Highlanders, at Narrow Water Castle in Northern Ireland. This was the largest loss of life in a single incident during the Troubles.

Battle of Tumbledown Hill by Terence Cuneo

Falklands, 1982: Lieutenant Lawrence was one of the unlucky ones. The casualties suffered by the Scots Guards on Tumbledown Hill were surprisingly light, given the rugged terrain and the unexpectedly firm resolve of the Argentinean defenders.

was passed down. After a few seconds about half a dozen shots came from different places, and then odd shots all along a line which we had not seen before, 250 to 300 yards away.

We began to charge and cheer, and the fire came over the earthworks in front in a perfect shower like the sparks from a Catherine Wheel. We all paused for a moment as if expecting to be mown down, but when no one was hit we rushed on and noticed that the bullets were all going over our heads. I only saw one man hit; he fell all in a heap and looked so beastly that we all seemed to hurry up to get out of the fire.

Fortunately the enemy were dazzled by their own fire, so could not see us to correct their aim, and their bayonets were not fixed, which would have lowered their bullets. We rushed on yelling, and I expected to run right up the parapet when suddenly we all went pell-mell into a broad ditch, which nobody had seen, being dazzled by the firing which came over in a perfect sheet.

The ditch was about 5 feet deep and 8 to 10 feet wide with perpendicular sides, and the parapet about 5 feet high, with a berm, and trench in rear. Just where I was there were some steps cut in the ditch and parapet, and to avoid being bayoneted by men falling on me I scrambled up the parapet as quick as possible, and getting on the top saw several rifles at once aimed at me, so I jumped down, half falling, among the enemy. I heard afterwards that they were Soudanese at that part of the line. I became engaged with an officer, who seemed very excited and slashed about wildly. Before I regained my feet he cut me across the back, but my brown belts took most of the blow. He also cut me across the sword-arm and just missed the artery inside my elbow. I hit him several times, but finding [found] the edge of my claymore ineffective.

I was trying the point when he tried to catch my blade, and

in doing so we closed; several of his men had gathered round, and one gave me a blow on the head, which came through my cork helmet to the skull, which it fractured. We struggled on the ground, and I fancy some of our men were coming at him, for he seemed to rise to try to get away, and I got my sword into him. I am not quite sure of this finish to our fight. We may have fallen at the same time, he from a cut I gave him across the neck, his only exposed part, and I from a blow by one of his men behind me with a clubbed rifle. Probably his men could not shoot me during this fight for fear of hitting him.

Our Sergeant-Major, going over the ground about two hours later, found an enemy officer just about the place where I went over; he wore brass spurs and a brass scabbard; he had a gash across his neck, which had sliced off part of his chin, but had apparently not died of it, for he had a koran in his hand with a bayonet thrust half through it; the thrust must have been made as he lay on the ground before taking out the koran from his breast. (I was the only one armed with a sword that crossed the trenches near this point in the first line, so he must have been my opponent.) My claymore was very sharp; I carried a stick of emery on purpose to sharpen it, as I had no revolver.

I afterwards had my claymore shortened by four inches and fitted with a sabre grip to facilitate pointing, but I have never tested it since. When I got up I felt not much the worse, and went down the trench to the left with a few men, chasing and killing a number who were still firing over their parapet at the 74th (HLI), who had had a check and had not yet succeeded in gaining the enemy's parapet. The 74th lost Major Colville, two lieutenants (Rays and Somervell) and fourteen men killed; five lieutenants and 52 men wounded, and eleven men missing in doing so.

I went on till I was quite tired, when, on turning round, one of two men who were following me fired so close past my face that it took the skin off my nose and chin. Private Murray was one of these two men. He had been connecting file with the 74th on our left. The 79th were then trying to form up on the ground a little to the right, but there was a heavy flanking fire from an earthwork and line of trenches on the left; at the same time the 74th were firing at the first parapet on our left, and many Martini-Henry bullets came amongst us from them, so most of us did not stay, but doubled on towards a battery above us.

From here there was a constant succession of lines uphill, with camps between and batteries on the commanding positions. Before one battery Sir Archibald Alison, our Brigadier, made us halt to let our guns shell it; our Pipe-Major Grant, did not hear this for his piping, and went on about 100 yards by himself till I ran after him and stopped him. We went on running and charging continually, with occasional small stands by the enemy and some firing, many of the trenches on our left facing our flank, and we firing up them.

I noticed that the enemy would often lie on the ground as if wounded, and start firing again when they thought they were not observed. I found it a good plan to rush at them with my claymore; that seemed to put them off their aim, and the point of my very sharp sword pierced them like butter. If I had a revolver and had paused to use it, either here or on top of the first parapet, I should certainly have been shot, as a revolver is no match for a rifle.

This went on till about 6 a.m., when we came in sight of the enemy's main camp near the station; it lay below us, and was swarming with fugitives, mostly mounted, and four trains were in the station. We were about 200, mostly Camerons, a mixture of the Highland Brigade, about one in six being officers; Sir Archibald was running at the front all along. The Colonel and Hamley now came up on horseback, just as an Egyptian officer approached, who said he was Rachid Pasha, the Governor. He was dismounted and kept a prisoner.

Three of the trains steamed out just as some of our guns came into action. They hit a carriage in the second train, but the detached half was carried on by the third train behind. We went on to the canal and bridge, where the flies were in myriads. I got some grapes and biscuit that had been brought in for the Egyptians and looted an umbrella, as I had no helmet. I had also lost my scabbard and knife. Everyone I met told me I was reported killed. I felt very done up, and after the regiment had formed up I had to lie down behind a large tent, where Admiral Sir Beauchamp Seamour had settled down too.

After resting I went to Surgeon-General Manley, who told me I must return to hospital or erysipelas would set up in my wounds. The surgeons were all out on the battlefield, but Corban dressed my wounds in the afternoon. The Brigade went on about 5 p.m., the 42nd by train for Zagazig. McCausland came back about 6.30 with our burying party, and had seen a Major, two Subalterns, one Colour Sergeant and a number of men of the 74th still unburied. My servant came in, having been looking for me all day on the battlefield. I joined Fox and Coveny of the 42nd, who were also wounded, in an empty railway carriage for the night. Sergeant Souter, who was on guard at the station, having given me some supper.

14th:
Various visitors came to our carriage, including the Duke of Connaught and my cousin, Tom Fraser RE (afterwards Sir

Thomas), who seemed very well, and several newspaper correspondents. We started for Ismailia in an Egyptian ammunition train full of live shells. The entrenchments looked very formidable as we passed through them. We reached the hospital there about 7 p.m., after many delays.

≡►◦◄≡

6
DARGAI, 1897

Lieutenant George Douglas Mackenzie DSO
(1st Gordon Highlanders)

In 1895 the 1st Battalion of the Gordon Highlanders were serving in the North-West Frontier of India when the tribes of some of the northern provinces rose in revolt. As part of the Chitral Relief Force they defeated the insurgents after a bayonet charge up a mountainside, relieved a beleaguered garrison and restored British rule. This meant that when the Afridis tribe rose in rebellion two years later, the Gordons were the obvious choice to spearhead the expedition sent to pacify the region. On 18 October they drove the Afridis from the hills around the village of Dargai, but when they left the enemy returned and reoccupied them. On 20 October the Gordons and the 3rd Sikhs were sent for again. They charged straight up the slope, as pipers played the regimental march, 'Cock o' the North'. When Piper Findlater was shot through both feet and unable to stand, he sat up and kept on playing. He won the VC for his actions, as did Private Lawson, who rescued his wounded comrades while under heavy fire. Lieutenant Mackenzie of the Gordons gave a brief account of this spirited engagement. He was later awarded the DSO for the part he played in the capture of the heights.

Of course all this time no idea of a check had entered anyone's head so we were surprised sometime after to be ordered to a village some distance up the hill, our order sobering to try to keep down the enemy's fire by long range volleys. This we did, assisted by the Maxim Gun of the 16th Lancers and our own, to the best of our ability; from as far as I can remember 11 a.m. till 2.30 p.m.; during most of which time poor little Ghurkhas [*sic*] pluckily 'sticking it out' were coming back wounded. The Derbyshire Adjutant came back for more ammunition, and looking through glasses it was evident that no progress was being made, but when at about 3 o'clock an order came for us to move up I fancy very few in the Battalion realised what they were 'for'. Well up we went, the accent being harried by an occasional bullet whistling overhead to show there was no ill feeling till, after an exceedingly stiff climb, we found ourselves in a little sort of glen under cover from fire from the cliffs at which the Derbys and Dorsets lying under cover just above us were firing volleys.

Here we lay for some time watching the 3rd Sikhs toiling up the way we had come, and then finally arrived up 'alongside'. The Colonel stood up and spoke to the Regt, the gist of his speech being 'Gordons, listen to me, the position in front has got to be taken *at all costs* and we are going to take it in front of the whole Division. Remember once we have started there is to be *no stopping*, the advance must be continuous. Section commanders *must try* and keep their sections together. Fix Bayonets and charge Magazines.' This was greeted with cheers, after which had subsided the man next to me remarked 'Well I'll have one other smoke anyhow.' When the 'Advance' sounded, the scene baffled description, men shouting and yelling, and more like a football scrimmage than anything else.

Personally I can remember very little. When I got to the ridge I found no one going over, some men staggering back wounded and some lying down under cover behind the Ridge. It was no good staying to be shot. So Sergeant McKay ('B' Company) and I took the plunge followed by many others. Sergeant McKay was knocked sideways by a bullet through his belt and I with ditto through my scabbard in the first minute, and as I went to retrieve my sword, which had flown out of my hand, received a similar attention through my kilt. After this time it was all scrambling, running and shouting (if one had breath to spare) till we reached the welcome shelter of the Rock where Colonel Travers and the remainder of the Gallant Ghurkhas, who had got across unscathed had found refuge and where they had been sitting for three hours awaiting relief.

Now there was a splendid push of tartan mixed with Sikhs, Ghurkhas, Dorsets and Derbys and the fire from above gradually slackening finally died away and scrambling up the precipitous cliff our boys' cheers told those below that the place was won. Now the sad business of counting the cost began. Word was first received, at any rate by me, that my Captain (Major Macbean), Dingwall and Lamont of the officers had been killed. About the latter I am sorry to report was true, but the other two, although most severely wounded (Dingwall's person and accoutrements having been struck by seven bullets!), I am glad to say they both quickly recovered. Dingwall afterwards rejoined us at Maidan, Tirah. Among the men casualties were of course far more numerous, but as I have no date I cannot give figures.

The official history of the Gordon Highlanders provides the casualty details which Lieutenant Mackenzie omitted:

The total casualties of the troops engaged were 3 officers and 33 non-commissioned officers and men killed, and 12 officers and 147 non-commissioned officers and men wounded, mostly in the space of about 150 yards across. The determined rapidity of their advance rendered the losses sustained by the Gordons less than might have been expected, but their success was dearly purchased by the death of Lieutenant Alexander Lamont, Corporal A. Bell, and Private Quinn, killed in action. Lieutenant-Colonel Mathias CB, Major Forbes Macbean, Captain H.P. Uniacke, Lieutenants M.F. Meiklejohn, Kenneth Dingwall and G.S.G. Craufurd, and 35 non-commissioned officers and men were wounded, of whom four died of their wounds: (Colour-Sergeant E. Pickersgill, and Privates Civil, Davie and McKinnon).

7
THE BOER WAR, 1900

Private Thomas F. Dewar (Imperial Yeomanry)

Decades of tension between the British and the Boer settlers in South Africa led to armed conflict in 1880–81. While this resulted in the creation of two independent Boer republics, tensions still remained high. The discovery of gold in the region increased the economic stakes, while repeated British attempts to gain administrative control over the Boer states caused widespread resentment. By late 1899 it was clear that war between the Boer republics and Britain was inevitable. In October the Boers took the offensive, invading Natal and besieging British garrisons in Kimberley, Ladysmith and Mafeking. British troops were sent to South Africa, and rushed into action. The Boers inflicted humiliating defeats on the British at Magersfontein and Colenso, forcing the British commanders to call for reinforcements and to rethink their tactics. The campaign of 1900 was more of a success, and by July a British column had cornered a Boer force commanded by General Prinsloo at Spitzkopf, near Bethlehem in the Orange Free State. The British force included a Highland brigade and Scottish detachments of the newly raised Imperial Yeomanry. Private Thomas Francis Dewar served as a medical orderly, with the dangerous job of tending the wounded on the battlefield. In his journal he describes the attack on the Boer position.

Camp, somewhere in the Bethlehem Hills,
Saturday 21st July 1900
Today we have been again in action, but this time the Cameron Highlanders and not the mounted troops have had to bear the brunt of things. Without a contour map or a series of views, it is impossible to convey even approximately the tactical plan of the day. Suffice it to say that from the plateau of the Orange River Colony, higher than Ben Nevis in every part, and in that part of it which lies between Bethlehem and Harrismith there towers up a conical hill some sixteen hundred feet high, called Spitz Kop or Spitz Kranz.

This hill is of an odd shape, somewhat like the hills shown in Japanese pictures and on the old willow pattern plate. Spitz Kop has two outlying hills as supporters, each some six hundred feet above the rolling veldt, and with the near or north-western side precipitous, the further side somewhat sloped. One of these, strongly held by the Boers, was the objective for the day, and General Bruce Hamilton's whole force was engaged in the attack.

The Yeomanry were on the left wing, and, early in the day,

advancing dismounted, their horses sheltered in a donga [gully], they made an attack at long range. After a time, one of the Ayrshire men having had his temple grazed by a bullet and another having had his helmet shot through, the order came for the Yeomanry to retire, and the Camerons, in widely extended line, took their place, and made a series of running advances in very poor cover.

From a safe corner behind some rocks I saw a couple of Highlanders fall, and, as they seemed unattended, I went forward to look after them. The first had a bullet in his calf, which was easily got out. By the time I reached the other, two stretcher-bearers were beside him, but one of them had already got wounded, and while we applied first field dressings a Mauser bullet went through the other's coat. At this point the surgeon attached to the Camerons came up, and we decided that it was neither necessary nor discreet to go forward at the moment! So we lay each behind an ant heap – no very efficient protection – till, the right wing, having turned the shoulder of the hill, the Boers began to show signs of moving, and their fire slackened and eventually ceased.

Then he and I made a zig-zag advance from one to another of the fallen men. The first I came to had a wound in the arm, the second a wound in the thigh, the third was dead with a bullet through his head, the fourth just dead with a wound of the heart, the fifth, a poor laddie, with a fatal wound from Martini or expanding bullet, through the right lung. The next case was that of a subaltern with a wound of the upper arm, who very pluckily disdained to be helped towards the ambulance; he set off with a rather unsteady gait. The Camerons had a total of about twenty casualties in the action, of which three, as I have said, were fatal, and all but one or two occurred on this, the left flank of the attack.

In the later afternoon having had my horse brought up, I rode round by the rear of the hill to its summit, noted the heaps of empty cartridges in the nooks and crannies whence the Boers had fired, but no positive signs of casualties on their part. Looking over the edge of the cliff, it was a matter of surprise to me that we had not suffered much more severely; for, from their coigns of vantage [defensive positions], the Boers, themselves unseen and unassailable, could completely command the plain. In spite of everything, however, we had attained our object; Spitz Kranz was in our hands, and tonight our picket will hold it.

Descending in the gloaming, I joined in a simple funeral service. Side by side, in a shallow pit, in their dusty uniforms and with their bare brown knees, lay these men who two or three hours before had been happy and strong and well. There was no opportunity for band or coronach, gun carriage or Union Jack. The chaplain of the Camerons performed a simple Scottish service, the graves were solemnly filled up by men of the company to which the dead belonged, and we saluted and rode home in the darkness, hailing with gladness the lights of camp as a beacon to tired men.

Camp, just under Spitz Kranz, Sunday 22nd July 1900
We have had a third day of fighting, without any very definite gain so far as I can see. This time the hills to the north and east of Spitz Kop furnished our objective; and, as a deep valley, in parts like a ravine, separated us from the Boers, a very difficult task had to be performed by our troops. This time it was the turn of the mounted men to face the music. The Boers were across the valley, well sheltered amid rocks and scarcely ever visible. On our side, the slope was gentle and grass-covered; so much the worse for us, but of course it was they, not we, who chose the position.

The Glasgow Yeomanry, advancing on the extreme left, were received with very hot fire. Very soon, one of their number, rising to make an advance, suddenly flopped down, evidently hit. He was some three hundred yards away, and to reach him I had to run transversely to the line of fire, occasionally lying down to recover breath. I thus furnished Mr Boer with an excellent mark, and the process was extremely unpleasant. However, nothing happened; I reached my man, found him shot through the foot, and applied first dressing. Our difficulties were not over, since we – the patient and I – were directly in the line of the fire intended for the men in front.

After some internal debate, I decided to try and get him back, so, crawling and then running towards the rear, I arranged with my man to bring up a led horse at a given signal. Then I returned to the wounded Brown, and we began our retreat.

Grovelling along in serpentine fashion, we traversed the first couple of hundred yards. Then we risked standing up, and Brown holding on to me for support, hopped another hundred yards with many intervals for rest. Then I signalled for the horse and got the patient mounted. As we retired, three men and two horses, we got a farewell salute from the enemy across the kloof; but, except for a graze of my man's horse, we escaped scatheless.

It happened that a strong crosswind was blowing all day long, and this, no doubt, accounts for the remarkably small list of casualties which characterised the engagement.

Having seen Brown on his way off to camp, several severe wounds to men of the Burma and Malta MI [Mounted Infantry], one through the neck and mouth, next required my attention. Thereafter I returned to the rear of the fighting line to be in touch with the yeomanry if anything should happen. I ensconced myself behind a protecting stone and read, as I waited, Jerome's *Thoughts of an Idle Fellow*, which I had purloined – borrowed, I mean – from the Bethlehem Library, and which I had brought in my haversack. 'Zip, zip, ping-ping: zip, zip, zip, ping'; 'hu-hu-hu-hu-hu-hu-hu-hu-hu', from the Vickers-Maxim, the 'pom-pom' of the Tommies, up behind: 'boom', from the field pieces. The bullets seem to be passing about two inches from one's ear; but for ten which are audible, only one strikes the ground within half-a-dozen yards. It is a most unpleasant, most disquieting sound; but, after an hour or two, one learns that the percentage of individual risk is much less than he had at first thought. While fully engaged or advancing, there is no time for thought; but to wait under fire, still more to have to retire, is, frankly, a trying thing.

Later in the day, after one or two minor casualties to the yeomen, I climbed a little kopje to watch our guns firing percussion shrapnel. There I met a man whom I knew, an officer of the Canadians. Between the rounds, he and I sat in a little kraal to shelter from the wind. Then there came another noise, new to me, as of a very swift bird, flying overhead, and flapping its wings two hundred times a minute. We left that kraal, without indecorous haste, I hope, but nevertheless promptly. The second shell also went high. The third hit the kraal and sent its walls flying. We had been well advised to move.

Soon after this, the fire on both sides slackened, and we could see, in the gathering gloom, the Boers leaving their sheltering rocks. Then back to a new camp just under the steep slopes of Spitz Kranz we wended, to enjoy our soup and tea and smokes. And therein, perhaps, is the oddest thing of all; to rise and have a nice breakfast, to go out and shoot at your fellow men all day, and then to return to camp in the evening with the surety of a nice warm dinner awaiting you – that is, if you do return.

≈≡➤◆➤≡≈

8

THE BOER WAR, 1900

Simon Fraser, 14th Lord Lovat (Lovat Scouts)

When the Boer War began in late 1899, it soon became apparent that one of the keys to success on the battlefield was mobility. While the Boers usually fought on foot, they used horses to move quickly, and to avoid pursuit. The British solution was to send cavalry of their own to South Africa, to counter the Boer's superiority in this area. The British raised units of Imperial Yeomanry, composed of volunteers who were already experienced horsemen. While many of these Yeomanry units were numbered rather than named, their ranks were often filled by men from existing Yeomanry regiments. An exception was the Lovat Scouts, raised by Lord Lovat himself, much as his ancestors had more than two centuries before. This time, instead of being raised from the tenantry, Fraser's men were all volunteers. As he lacked suitable experience, Lord Lovat assumed the role of second-in-command of the regiment, but fought alongside his men during the Boer War. Here he writes a letter home to a friend, outlining the way the Boers operated, and describing a small skirmish where his men emerged victorious.

Letter to Sir Francis Linley, 21st May 1900

My dear Wipe,

You old scoundrel, never to have written a line. We have

had a great time and really done rather well, been complimented by three Generals and had six men mentioned, besides being told by Hunter that a very large share of the Retief success was due to our reconnoitring maps and on the day of fight seizing two important kopjes. To give you news is absurd, but let me clear your intelligent mind of one or two paper errors. Firstly, to a man with eyes and capable of using them the Boers are always in sight. They wear dark clothes and can be seen for miles. They never take cover till one gets nearly within 'naked eyesight' range and therefore are easily picked up by the intelligent spyer.

Secondly, the Boer shelling is good, much better than our own. Their shrapnel, it is true, usually bursts high; but then as ours never goes near the mark, through entire lack of range or accuracy, the advantage lies with the Boers.

Thirdly, fighting is devilish good fun before the bullets begin and as soon as the show is over. I personally have only once got sufficiently excited to get over that feeling of internal chill, irritability and anxiety to make water which used to precede my efforts in the pig-skin. On that one occasion on which I got really angry I thoroughly enjoyed myself.

As a corps we have been very lucky. One company came in for Roberts' march, saw Doornkop and Diamond Hill, besides lesser engagements, the other company came in for Methuen's doubtful victories and good steady picket fighting round Heilbron. I was with the latter and was lucky enough to see the three fights on the Railway as adjutant to 1,000 details on my way up from dysentery to join my company.

On July 1st, our two Companies joined and we had some good fighting at Bethlehem, Retief, Nauport Hill and Golden Gate, being very lucky in being the only company who saw all four. Our casualties have been extraordinarily light as yet;

only 14 men since the start though we lost four horses out of 50 one day and 9 another. Poor Brodie was wounded in his leg and is to go home. As far as one can judge, we shall go south to round up Olivier when we have refitted here and given time to Rundle on the east of Rietz and Bruce Hamilton at Rietz to make good their positions.

The men are enjoying themselves and like the work. John Dewar and Paterson have done extraordinarily well, especially at night visits to Boer laagers [defensive encampments]. I don't think you know any of the others except McKillop, but you would recognize a good many faces of the Beaufort beaters.

Two of our men did rather a smart thing the other day. Were doing extreme right flank to 'Yeodogs' [Imperial Yeomanry] when they bumped into seven Boers, who made signs to put down their arms. Our lambs, with no thought of surrender, thought the Boers wanted to come in and yelled out 'Well, put down your b—y arms!' Then Mr Boer fired and missed, and our fellows downed a brace and while one led back the horses the other took cover and guarded the rear. The Yeodogs not arriving as expected, a bolt was determined on, but one horse disabled made this difficult. Things began to look black for our men, when fortunately the Boers, finding the fire too hot in front, tried a turning and cutting off movement to the rear with the result that our lambs tumbled up on one horse, headed straight for the Boer laager, skirting wide as soon as clear of the immediate enemies and getting off without a scratch with at least two bagged.

Alastair has got back with only slight go of fever. No news yet as to result.

Post off.

CHAPTER 5

THE GREAT WAR

The origins of the Great War (or First World War) can be traced to the international tension created by the unification of Germany in 1871. For the next four decades an uneasy peace existed in Europe, the apparent tranquillity endangered by the expansion of Germany's industrial and military might, French resentment over her loss over territory to Germany in 1871, colonial ambition, and a dangerous naval arms race between Britain and Germany. A complex web of alliances developed, where one country would aid another in time of war.

The diplomatic web fell apart when the Archduke Franz Ferdinand of Austria-Hungary was assassinated in June 1914. The Austro-Hungarians blamed Serb nationalists, and declared war on Serbia. As a result Russia mobilised against Austria, causing Austria's ally Germany to declare war on Russia. France promptly declared war on Germany. As an ally of France, Britain was dragged into the conflict, and declared war on both Germany and Austro-Hungary.

The outbreak of the Great War in August 1914 was met with spontaneous enthusiasm in Scotland. Thousands queued up outside recruiting offices, answering Lord Kitchener's plea for volunteers. In fact, in proportion to the total eligible male population more Scots volunteered for the army during the first year of the war than the totals of England and Wales combined. During the four years of war, more than half a million Scots enlisted in the army – a quarter of the male population, and a little under half of those within the eligible age band of 25 to 49. The majority of those who remained were employed in vital reserved occupations – working the farms, producing munitions and building warships.

This great wave of volunteers – Kitchener's New Army – had to be organised, trained and equipped. This meant they would not be ready for active service until the following spring at the earliest. Meantime the Scottish battalions of the standing army were sent to France, as part of the British Expeditionary Force (BEF). At the time, most Scottish regiments consisted of two battalions, one of which served overseas, while the other remained at home. For example, in the Royal Scots, the 1st battalion was in India when the war began, but it was shipped home before the end of the year. That meant that only the 2nd battalion was immediately available to serve in France. These home service battalions formed the 'Old Contemptibles' – the professional British army that fought the Germans at Mons, on the Marne and at the First Battle of Ypres. In most Scottish regiments, the 3rd battalion was a depot unit, used to fill the ranks of the two regular battalions. They certainly needed the replacements – by December most of the regular Scottish battalions had suffered almost 50 per cent casualties.

By October, what remained of these veteran battalions were joined by new battalions (usually numbered 4 to 6), made up of men from the Territorial Army. Many of these Territorials had their first taste of battle during the terrible bloodletting around Ypres. The following spring they were joined by the volunteers of Kitchener's New Army, supported by the men of the seven regiments of the Scottish Yeomanry Cavalry. For the most part, these men were formed into six Scottish divisions. The 51st (Highland) and the 52nd (Lowland) divisions were formed from the Territorial units, while the ranks of the 9th

(Scottish) and 15th (Scottish) divisions were filled by Kitchener's volunteers. Two additional divisions – the 64th (2nd Highland) and 65th (2nd Lowland) divisions – were raised from the volunteers. Without these men the British war effort would have crumbled.

Rather than send them to the front in penny packets, the British High Command planned to use these volunteers as a strategic weapon, unleashed *en masse* on an unsuspecting German army. The decision was made to launch them into the attack at Loos in Flanders, where it was hoped a short, sharp assault would puncture the German line. What is remarkable when you read the letters and diaries of these volunteers, is that for the most part they were filled with optimism. While few would have dreamed of martial glory, they felt they were playing their part, and that their commanders knew what they were doing. These personal accounts stand in stark contrast to those written later in the war, when the survivors of these battalions harboured no illusions about the horrors of trench warfare.

The Battle of Loos, which began on 25 September 1915, was meant to be the assault that would win the war. The British even had a secret weapon – gas – which was being used in action for the first time. It proved a disappointment. Not only had the Germans been issued with gas masks far superior to those used by the British, but the gas itself proved almost as dangerous to the attackers as it did to the defenders. Like thousands of others, my grandfather, a subaltern in the Royal Scots, was incapacitated and injured by the gas dispensed by his own side. Then came the machine guns. The gas, coupled with a fearsome artillery barrage, was meant to neutralise the German defences. Instead the Germans rode out the storm in their deep shelters, and emerged to mow down Kitchener's volunteers in droves. By the end of the day over 10,000 Scots lay dead or dying, all for the gain of two miles of mud and rubble.

The importance of the Battle of Loos (1915) was that it was the first real slaughter of the volunteer battalions – the so-called New Army. Before, casualties had been inflicted on regular soldiers, or the Territorials. Loos extended the 'roll of honour' to include those who had flocked to the colours out of a sense of patriotic duty. It was the battle where the misplaced optimism faded and died. After the war, all those official histories written by staff officers seemed reluctant to mention casualties. They had no place for the grim realism of some of the eye-witnesses included in this book. Instead they preached the importance of sacrifice and heroism, singling out deeds of bravery, or claiming that it had all been somehow worthwhile. *The History of the 9th (Scottish) Division*, written in 1921, claimed of Loos that 'The lessons deduced from it laid down the lines upon which British tactics and strategy were based.' By that, the author probably meant that the same bloody mistakes would be repeated over and over again – at the Somme and Second Ypres in 1916, and at Passchendaele in 1917. Despite this, an equestrian statue of Field Marshal Haig surveys the esplanade of Edinburgh Castle.

Of course, not all Scottish soldiers were fed into the mincing machine of the Western Front. Several regiments fought at Gallipoli, the ill-planned offensive designed to capture the Dardanelles and knock Turkey out of the war. The Turks were no pushover – casualties were heavy from the start – the 1st King's Own Scottish Borderers alone losing half their strength as they tried to make it off the beach. Other Scottish battalions suffered almost as badly, although the first-hand account from Gallipoli included here is less gory – an account of life in the trenches, waiting for 'the big push'. Scottish soldiers served even further afield – in the deserts of Palestine, in the fertile crescent of Mesopotamia, in the mountains of Salonika and Macedonia, and in the veldt of East Africa. One of our first-hand accounts gives details of an attack launched by the Black Watch north of Baghdad, where Private Charles Melvin from Kirriemuir won the VC. As the residents of the town said afterwards, they felt sorry for the Turks 'faced wi a fu' Charlie comin' towards them, kilt flyin'. Before and after the war, Melvin was best described as 'a local character', but at Istabulat, in what is now Iraq, he came into his own.

The slaughter at Loos meant that the army was once again short of men. Consequently conscription was introduced in January 1916, and by the following year a new wave of soldiers began to appear – ready to participate in months of slaughter around Ypres and Passchendaele. By the end of the war most Scottish regiments consisted of more than a dozen battalions. The Royal Scots mustered 35, including three battalions of Canadians. It represented an enormous and costly enterprise, but perhaps because of the sheer scale of the casualties, it became frowned upon to question the point of it all. Despite the collapse of the German army in the autumn of 1918, the killing continued right up until the armistice on 11 November. The official death-toll within the Scottish regiments was 147,000 men – roughly one in four of those Scottish soldiers who served in the army, or one in nine of Scotland's eligible male population before the war. It is little wonder that for decades afterwards, war widows would be a common sight in Scottish towns.

At the end of the war the greatly enlarged Scottish regiments were reduced to their prewar strength, and those who could simply got on with their lives. After the victory parades came the building of the war memorials, now a feature of almost every Scottish town or village. In dozens of Scottish high streets, cemeteries or churchyards, the stone figure of a kilted, tam o'shanter-wearing soldier now stands sentinel over the names of his fallen comrades. Many thought the immense sacrifice had at least bought a lasting peace. Few imagined that less than three decades later, a new list of names would appear on these war memorials. In many cases the names would remain the same.

———◆◆◆———

1

JOINING KITCHENER'S ARMY, 1914

Private Charles Forman (8th Battalion, Black Watch)

While optimists and newspapermen predicted 'it would all be over by Christmas', Lord Kitchener, the Secretary of State for War foresaw a long and brutal conflict. He realised that the regular army was too small to fight a protracted European war, so he issued a call for a new army, composed of the thousands of volunteers who were clamouring to fight. These men would be formed into service battalions, which would be attached to existing regiments, but retain their own battalion identity. Charles Forman, a 25-year-old from Leeds, was one of these volunteers. Unusually for a Yorkshire man, he decided to join a Scottish regiment.

Things were very bad around 1914. I was out of work. On August 4th war was declared, and on November 5th I joined the Regular Army. I asked my eldest brother Jim (who was later killed in France, 1918) what regiment I should join. He told me, 'Join the Black Watch! You'll see some fighting with that lot.' He was quite right. I did.

I volunteered for 7–5 [seven years, five months' service] in the Black Watch at the Army Recruiting Office in the High Street. I happened to know the officer in charge, and when I told him the regiment I wished to join he said, 'You're not a Scot.' I said, 'You know I'm not' – he replied 'Oh yes you are – born in Glasgow. Sign here'! That was how I was able to join the Black Watch.

The Orderly Sergeant said, 'Fall in outside, and we will march to the station.' There were about ten of us. 'Let us walk there on our own,' I suggested. 'You do as you're told – you're in the army now'! He never said a truer word. And so I started my great adventure.

First, to Lichfield Barracks, and from there I was sent to Perth, in the north of Scotland. I was the only one going north – all the others went down south. I arrived at Perth after midnight. It had been the longest distance I had ever travelled – other journeys I had made were work trips, or to the seaside. In Perth heavy snow was falling. My dress: low shoes, blue suit, stand-up collar and white shirt, cloth cap, and I had about two shillings in my pocket.

I arrived at the barrack gate and they rang the bell – one clang – I should say they could hear it all over Perth. I waited awhile – and then footsteps, a creaking bolt being drawn, and a voice: 'What yer wanting?' 'I've come to join up.' 'Come with me to the Guardroom.' There was a guard lying on the floor covered with a blanket. Over the door of the cell a sign read 'Prisoners'. The Sergeant threw a couple of blankets to me and said, 'This way.' He led me into the barracks, up two flights of stairs – no lights. He said, 'You had better sleep here' – on the concrete. He told me what time Reveille was, and went. Well, it didn't break my heart. It would take more than that in those days – I was very fit.

Fall in, on the Parade Square – 7–5s in the front, Duration of War in the rear: three of us in the front, and about 80 in the rear. Then we were detailed for fatigues. We three were detailed to the Sgts. Mess. Arriving there I was given six spittoons which had been in use the night before, and told to clean them. That was my first job in the British army for King and Country. I little thought then I should be using them myself two years later as a Sergeant in the Mess!

I stayed about three days in Perth, getting my khaki, etc., and then I moved down to Aldershot to join the 8th Battalion, Black Watch – the first of the first 100,000 – Kitchener's new army. Maida Barracks was our HQ there. We then moved to Alton, Hampshire, where I was to become an NCO – Lance-Corporal one stripe on 9th May 1915. I was an Orderly in the Officer's Mess there, and I received orders to pack my kit, and proceed to the front: France, via Southampton to Le Havre, under Major D.A. Steward, for whom I was batman.

⇒◆⇐

2
THE BATTLE OF YPRES, 1914

Captain Axel Krook (1st Battalion, Black Watch)

The 1st Battalion of the Black Watch formed part of the British Expeditionary Force – the 'Old Contemptibles' who marched into Belgium, only to be met by overwhelming numbers of the German army around Mons. The BEF retired over the French border, and alongside the French they halted the German offensive along the River Marne. Then, as the Germans began probing towards the coast, the British moved north and west in a race for the sea. By

September the two great armies lay facing each other, from the Swiss border to the English Channel.

The new German commander, General Falkenheyn, determined to pierce this line, by attacking the junction between the British and French armies at Ypres, where a prominent salient in the line left the BEF vulnerable to a determined German attack. The brutal fighting which followed virtually destroyed the regular British army, but the line held, and the Germans were repulsed. The 1st Battalion of the Black Watch reached the Ypres salient on 21 October, and was immediately thrown into the line. Captain Krook was one of the battalion's company commanders, and in his diary he told of the confused fighting to the east of Ypres, where part of the battalion was overrun, and Krook himself captured by the enemy. This extract begins on the eve of the battle, when the battalion was quartered in a hamlet two miles east of Ypres.

27th October 1914

As soon as it was light, the Germans started shelling, and one of the first shells knocked out the two machine guns – bursting just between them. Shelling went on all day. 'A' and 'B' Coys prolonged our line to our right. 'A' suffered severely having three officers wounded and about one hundred men killed and wounded. I lost about fifteen men. When it was light enough to see I discovered that there was dead ground in front of my position where enemy troops might assemble without being seen and then rush us. I chose what I thought was the best place as an observation post, and sent Corporal Whitecross with six men to take up this post. He lost one man killed and another wounded on the way there. He took on the remainder and stayed all day in observation, only coming in once – under fire – to report.

At night the Bedfords relieved us. They were very jumpy, and would not wait for my men to get out of the trench before they jumped in, which made it very difficult to keep order and silence. It appears that they had had a very bad time.

We were ordered to Battalion Headquarters. 'A' and 'D' were sent to reserve; 'B' and 'C' were lent to the Coldstream [Guards]. West remained at HQ. The move to the Coldstream line, between Bercelaer and Kruseik, was ordered the very moment that we got to HQ. The men had not even time to get their packs off. I reported to the Coldstream, and was sent to the extreme left of the Coldstream line. This was all done in the dark, and in complete silence. I joined up with Coldstream Nos 1 & 2 Coys (Captain Evelyn Gibbs) on my right, and got into touch with the Scots Guards (Captain de la Pasture) on my left. Their right was about 120 yards from my left. This space had to be watched.

28th October 1914

We found the trenches that we were told to occupy were in a shocking condition – full of litter of all sorts and one or two dead bodies. We cleared up as best we could, buried the dead, and tried to improve the trench. We had very few tools, no ammunition except what was on the men, no means of communication except by runner. After making a fuss, we were told that there was a heap of boxes of ammunition at the Krusiek crossroads, and eventually two boxes arrived, but they were marked 'For Practice Only', which did not sound too good. We then found another box buried in the trench, also marked 'For Practice Only'.

That night Gibbs and I had a notice that an attack was expected by the XXVII German Corps from [the] direction of Menin. I went and saw Gibbs. There was nothing for us to do but wait. Wavell Paxton was with Gibbs, and we had a glass of excellent brandy. We were then informed by messenger that a counterattack was to be delivered the next morning (29th October) across our front, and that we were to hang on.

29th October 1914

A foggy morning. Heavy firing began on the right of the Coldstream line, and very soon extended to our line. On the left of my line my trench curved round in a semi-circle, and then came the 120-yard space between us and the Scots Guards. At this part of my trench the Germans made three charges, but they were all repulsed with severe loss to the enemy. We now had to open the boxes of ammunition marked 'For Practice Only' and issue it. It was maddening; the cartridges burst in the chamber after firing, and it was almost impossible to get the breach open again. The men were cursing and using their feet to kick the breach open.

At about 6.30 a.m. Gibbs informed me that their HQ had gone [wiped out], and a little later that Nos 2 and 3 Coys had been overwhelmed. I said that I would hold on and support him, and I kept sending messages for help via the Scots Guards. Gibbs asked me to send a section to join two of his sections to guard our right rear, as after the breakthrough at the Kruseik crossroads, the enemy were getting round behind us. I sent a section under Corporal Williams, who was killed after he had gone a few yards, and Corporal Whitecross immediately went out and took the section to its position.

No help came – no counterattack. Then came a message that a section of the Gloucesters had arrived, and wanted to know where to go, and that they had an officer with them. McNeil told me that he knew where they were, and after receiving instruction from me as to where to place the Gloucesters, he disappeared into the wood at the back of the trenches. I never saw him again, nor the Gloucesters. I sent a messenger to HQ via the Scots Guards. I never saw him again either.

I then went to the right of my line to be in touch with Gibbs, and remained there until another message came to say that three platoons of the Gloucesters had arrived, and wanted to know where to go. I went down to the left, and some men left their firing positions and began to follow me. I sent them back, and told them to keep on firing.

All this time we were being fired at from behind as well. I saw no sign of McNeill nor of the Gloucesters, and on getting near the left end of my trench, saw that there was no one left of my left section, and it was difficult to get along, as there were dead and wounded lying in the narrow trench.

I turned to go back to the right, and (about 10.30 a.m.) came face to face with a lot of Germans. I had my notebook and pencil in my hands – and I must admit that I was taken by surprise. They fired at me, one downed me with the butt end of his rifle – and that was the end of the fight for me. Angus McNaughten was with me until the last moment when I went to the left of my line to try and get into touch with the arriving Gloucesters. He stayed to keep in touch with Gibbs. Then, what remained of the line was attacked with the bayonet from the rear. The sections sent out to guard our right rear were overwhelmed without having the chance of even warning us.

━━◆◆◆◆━━

3

THE BATTLE OF LOOS, 1915

Lance-Corporal Charles Forman
(8th Battalion, Black Watch)

Lance-Corporal Forman wasn't concerned with the larger picture – only the grim reality of his first big offensive. British hopes rested on the effectiveness of poison gas, which at the appointed hour

(5.50 a.m. on 25 September) would be released from canisters sited in the British trenches. The idea was that the light westerly wind would blow this cloud of chlorine gas over the German front line. As Lance-Corporal Forman points out, the gas was less effective than the generals had hoped – one of many disappointments and blunders which rendered the offensive a costly failure. Among the 40,000 British casualties at Loos were over 500 men from the 8th Black Watch. Lance-Corporal Forman could only steel himself to write this account of his wartime experiences some six decades after the battle.

5.30 a.m. (Zero Hour)

Before we left the trenches we had our first casualties. A German shell had dropped in the trench and killed Captain Murray of 'D' Coy, and three or four. Then over the top, with the best of luck!

Our headgear was a glengarry. We didn't have tin helmets in those early days. We had 120 rounds of ammunition, entrenching tools, iron rations and other odds and ends. Our training for moving forward in those days was by short rushes of about 30 yards, and then drop down. The Germans soon got the hang of that. He would wait until we got up again, then sweep us with machine guns. Each time some would fall, never to get up again.

The order came to wear gas masks as the gas we had released was hovering about in no-man's-land. We carried two issues – 1st and 2nd; 2nd being more up to date, having a rubber mouthpiece valve, and glass eyepieces instead of celluloid. Now, these masks was just a flannelette bag affair you wore over your head, and tucked in your collar, breathing in through the bag and out through the mouthpiece. Scotch regiments carried these masks in a big front pocket on their kilt aprons, and the rain washing chemicals out of the masks left each man with a reddish-purple stain down the front. I put on the 2nd issue, and then one of my men said: 'You've no eye-glass in, Corporal.' I quickly exchanged it for my 1st issue, and this mask rolled up like a turban was my headdress for a good many days after, my glengarry being lost.

As we moved forward I saw Sergeant-Major Hamilton lying shot. I went to see what I could do, but I could do nothing. He had been hit in the stomach, and would not live. He was rather a stout man, and as I opened his kilt to use his field dressing, [I saw] he was burst right open. Bullets were hitting all around, and I had to carry on. He must have been reported as 'missing', because his wife had written, asking what had become of him, and I had to give information to Battalion HQ that I had seen him.

We reached the German front line, and the first thing I saw was a German gas mask – the same type civilians had in the Second World War, 25 years after! Before the battle we were told that there would be no resistance for five miles, as the Germans would all be gassed. What a hope! There were dead Germans about, but they was not gassed, and I never did see a gassed German! The trenches we had left had no proper shelter or cover, but here were well-made dugouts about a dozen steps down, with wire beds to sleep on, and all the comforts.

We spent the day in these trenches. The Germans had fell back to their support line. It was then left for our reserves to carry on through us – but where was the reserves?! There was even cavalry supposed to follow through, but no sign of reserves till night-time. Field Marshal French was asked in Parliament later on – where were his reserves at Loos? He said: 'They were there – but not where they were wanted.'

Now it began to rain, and with the darkness things were quieter. No officers left in my Company to give us orders – a Sergeant and myself – Lance-Corporal, and about 30 men. The Sergeant took command, and I was second-in-command – we were very inexperienced. We decided however to send a man back to Headquarters for instructions, and about 2 a.m. we had orders to fall back to our original front line trench. What an awful night, for dead and wounded shouting 'Stretcher Bearer! Stretcher Bearer!', and as we were going back we passed the reserves going up – English regiments. They could hardly make a go of it – they had been marching all day. What a mess!

These English regiments were part of 21st and 24th [Infantry] Divisions ordered up to the front at short notice, having been in France only two weeks. Being a fair distance from the front they had marched most of the day, and wandered in the confusion most of the night, soaked to the skin and with no hot food available.

They made their attack at 11 a.m. next morning: no maps, no artillery support, no smoke screen, uncut barbed wire. Their object was to continue the advance made the day before from the old German front line, through the second line and beyond. But, the Germans had had time to re-form, and were as strong as when the battle began.

They moved forward in perfect order in extended lines, each about 1,000 strong, offering a target never seen before – across open fields of grass. German artillery and machine guns annihilated them. There had been twelve battalions – about 10,000 men. Their casualties: 385 officers, 7,861 men. It lasted 3½ hours. German casualties: Nil.

During the day of the 26th the Germans counterattacked and was driving the regiments that had relieved us back from the ground we had taken. Orders came that we had got to go forward again, to hold the line, and rally any men falling back. We were about 70 Black Watch and 30 Cameronians, under the command of Captain Bowes-Lyon [the Queen Mother's brother] in this action. He and a Lt Mackintosh were both killed by German grenades.

As we moved forward, the enemy had a heavy gun hitting the communications trench, and it was a proper death-trap. You had to wait till the shell had burst and then make a dash for it. Quite a few got caught, and pieces of men were lying around – heads, arms, legs and torsos – one of the worst things I saw during the war, in such a short space.

The German advance was halted, and about 9.30 p.m. we were relieved by 85th Brigade, and so we withdrew back again to our old lines. At 5 a.m. on 28th September the Battalion was withdrawn to the Reserve Lines.

The order came to assemble in 'Railway Trench', and there we numbered off left to right. It stopped at 113. We moved out onto the road, and the order was given to 'unload'. While doing so, someone fired a round off – he could have shot someone! Imagine going through that lot, and then get pipped off like that. The RSM came marching down. Oh, for about a minute the air was blue as he stood and swore at this chap. Now we marched off out of range of fire. One Jock had some bagpipes he had picked up. They belonged to the Royal Scots, and he struck up a tune, 'Eh, Jock, are ye glad ye 'listed! How do you like the soldiers noo!'

The rifle I was carrying belonged to the Royal Scottish Fusiliers. I had two or three different rifles during the action. At last transport Lines was reached, and we piled arms and were served out with tea and Bully Stew – the first meal since the start of the battle. Now, on lifting rifles the one I should pick up was my own – remarkable!

And that was the Battle of Loos. History gives the losses for the Battalion as 19 officers, and 492 other ranks, killed or wounded. Col. Lord Semphill (CO 8th Battalion) was wounded, Major Collins (Second-in-Command) was killed, and Major Steward (my Company CO) was wounded – naming but a few.

4
THE BATTLE OF LOOS, 1915

Lieutenant-Colonel J. Stewart
(9th Battalion, Black Watch)

At dawn on 30 September 1915, the 9th Battalion of the Black Watch went 'over the top', and assaulted the German positions around the village of Loos. The hope that a massed artillery barrage and a gas attack had softened up the defences proved wildly optimistic. Although the battalion seized its objectives, casualties were horrific – almost two-thirds of the 900-strong battalion were either killed or wounded during the day's fighting. We will meet Lieutenant-Colonel Stewart again. At Loos he was the deputy commander of the battalion, and was therefore able to combine an appreciation of the attack as it happened with the bigger operational picture. The following diary entry was written in the immediate aftermath of the battle. The entry is decidedly matter-of-fact – a stark account of a brutal day.

Thursday, 30th September 1915
Years seem to have passed since I last wrote in this wee bookie. I must try to give some sort of account of our fight now. We

went up into the trenches on the Friday afternoon, the first company moved out of M— at 4.30, and the last company at 7.10. It was a long and trying job, and the last lot were not reported in 'till well after 2.30 a.m. All reported present.

'T' & I occupied a small dugout under the Loos road. 'T' took first watch, and I tried to sleep, but didn't do very much that way as people were coming and going in and out all the time. I got up at around 2.30 and 'T' took his turn. At 5.05 a.m., a message came that 'Zero Hour' (i.e. the time the gas was to start) would be 5.50 a.m., so I woke 'T', and we both had a shave and a cup of hot soup. It was rather cold, raining slightly, and a soft wind from the west.

The intense bombardment and gas started at 5.50 punctually. It was the devil's own row, and of course soon the Huns got busy, and things became pretty warm. We got a touch of a German gas shell in our dugout, so moved up to the frontline trenches. Just at 6.30 our first line left the parapet. Alas, casualties began directly we showed ourselves. The enemy's machine guns got to work and our men dropped right and left, but they never wavered for a second. On they went, line after line, into and over the German front line trenches, on into the second and third lines, and bang into Loos itself. Nothing stopped them. It was a perfectly magnificent show, but – alas, alas – it was only a remnant of a regiment.

I had been sitting on the parapet when the show started, and 'T' came up shortly afterwards. I saw Scott Pearse and Sterling lying just outside our wire, both wounded, so I went over and helped to dress their wounds, and gave them morphia, and helped Pearse down into the trench, before we ('T' and I) went over ourselves. We went with (I think) the fifth or sixth line, but I am not sure. Anyhow, it was a pretty darned rough time, as the enemy were shelling the field in order to deter reinforcements from coming up, but it was no good. The Gordons and Camerons followed close on our heels, in spite of the terrific fire, and we thus proceeded over the historic 'hay field'.

The Black Watch by this time (7.25) were well into Loos, and at 7.50 'T' and I were at the corner house in the village, where we had arranged to be in case messages had to be sent back. It was near this spot, whilst we were waiting, that a bevy of shells came whistling along, so I dragged 'T' into a little trench, and we had hardly time to crouch down when – bang bang bang bang bang – came five HE shells. We were lucky to have taken cover, but unfortunately the trench was full of gas, and I got a real good sniff which very nearly laid me out, so I shoved 'T' unceremoniously out of it and we just got out in time, but felt the effects all day.

We moved on (by that time, Colonel Wallace of the Gordons had joined us), and at 8.30 'T' and I having had no reports at all, decided to move on through the village. Just as we were starting we were met by a wounded man – Black Watch – who told us that the Black Watch were there on Hill 70, so we pushed on through the village, meeting Wattie Campbell of the Royal Scots in the square by the church. There were many men, of all sorts of units, hunting through the cellars and houses of the village for hiding Germans, and all Black Watch men we met were rounded up and sent on. There were and probably still are many Germans still hiding in Loos, but it was not our job to clear the place.

At the church 'T' and I had an argument as to which was the right way to go, to get to Hill 70, and so we had our maps out, and there, under the hail of shells, we squabbled over the way. We were both of us strung to the highest pitch, and looking at it now in comparative quietude it is really rather comic. Having fixed up the route we went on, and just as we were moving – bang – came a very big shell, which landed within 20 yards of us, and fairly blew us into a passageway close by, covering us with dust.

We went on, and eventually (rounding up a few bombers etc. on our way), we got to the last houses of Loos, about 250–300 yards behind Hill 70, at 10.26 a.m., and there we saw the remainder of the Highland Brigade holding on to the crest of the hill. Our right rested on the extreme ESE edge of a 'crassier' (or slagheap) and was very lightly held by a few men of the 9th Black Watch. By this time a few men had rolled up who had been acting as escort to prisoners. I ought to say, that during our advance, we must have taken at least 600 prisoners. They came out in droves and all the way across the hayfield we passed whole companies of them going back. (I now hear we got a General among them, but I do not know who he is.)

I sent what men I could up to reinforce our right, and 'T' and I just waited for news. Our left was up against a half-finished enemy work on the top of the hill, and advanced several times from this towards the Dynamitieve [location of explosives], but had to go back each time owing to machine gun fire. Eric Wilson passed down, hit by a bullet through the shoulder. He had it dressed, and pluckily came back, our only officer left. We then heard that all the remainder – 18 – had either been killed or wounded, crossing the field.

Matters remained like this, at a complete standstill all day. No reinforcements came up, as we had been led to expect, and we did not know what to do. You see, we couldn't see what was going on the other side of the infernal slagheap. The London Division on our right *ought* to have been up with us, at least part of them ought to have been on the north of the heap, but bar a very few men on one of their battalions, there was absolutely nobody belonging to them with us, and it was a very long time before we saw any of them. About 12 noon 'T', who was senior officer, after consulting with Sandilands and Wallace, sent an urgent note asking for reinforcements, and at 1.25 p.m. a message came that our guns were in their new forward positions, and that reinforcements were coming up. This cheered us up a little, but they were a *very* long time coming, and it was 4 p.m. before they arrived.

Meanwhile, the Germans repulsed all our attacks on our left, and brought up a machine gun on our right, with the view of enfilading our whole line, but we foiled this move by the skin of our teeth, and hung on. About 3 p.m. two motor machine guns came up, and I sent one to our right, and one to the centre. At 4 p.m. I saw the promised reinforcements coming up on our left, and none at all on the right, so our anxiety was doubled, as I could see it was our weak spot. Ah, by Jove, if the enemy had only known that the right of the hill was only held by, at the most, 30 men, and that the only support or reserve at our disposal was 14 men of the Black Watch, 'T' and myself, the story would have been a very different one.

At 4 p.m. the CO decided to send a message asking to be relieved, as we were then only a couple of hundred strong – [in] the whole Brigade – and at 5 p.m. we got back a reply to the effect that we would be relieved by 62nd Brigade during the night. Meanwhile, things had assumed a better aspect, for at or about 4.45 p.m. I saw some men dribble across the infernal slagheap and join our right front line. These proved to be men of the London Division, who had been held up on the other side of the 'crassier'. A fair number came up, and I then began to think that things were better, but I dreaded a strong counter attack during the night, and as things went on that dread got worse. Surely the enemy would not sit quiet after the hammering they had got. Their marvellous rail system must help them, and we, a few poor hundred, could easily be wiped out.

That waiting was awful, but about 1.30 a.m. we were relieved by half a company of the Northumberland Fusiliers – Arthur Paines' Battalion. Just think – the remnants of a battalion who went into action over 900 strong, to be relieved by a half company. We got our men together and found there were about 95 all told with 'T', that gallant boy Eric Wilson, and myself. We marched back through Loos, over the hayfield, and back through Quality Street to Philosophe, which we reached, dead done, too tired and anxious even to sleep, about 3.30 a.m.

All the way, at least through Loos, we were exposed to the fire of the enemy's heavy guns. They seemed to be wild at losing the village, and just shelled it out of pure cussedness. Such is the bald and unvarnished tale of the day. I have said nothing of the hail of machine gun fire, and shells that we were given. That, of course, is understood, and only part of the day's work, but the nervous strain was almost more than one could stand. By God's good grace alone we stood it.

⟫◆⟪

5

CAPTURED, YPRES, 1915

Lance-Corporal William Anderson
(9th Battalion, Black Watch)

Lance Corporal Anderson was captured on patrol while serving with the battalion in the vicinity of Ypres, during the months before the Battle of Passchendaele. Until well into 1916, British soldiers who were captured by the enemy were officially listed as 'missing'. It seemed that the anguish and uncertainty this caused their families was less important than maintaining the impression that British soldiers never surrendered. Anderson kept a record of his experiences, from the moment of his capture until the end of the war, when he was being held in a prisoner of war camp in Germany. This passage recounts what happened to him during the hours immediately after he was taken prisoner.

The time of my capture was around 4.30 in the afternoon, and we had to make our way back to the German reserve lines through a considerable barrage of shell and searching gunfire. The going was rather tough and treacherous. At one time up to the knees in mud, and another hopelessly entangled in the none too tender embraces of barbed wire. Ditches running deep with dirty, evil-smelling water had to be forded, and masses of hydrogenous material overcome in our scramble across the battlefield.

On reaching the German reserve line the first thing demanded of us was to hand over our rifles, ammunition and equipment. Following this we were carefully searched through our personal clothing, and anything in the form of diaries, photos, etc. were confiscated. This part of the proceedings was carried out by a few officers and soldiers, who then proceeded to question us about conditions on our fronts.

In entering the hut to endure the questioning we were greeted by an outsized German wildly brandishing a hand grenade, and shouting imprecations on us, in the purpose, I am sure to instil fear of the consequences of our failure to answer the questions truthfully. I'm afraid the German and his potato masher failed to intimidate us much, as his questioning would produce very little information of value to the Germans, for obvious reasons, chief of which being that we knew very little ourselves about conditions in our front. The Germans however were able to tell us a good deal about our own selves, the dispositions of our regiments, etc.

Having got over the searching questioning and examination, we occupied the remainder of the day collecting wounded and carrying them back to the dressing stations. Friend and foe got similar treatment, and Jerry gave our wounded as good a treatment as his own. The transport of wounded was no easy matter, given the condition of the ground, and the distance to the dressing stations, which was some three or four miles. Also, most of the stretchers used were improvised from anything available, and made suitable for the transport from anything lying around. We were now thoroughly tired out, and beginning to feel the want of food, but we only had a rest of about a couple of hours that night before we marched off on the next stage of our journey.

By this time our numbers had grown to around 200 prisoners from various regiments, and we had no idea where our next billets would be. We were still without food, and having had little in the way of sleep for the past eight to ten days, one can imagine how miserable and weary our band was. After marching for hours we were halted at a Divisional Headquarters, and were told we could rest for a few hours to await orders for our disposal. The smells and signs of cooking raised our hopes, which, however were soon to be dashed, and for us food was not yet. Rain helped to add to our discomfort, we had no shelter of any kind.

Here we had to submit again to more searching and questioning by a swell officer who spoke perfect English and who was well informed. It was obviously one of the Germans who infested our country in prewar days. We came across them at every turn in Germany, and at one of the camps where I was interned there was an officer who boasted of having carried on a business in Manchester until June 1917 – almost three years after the war had started. Two Manchester lads amongst us actually recognised him, but how he was able to get back to Germany I can't tell.

After a delay of a few hours we were on our way again, still without food. We had a long march in front of us. A few miles along our way we were held for a few minutes for the purpose of changing our escorts. Our journey continued with a couple of fully-fledged Ulhan lancers, one riding at front and rear. We began to feel ourselves of some importance now – we could imagine making a grand entrance into some place of importance. Alas, hunger is a sure leveller, and we would really have given up a reception and welcome by the almighty Kaiser himself for a piece of bread and a drink of good water. For hours and hours we tramped, until we arrived in a compound of huts. Here we thought we'd find a resting place for the night, with something in the way of food and drink. Alas, again disappointment comes our way, and we were off on the march again without either rest or food. Another two hours' march and at last we arrived at a resting Halluin, a small French town on the border of Belgium, and quite close to Menin.

6
LETTERS HOME, 1915

Sergeant Jack Barbour (9th Battalion, Black Watch)

While mail was censored, and soldiers were often reluctant to share much of their experience in the trenches with their families, a few managed to write something about the conditions they experienced, the morale of the men in the trenches, and the importance of letters from home. Sergeant Barbour was a loving son, who wrote to his family in Dunfermline whenever he could. In these letters he mentions his brother-in-law (Patterson), who served in the same battalion, and his high hopes for the coming offensive. Jack Barbour was killed the day after the last letter was written, during the opening minutes of the Battle of Loos, 25 September 1915.

BEF
2nd September 1915

Dear Father and Mother,

We are again billeted a few miles behind the firing line, after another spell in the trenches. The part we occupied was quite close to the enemy's lines – a matter of 100 yards, and this fact alone helped to make things much more interesting. Whenever it became dark, doubtful compliments were shouted across from either side, accompanied by the occasional round or two. The Battalion suffered four casualties, a Captain and three men. Unfortunately the former only lasted 24 hours or so after receiving his wounds. He was second in command to our own Company, and very much thought of by his men.

In your letter, Father, you were asking for details of the life in the trenches, but I cannot think of much to say. The feeding is good, and such things as stew, tea, etc. are always to be had quite hot, which is a great thing in itself. Needless to say there is a constant watch kept when in the front line, more so at night than by day. It is, however, chiefly in the daytime that one gets a sleep, and there are dugouts for that purpose – they serve the purpose very well, and are quite comfortable. At night, sleeping in dugouts is not allowed, for a very good reason, so that if one wishes to woo Morpheus he must stretch himself out on one of the fire steps, cover himself over with his waterproof sheet, and trust in nothing heavier falling on him than rain!

There seem to be mistakes in regard to that part of my affairs which I did not tend to [*sic*] in person; a government parcel is quite out of the question. I also received a form to fill up, but will have to give to the C2MS to explain. Your lot, mother, arrived here quite intact. The cake was splendid, and not the least bit broken. The eggs were however, all but two in bits. Just like to say that they were quite soft and could have done with a little more boiling. Catherine's letter with Patterson's enclosed got off today. Pat seems to be a bit downhearted, and no wonder.

I'm pleased to report that my health is good; the weather so far has been all in our favour, but now the days are darkening, and the nights are becoming rather cold. I've got to go now – will look for letters soon.

Lots of Love,
Jack.

BEF
24th September 1915

Dear Father and Mother,

Just a few lines to report good health as usual. The opportunities for writing are now few, and may be for a few days to come, so if the letters are few and far between, don't become alarmed. We are expecting great things, and everyone is in great spirits. Catherine's parcel arrived

last night, and I'm glad to hear Mother is enjoying a
holiday in Dumbarton.

Your Loving Son,

Jack.

———◆———

7

LOOS, 1915

Second Lieutenant Alexander Gillespie
(4th Battalion, Argyll and Sutherland Highlanders)

Like many Subalterns in the Great War, Alex Gillespie was a teenager
when he went to war, and didn't live long enough to pass out of
his teens. He was a Territorial Army soldier, but he was attached to
the 2nd battalion – one of his regiment's two regular battalions. The
young man clearly missed his family, who lived at Longcroft, outside
Linlithgow, and he wrote frequent letters home. These letters, written
during the relatively peaceful early summer of 1915, recount the
arrival of his battalion at La Bassée, near Loos, and their general
cheerfulness is infectious. While young Gillespie tried to shield his
parents from the worst of the war surrounding him, his letters still
contain valuable insights into the nature of conditions on the front
line. Gillespie was killed in action on 25 September 1915 – the first
day of the Battle of Loos. He died leading the veteran soldiers of
his platoon in a charge against a German trench. His elder brother
was killed in similar circumstances the following year.

Billets: June 12, 1915
Your bog-myrtle came today, still very sweet, and a scent like
that always stirs the memory more than any writing, or talking,

or sketching can do. There's a passage in Homer which I'm very fond of, where he casts about for something to give the idea of swiftness, and instead of taking lightning or the flight of an arrow, he says, like the thought of a man who has travelled to many places, and sits at home thinking to himself, 'I wish I was there or there.' But I shouldn't be at all happy at Rhuveag just now, so I don't really want to be there, except to see you. I have just come in from a walk with the doctor, along a road which runs south parallel to the firing line, and a mile behind it.

We should have been in La Bassée before evening if we had followed it along. The country was very pretty; tall hedges with wild roses in them, grass very long and green, and pollard willows standing beside the black ditches, which are now mostly covered with duckweed and water crowfoot. The willow is a prettier tree than the olive, I think; it has much the same grey-green colour when the leaves turn over, but the branches are more graceful. The farms were mostly deserted, and shell holes through the roof and walls, showed the necessity; but of course there are soldiers, gunners especially, billeted everywhere, and one or two stray inhabitants, who have escaped so many times that now they feel they can't be hit; curious how a lot of narrow escapes either break a man's nerve altogether, or give him ten times the confidence that he had before.

There are no vineyards so far north as this, but vines climbing all along the cottages and houses, as they used to do in the villages round Winchester. I saw one artilleryman busy building an observation post, just like a large bird's nest 60 feet up in a poplar tree; that is the great difficulty in this flat enclosed country, to observe the fire of modern long-range guns. Little shops are springing up everywhere, and there are notice boards in windows to say that eggs and milk and chips are sold . . .

We go back into trenches tonight, to a new bit of trench; that means dining early, so I must get ready.

Trenches: June 13, 1915

We were a very long time in getting into our new trenches last night, for the guides had been sent to the wrong place; the night was very dark, and we wandered about in a perfect rabbit warren of trenches, where even the occupiers did not seem to know the way. Luckily, the Germans were unusually quiet, for if they had started shelling us when we were blocked in the communication trenches, or had showered grenades over the parapet as they had done the night before, they might have made a large bag.

This used to be the hottest corner in this part of the line, but it's only lukewarm now. My trench is only 70 yards from the German front trench, so we can only use loopholes and cannot put heads up by day. I think I described the place to you once before; it's very like the lower deck of a ship, for the trench is roofed over, to give protection against rifle grenades, bombs, and trench mortar 'sausages', which are freely offered at times, and in place of portholes, there are iron plates with sliding shutters, in case we have to fire. The parapet is very thick, but it could not have been built at all, if it had not been begun and finished in the days of peace which followed the New Year, when both sides were too wretched with mud and water to bother about firing. Then, when both had made themselves reasonably comfortable, they went at it again.

There are a great many graves scattered about just behind the trench, for the Germans are really on three sides of us here, and it takes [a] long time to get in and out. But there is one advantage of being so near, that they can hardly shell us for fear of hitting their own men. We have to keep boots and equipment on day and night, for the trenches are too close together to make it possible to put up wire, and now, of course, there is always the chance of gas, though we are well provided against that. Perhaps all this sounds a great deal worse than it really is, for we have had a very quiet day, with very little firing, and I don't think it's any worse than our old lines used to be. I had one piece of luck, for the 91st have moved along a little to our left, and I found Sholto there this morning, very brown and big . . . I wish he had come to this battalion, and I think he misses some of his friends in the 4th. He has been in the trenches a fortnight without a break.

We have two bomb catapults, but I think the elastic is wearing out, as it does with all catapults. I wish I had something which would destroy Bombilius Major [the bee-fly], who is holding this trench in great force, and seems to think the sand-bags are put there for him to bask on them. There is a kind of biting house-fly too . . . There are no gardens here [some soldiers tried to grow vegetables in their trenches], there has always been too much to do, and much more than rain used to fall from the sky . . .

<hr />

8
FIELD DRESSING STATION, YPRES, 1915

Revd A.M. Maclean
(Chaplain, 1st Gordon Highlanders)

The role of an army chaplain is to offer moral support to the men, tending to their spiritual needs, and looking after those who were wounded. For many, a figure representing the Church of Scotland was a valuable link to home and family – a reminder of the life they had left behind. Then came the business of burying the dead, or consoling the dying. The Reverend Maclean was from Paisley, but before the war he studied divinity at Aberdeen University. When war broke out he naturally offered his services to his local regiment – the Gordon Highlanders. This passage, written after the war, suggests that when faced with the carnage of Ypres, the minister still retained his faith in the humanity of his fellow Scots.

All that day I was engaged in burying the dead. Through the following night the wounded came, streaming in faster than they could be evacuated. Their condition was pitiable, for a cold, clammy rain had fallen persistently all day. Yet I never heard a murmur. Yes: I heard one. A young Aberdeen student, with a finely chiselled face, lay on the table while the surgeon tried to give him unavailing relief, and as I held his hand he moaned out his sorrow over the failure of his battalion to hold the trenches they had won. I saw a Scot lying on the ground, plastered from head to foot in mud as with a trowel. I thought I recognised the yellow stripe in the tartan, and stepping gently over an unconscious form between, I touched him and said, 'Are you a 1st Gordon, my lad?'

His arm was crushed, his leg was twisted, but the white of his eye gleamed through the mud that caked his face as he answered with an unmistakable grin, 'A wis this mornin', and a think a'm a half yin yet.' And then in a moment he knew me, and reaching out his only hand, he gripped me tight, and said, 'Oh! minister, it's you. You might write to my wife, and dinna frighten her. A'll be a' richt yet.' What a superb spirit! A jest for his own misery, and the tenderest consideration for those at home. Such are the men who are bearing all for you on these grim fields of Flanders.

A cheerless dawn was breaking as I left that dreadful place. I noticed the stains upon my boots, and thought of Barbour's terrible phrase – 'reid wat shod'. And so I went to meet the Gordons returning. Grim and stern and silent they marched in, still they held their heads high, as well became the 'Gay Gordons'. At the head of the column strode a young captain, with purple and white ribbon of the Military Cross gleaming on his breast (a year ago he was a divinity student of the Church of Scotland), and as I listened to him speaking a last word to the men as gently as a mother putting her children to bed, there revealed to me something more of the nobility of the men with whom I had to do.

⊰•⊱

9
GALLIPOLI, 1915

Lieutenant P.M. Campbell (Ayrshire Yeomanry)

Scotland's Yeomanry Cavalry regiments were Territorial soldiers, but were kept in Scotland until the spring of 1915. By that time it was clear that cavalry were of limited value on the Western Front. Therefore, most Yeomanry regiments spent the war as dismounted troops, serving alongside the infantry in the trenches. In October 1914 Turkey joined the Central Powers, and declared war on Russia. The Allies devised a plan to knock Turkey out of the war by capturing her capital, Constantinople. First they had to secure the Dardanelles, the narrow waterway that separated Europe and Asia, and which formed the maritime gateway to Constantinople. The western side of the channel was formed by the Gallipoli peninsula, and in April 1915 a force of Anzac and British troops were landed on its western shore. The Turks held their ground, inflicting heavy casualties on the Allies. By October the fighting had developed into a stalemate, with lines of trenches stretching across the narrow, rocky peninsula.

This extract from a letter provides us with a vivid account of life in the trenches of Gallipoli soon after the initial Allied landings there. The Ayrshire Yeomanry were attached to a battalion of the Scottish Rifles, where it seems Lieutenant Campbell felt at home, as its ranks included many of his old schoolmates from Fettes College. It also shows that the social divisions which existed in prewar Scotland were maintained, despite the privations of the trenches.

To E.M.C.

First Line Trenches

Tuesday, 26th October 1915

Sorry to have been so long in managing a letter to you. No doubt you will have seen the few I have been able to send to father and Joy, so I won't bother about repeating things. Suffice it to say we have been on land since the 11th October, and have had a wonderfully safe and peaceful time ever since.

Of course, the living is rough in the extreme. Our Squadron officers messed together at the rest camp round a fire in the open, like so many gypsies, and each slept in a 3 yard by 1 yard by 4 foot deep trench. But the nights down there were very peaceful, and on the whole very comfortable, and I slept very well. Very little shelling at night has gone on here since we landed.

We came up for a prolonged spell in the firing and support lines on the 24th. I, in sole charge of 61 men, have been attached to an experienced regiment (combined Battalion of 7th and 8th Scottish Rifles), and we are doing duty in the firing line, mixed up with them. As you can imagine with detached groups all along the line, and bombers, snipers, etc., each in his special place, it is taking a bit of work to manage them all. You will understand, of course, that our men are spread out among the old hands.

Thursday, 28th October 1915

Since 26th have had no time for writing – things have been very peaceful for all that, but of course there are innumerable duties to be performed, and other officers are always coming along to visit you in your dug-out, which is very pleasant, but not conducive to correspondence. When I say dug-out, it is only a small section of open trench behind the firing line.

There are no proper dug-outs here, as there is no timber or iron to be had to support roofing, so if it came to heavy shelling by the Turks, or bad weather, there would not be much protection for anybody. In the meantime the enemy have very few shells, and generally do not risk shelling the front line, although a section immediately on my right here had 18 shells into and about it yesterday morning. We have orders to be prepared for a good supply of enemy shells in future, as Bulgaria is undoubtedly going to be a means for this. If the Turks had a really big supply of ammunition and guns, the general opinion is we could not exist long on the peninsula, as every inch more or less of ground is at their mercy in that direction.

Their firing line is very close, normally 75 yards – in some places 15 yards only – but we suspect not very strongly held, their main resistance line being 600 yards away – a mass of barbed wire, with many redoubts. Last night two men went out immediately on my right, and found the enemy trench unoccupied for 30 yards. They got inside, collected some booty, and returned safely. Patrols of this kind are practically the only activities in the firing line at the moment, and they of course go on continually. The Turks had decidedly the best of the sniping the first two days I was up, but we gave their posts such a devil of a bombing two days ago that we imagine they were wiped out, as they have been practically silent since.

Catapults, of course, do most of this, and they are great fun – the Turks have nothing with which to reply. In such times life is quite enjoyable here, and there is no strain, except possibly in lack of sleep, or excitement about it whatever. Sleep is short, because at night you have to take your turn of patrol duty (2½ hours or so, between 9 p.m. and 5 a.m.), and there is a general 'stand to' for an hour before dawn – at present 5.30 to 6.30 a.m. And during the day duties of various sorts don't give you much time for napping. Up till last night I had not managed more than eight hours in four nights, but last night got six or so hours, so feel quite fresh today. You don't seem to need so much sleep with the continual open air.

I sleep on quite a comparatively broad ledge in my dugout, and have a fleece-lined Burberry 'British Warm' coat, waterproof cover (6 feet by 3 feet) and three blankets to keep me warm, so don't do badly. Of course you also sleep with Balaclava helmet and gloves on. Against a spell of wet weather I should be very glad to have a good-sized oilskin cover. They are very light, and easily sent by post, so if you would get the N.B. Rubber Co. [North British Rubber Company, Edinburgh] to send me one as soon as possible, shall be much obliged. See that it is made without holes – one complete sheet.

We have had a west wind and mild weather for the past two days. I am at present (12 noon) writing this in my dugout in my shirt-sleeves in very pleasant sunshine, an atmosphere *almost* free from unpleasant reminder of the ever-present decaying corpses, and nothing more troublesome than a mouth and nose covered with flies. At the moment there is hardly a shot being fired, and it is almost possible to forget the war. We get a sufficient supply of good drinking water daily, chiefly in old petrol tins from water-tank steamers, and about 10.30 a.m. I have time to boil myself some water and enjoy a very pleasant wash and shave – a luxury hardly expected. Of course occasional casualties occur all along the line, but we have been lucky so far.

Friday October 29th, 1915

We all enjoyed receiving our first mail yesterday evening. I got a letter from Joy (October 1st) and one from Jack (September 30th), for which I shall thank the kind sender personally. Also three *Times*, one *Scotsman*, and some *Illustrated*s from Joy, all most welcome reminders of civilization. The casualties in the fighting in France about September 25th have obviously been infernal. In the *Scotsman* obituary of October 5th there were several fellows I knew, and there must be many more dead. We don't seem to be able to make anything but small advances at enormous cost.

Forgot to state that the second instalments from Lambert, Gibson and Stewart reached me also last night, and no doubt Joy's parcel shortly follows. The rationing here is wonderfully good, and officers feed in small messes (Company, Squadron, etc.), and do themselves quite sufficiently well. In colder weather, I daresay, we shall get hardly as much as we would like, but in the meantime we grow fat on plenty of food and little exercise. About 10% of the men are already down with dysentery, but so far no officers.

I hope all the letters I wrote from Malta, on board ship, etc., were received. We were told to censor our own, so I said practically all I wanted to say, and if any were opened they might have been stopped. I shall write direct to Gibson if there are any additions or changes in what I want him to send me.

Most of one's work in the trenches at present is clerical. Endless returns have to be made about one's men – health, clothing, equipment, arms, ammunition, etc., and of course censoring letters takes up a bit of one's time.

4 p.m. (about 2 p.m. with you)
Since writing above our first casualty has occurred – a sergeant hit on the head by a fraction of one of our own bombs – nothing serious in the way of a wound, but enough to give him a fortnight or so in hospital. The bombs we use here are chiefly 'Double Cylinder', 'Maltese' or 'Mills', and fragments, of course, are always coming back. The chief entertainment here is when our Monitors shell the Turkish trenches in front of us with 14-inch shells. They fire from a range of about 15 miles in order to get high trajectory, and the shells seem gently to remove half an acre of Turks and Turkey every time they burst.

Saturday October 30th, 1915
When you see the country here one's chief wonder is how our good fellows ever did as much as they have done – especially at the first landings. The 8th Scottish Rifles, to whom I am attached, in half an hour's action lost 15 officers killed and 8 wounded. Among those killed were six Fettesians – Eric Young, Cecil McIndoe, Ronald McIndoe, Hugh McCowan, T. Stout and another. A. Tullie and R. Humble were among the wounded, so you can imagine the sort of work they had to do.

p.s. Forgot to say that I have seen Turks all right – in fact fired at a great big fellow 100 yards away outside his trench in the moonlight the other night. He disappeared of course, but

whether dead or alive we could not tell. He was as good a
target at night as I could ever hope to get.

– p.p.s. In case anybody is anxious, I feel as fit as I ever did,
and quite on for an attack at any time.

———⸎———

10
THE DRILL SERGEANT, 1916

Private Tom Lyon
(16th Batallion, Highland Light Infantry)

Few of the conscripts and late volunteers of 1916 onwards shared
the optimism of the initial wave of volunteers. They had seen the
lists of dead in the newspapers, and harboured few illusions about
what lay in store. Private Tom Lyon went on to fight at Passchendaele,
and wrote a moving account of what he went through. However, as
a piece of light relief, he offered this account of his Glaswegian drill
sergeant. Before teaching the arts of war, men like the drill sergeant
were expected to 'square bash' their charges until they learned to
operate as part of a team – a business of crushing the individual,
and building the soldier. His means of achieving this may sound
familiar to many who have encountered drill instructors in the decades
since this HLI drill sergeant put his charges through their paces.

'Yah!' jeer the vulgar little boys as we march to and from the
parade ground. 'Yah! luk at the tin sodgers wi' their badges –
H.L.I. – Harry Lauder's Infants, – Heluva Long Idle!' Our
'idleness' is more apparent than real. From foggy morn to ink-
black eve we wear down our shoe leather and our energies on
Glasgow Green, all for the cause of King and Country and

one-an'-tuppence a day. I'm willing to bet a silk hat to an Iron Cross that not many men in our battalion ever worked to such excess that they fainted from sheer exhaustion – that is, until they joined the Army. But fainting has become quite a hobby with us, especially when engaged in that gentle pastime known as Swedish drill [gymnastics].

'That's them bleeding cigarettes again', says the Sergeant by way of sympathy when the matter is carried out of the ranks; and, 'The Lord help you when you run up agin somethin' really severe in the way of work or 'ardship', he says tenderly, as he wipes globules of perspiration from his own forehead.

The Sergeant is not a lily-lipped or honey-mouthed individual, but he does know his business. As our transatlantic neighbours would say, he sure can deliver the goods. In his own person there is compassed more authority than was ever dreamed of by Wilhelm, the Imperial Pooh-Bah, in his most ambitious moments. 'If the General or Sir John French himself were on parade in this squad just now,' he told us the other day, 'he'd have to ask my permission before he could fall out, for I'm in command here, an' don't you forget it. Squad – 'Shun!' And obediently we 'shunned', duly impressed by his omnipotence.

He kept us ''shunning' and 'stand-at-easing' for ten full minutes, and until every man's back ached as under an Atlas-like burden. ''Shun' he roared . . . 'Oh! keep yer heads up an' yer chins tucked in . . . Ye would think that some o' you fellers had the weight o' the National Debt on your shoulders . . . You in the front rank – straighten yourself, man! Don't stand there like a half-shut knife. Throw your chest well out – you've got a hump like a camel . . . Your chest, man, your chest – don't you know your chest, you skilly-holder? An' keep yer eyes off the ground – there ain't no threepenny pieces lyin' about here. Here, you with the brown jacket in Section Four, who the hell told you you could blow your nose? If you weren't a blasted fool, and didn't know no better, you'd get two weeks' C.B. [Confined to Barracks] for that. Keep your hands down and stand to attention. Wait for the command "stand easy", and then you can blow yer nose to Jericho if you like.

'What are you laughin' at, you in the rear rank? D'ye think ye're a bloom' row o' ballet girls? An' what are you grinnin' at, pantomime-face? Ye've got nuthin' to laugh at. It's me as should be doin' all the laughin'. I see lots o' funny things afore me, but I'd kill myself if I were to laugh at 'em all. For Gawd's sake remember that ye're soldiers, an' keep yer mugs straight an' yer backs straight, an' yer mouths closed an' yer heels closed, an' stand at attention and do what I tell you . . . Move to the left in fours – Form Fours! . . . As you were! For the love of Mike, what's happened to ye? Are ye nailed or froze to the grass? Do ye think ye're a bloomin' waxworks or a collection of statues? When I tell ye to form fours ye should jump to it so quick that I shouldn't see ye movin', but instead o' that ye hobble into yer places as though you was a home for the aged an' infirm. Now jump to it – Form Fours. As you were!'

And we'd have to do it a dozen times before 'His Mightiness' was satisfied. When we had marched round the park several times in different formations we'd get the command to halt. 'Dress by the right!' Immediately we hopped, skipped, and jumped in an endeavour to 'touch in' to our neighbour and to form a straight line. 'Huh!' snorted our Instructor. 'Call that a straight line! Ain't ye never had no mathematics, an' don't ye *know* what a straight line is? Look at the distance you've lost in the marching. All together now, jump to it lively, dress up. Heavens! You fellers need to do as much dressin' up as a woman, an' even then ye don't look nice. It's a good dressin' down some o' you needs. You! . . . fat one in the centre! . . . back a bit. You're puttin' the whole line out. You better dress by yer belly instead o' yer face.'

Soon he'd give the order, 'Hats, coats, an' weskits off an' lay 'em on the ground', and we'd know that we were in for a stiff hour of Swedish drill, and some would begin to wish that they'd put on a clean shirt that morning, or that they'd got that missing button sewn on to their trousers, or perhaps they wondered if their old braces would outlast the hour.

'Look sharp, there,' said the sergeant. 'I asked ye to take off yer coats an' vests; I didn't tell ye to make yerselves look pretty. Never you mind smoothin' back your hair, you in the rear rank! I'll put it out of curl for ye before the hour's over; I'll bet.' Then away he took us at the double. And after ten or twelve minutes' running, and when we were all breathless and perspiring, he put us through a series of exercises that lacked nothing in strenuousness, his commands the while being interlarded with priceless gems of criticism and comment. At one exercise our hands were placed on the ground and the entire weight of our outstretched bodies rested on our arms and our toes. 'Now, keep yer bodies perfectly straight,' said the Sergeant. 'I don't want to see a row of Ben Nevises up in the air, and there's a feller with 'is knees on the ground! Get up off yer knees, you! This ain't a bleeding synagogue or a Hindu Temple.'

How I wish that Kaiser Wilhelm of Germany could have the privilege of being under the Sergeant's tuition for a single week! At the end of that time, I venture to predict, even the road-hog of Europe would feel himself to be but a poor, contemptible worm, having neither merit nor worth nor soul to call his own, and having lost even that which is the proverbial prerogative of worms – the ability to turn.

———◆———

11
ISTABULAT, MESOPOTAMIA, 1917

Lieutenant-Colonel J. Stewart
(2nd Battalion, Black Watch)

The 2nd Battalion Black Watch was serving in India when the war began, and went on to see service in France before being shipped east again, this time to Mesopotamia. After the fiasco at Gallipoli the war against the Ottoman Turks was fought on four main fronts – in northern Greece, along the Russo-Turkish border, in Palestine, and in Mesopotamia. This last theatre was fought along the banks of the rivers Tigris and Euphrates, with the British pushing inland from the coast. The Black Watch arrived there in November 1915, and took part in the drive on Baghdad, which was finally captured in March 1917. By that time Lieutenant-Colonel Stewart had joined the Battalion from the 9th Black Watch, and during the operations in upper Mesopotamia he assumed command of the old regular battalion.

By late April the British had reached Istabulat, on the River Tigris, where they found the Turks had dug in. A brigade-sized attack was ordered, with the 2nd Black Watch and the Seaforth Highlanders advancing up either bank of the Dujalil Canal, which bisected the Turkish position. Indian regiments supported the Highlanders on both flanks.

This account by Lieutenant-Colonel Stewart shows just how far he had developed as an infantry commander since the Battle of

Loos two years before. He launched a textbook attack, which he recounts with military efficiency. He also pays tribute to Charlie Melvin, a rowdy private from Kirriemuir, whose winning of a Victoria Cross made this otherwise insignificant little action one of particular significance to the story of the Scottish soldier. It is reputed that Private Melvin was sent a congratulatory telegram by J.M. Barrie, the creator of Peter Pan, and 'Kirrie's' other famous resident, but the veteran soldier never told his mother of his award – she had to hear the news from her neighbours. Lieutenant-Colonel Stewart picks up the story;

21st April 1917

At Zero [Hour], the whistles of the Company commander blew quietly, and we started off. It was just getting light, but not a sound came from the Turkish lines. I should have said that, owing to our not having any long-range artillery, it was impossible for our gunners to give us any efficient covering fire, but they had to wait until we had taken the redoubt before moving forward and engaging in counter-battery work, in doing which they lost heavily alas, owing to lack of cover, as they had to take up positions on the plain. It was here that the late Lord Suffolk was killed.

We had advanced some few hundred yards before I heard any rifle shots at all, and these were only caused by our front line stumbling on one or two Turkish listening posts which were dealt with by our first line in their advance.

The Dujail bank affords an excellent guide for marching by, and the hillocks gave more cover than we had dared hope for, but as we approached the redoubt the men on the plain, i.e. on the right of our line, began to suffer from the fairly heavy fire of the enemy. It was not for long, however, as the surprise was complete and our first four lines reached the redoubt with comparatively few casualties and speedily drove out the Turks who took refuge in some trenches further back.

Just as the sixth line came up the Turks made a very heavy counterattack and drove our men out, but luckily the seventh and eighth lines appeared on the scene at the psychological moment and again the enemy were driven out of the redoubt. By this time the Gurkhas had made their appearance on our right, and, having cleared the plain, swung round to their left, and made for the redoubt. The Turks made one attempt to counterattack but without success, and by 6.30 a.m. we and the Gurkhas were firmly fixed in the Turkish position. Extra ammunition came up, and all was well.

It was just before the first attack that Private Charles Melvin performed a deed that won him the Victoria Cross. In official language the episode was as follows:

For most conspicuous bravery, coolness and resource in action near Istabulat, Mesopotamia on 21st April 1917. Private Melvin's Company had advanced to within sixty yards of the front line trench of a redoubt, where, owing to the intensity of the enemy's fire, the men were obliged to lie down and wait for reinforcements. Private Melvin, however, rushed on himself, over ground swept from end to end by rifle and machine gun fire. On reaching the enemy trench, he halted and fired two or three shots into it, killing one or two of the enemy, but as others in the trench continued to fire at him, he jumped into it and attacked them with his bayonet in his hand, as owing to his rifle having been damaged it was not 'fixed'. On being attacked in this resolute manner, most of the enemy fled to their second line, but not before Private Melvin had killed two more and succeeded in disarming eight unwounded and one wounded. Private Melvin bound up the wounds of the wounded man, and then driving his eight unwounded prisoners before him, and supporting the wounded one, he hustled them out of the trench, marched them in, and delivered them over to an officer. He then provided himself with a load of ammunition and returned to the firing line, where he reported himself to his platoon sergeant. All this was done, not only under intense rifle and machine gun fire, but the whole way back Private Melvin and his party were exposed to heavy artillery barrage fire.

It is not often that a Commanding Officer has the opportunity of recommending one of his men for that coveted honour, and sometimes his recommendation is 'turned down', so it was with a very great satisfaction indeed, when about nine months afterwards, at Ismailia on the Suez Canal, news reached me that Charles Melvin had been awarded The Cross he had so thoroughly deserved.

━━━▻◆◅━━━

12
PASSCHENDAELE, 1917

Sergeant John Jackson
(1st Batallion, Queen's Own Cameron Highlanders)

The British offensive at Passchendaele (also known as the Third Battle of Ypres) was the brainchild of Field Marshal Haig. Unfortunately the Germans were ready for him, and the September offensive soon bogged down in a sea of mud and blood. After the war the very name of the place became a byword for the futility and carnage of trench warfare. Two months later the British were still clinging to their meagre gains on Passchendaele Ridge, and launching small attacks, designed to strengthen their position. On 16 November 1917 Sergeant Jackson's battalion staged one such operation.

At Passchendale the gain of an isolated farmstead or a few yards of trench was regarded as an achievement of some merit, so great was the contest for every inch of ground in this sector. The very name of the place was sufficient to cause cold shivers to run down our backs. Little wonder that we congratulated ourselves on missing at least one spell in the trenches. Unfortunately our good luck did not last long, and before we had been two hours in camp, a message was received saying that if either Sergeant Walker or myself were returned from leave, we had to proceed to Irish Farm, and join the battalion in readiness to enter the front line. What a reception for men newly back from leave – straight from our own firesides to this inferno! However, we had no choice in the matter, and we both went forward next morning.

Arriving at Irish Farm, which was the name given to a collection of old ragged tents surrounded by a sea of mud, we found the position so acute, that the regiment was 'standing by', and ready to go into battle at 30 minutes notice. Next morning, just as the piper was playing 'reveille', our camp was bombed by enemy aeroplanes, and artillery also opened out on us. We sought what shelter there was in some old trenches, and as we stood there a piece of shrapnel missed my head by a hair's breadth, and buried itself between my feet in the bottom of the trench. By and by, things quietened down again, but with the heavy rain which fell and being very wet and cold, not to speak of the quagmire in which our camp was situated, we were in a most miserable state.

On the night of the 15th November, the Camerons relieved the 2nd Royal Sussex on the left position of the 'Ridge'. Only about half of the regiment went into action as the accommodation was limited. Battalion Headquarters were situated in a captured German 'pill box' at Meetcheele, but this was so small that only the CO and the Adjutant, together with two telephone operators, could get inside. The remainder of the headquarters had to take what shelter we could find behind a wall, which was really no shelter at all. This was our first time in action since I took charge of the telephone lines, and I found little or no communication between companies.

It seemed impossible in the constant shelling that was going on to keep telephone wires 'through'. Without any help, my partner had been left behind, I knew I had a big task on hand to arrange any lines of communication. I searched around till I found a wire leading to our support company some distance in the rear, and was able to repair this, and keep it in working order. From the support company, contact with brigade headquarters was made with lamp signalling, all contrived so that the enemy could not detect it. The line to the support company was therefore very important, and acted as a sort of back-door through which reserves could be summoned when necessary.

The biggest puzzle was the left front company, to which there was no line at all. Having salvaged as much wire as I thought would be required, I commenced to lay a line to 'C' Company. It was all work in the open and mostly in view of the enemy. Shells and bullets were everywhere and many times I must have been very nearly hit. The ground I had to traverse was a gruesome swamp stinking with dead bodies, and often I sank to the knees in what I thought looked solid ground. Now and then the wire I was laying would go up in the air on being hit with a shell, and then I had to retrace my steps, and repair the damage.

My thoughts must have been too much occupied in laying the wire to notice the majority of the shells, for now I sometimes wonder how I managed to get that line out, working all on my own. At the time I thought nothing of it, it just seemed to be all in the day's work. When I finally got to 'C' Company, and found the wire was through, then I knew I'd done something worthwhile. The lives of the men of the left company might depend on that wire to headquarters. Although only a short distance, probably ¾ of a mile, it had taken me nearly three hours to get there, and I yet had to get back again.

After a rest, I set off, and on my way back I had the experience of being hunted by shells. They were too near and too exact to be random shots, so I adopted a zig-zag course, and through this and by doubling on my tracks I got safely back, and in this I considered myself more than lucky. Soon after I had left 'C' Company signal office on my way back, it had been hit with a shell and the two men there, Henderson and Tingle, were both badly wounded. Poor Jimmy Henderson died of his wounds, but Tingle recovered and rejoined us later.

During our short spell in the line, we suffered enormous losses, and there was a constant stream of stretcher bearers with wounded passing down to the dressing stations in the rear. A large number of German prisoners assisted in the work of carrying. They were big hefty fellows, but meek enough now as prisoners of war, and giving credit where it is due, they did sterling work among our wounded, and were very gentle in their handling of the poor fellows they carried so carefully. Without their help our stretcher men could not have coped with all the casualties, and many more men would have died failing the necessary attention to their wounds. Their job too was a dangerous one. The sector was being literally swept with bullets and shells, and it was not uncommon for a stretcher party to be knocked out while proceeding to the rear with wounded.

There were many pathetic scenes regarding these white-faced, blood-stained fighters, which caused lumps to rise in our throats, and made us set our faces in grim determination to have revenge. One of the most pitiful sights, I saw, was that of one of our own men, Gaelic bred and born, who, not being able to speak a word of English, lying on a stretcher badly wounded internally, could not tell us how to ease him in his agony. On our right flank lay the 1st Canadians, this being the first instance during the war that the two 1st Divisions had fought shoulder to shoulder. Like us, the Canadians were losing heavily. Blood and mud were mixing freely on the shell-battered ridges of Passchendale [*sic*], good men 'falling as the leaves fall in autumn'. Trenches were knocked to pieces, and we lay in any sort of holes in the hope of escaping the hail of high explosive and machine gun fire.

On the night of the 16th November, our second night in the line, the Camerons went over the top and captured two fortified farms, held by the enemy, together with 25 prisoners. It was a successful attack carried out under a murderous fire. The farms proved hard nuts to crack and their defenders sheltered in their concrete emplacements caused us many casualties and it was not until we could reach them by bombs through loop holes in their defences that the garrisons gave in, and cried, '*Merci, Kamerad.*' What a night of fighting that was for all of us.

I was fortunate during the bombardments in keeping my lines in fairly good condition, but to maintain them meant ceaseless work for me. We had no chance of a meal since we came into the line, just a bit of biscuit from our haversacks, and all the time it had rained and was bitterly cold. Under these awful conditions it was impossible to stay long in the line, and so after 48 hours of hard fighting, we were glad to be relieved by the Black Watch. We trooped wearily out again to the camp at Irish Farm, and here we had a chance to look round and see who had come through alright, and who was missing. It reminded me of the roll-call after Loos. Our ranks were sadly thinned and many good men had made the supreme sacrifice. We left Irish Farm on the 18th, and returned to Dirty Bucket Camp. There, we enjoyed hot baths and clean changes, which we were all sadly in need of, after our experiences in the mud of Passchendale Ridge, though it was long before we were free of the effects of those two terrible days and nights. For my share of the fighting at Passchendale I was recommended for the Military Medal.

———⟫◆⟪———

13
THE ADVANCE, METEREN, 1918

Lieutenant Douglas Wilson
(5th Batallion, Queen's Own Cameron Highlanders)

On 10 April 1918 the German army launched a major offensive, which drove the British back from Passchendaele, and forced them to abandon their hard-won gains on Messines Ridge, to the south-east of Ypres. However, by the end of the month the Germans had been forced to a standstill, and disaster on the Western Front had been averted. Reinforcements, many of them from Canada and South Africa, were thrown into the line, and plans were made for a series of counterattacks, designed to coincide with French and American offensives further to the south.

From 16 to 19 July the British attacked the German positions around Bailleul, south of Ypres, and succeeded in driving the enemy back for more than a dozen miles. As part of the Highland Brigade of the 9th (Scottish) Division, the 5th Camerons formed the leading wave in the assault, launched on the morning of 16th July. Lieutenant Wilson described what happened next as his 'mad half-hour'.

Now the sun was bright and strong, ushering in a warm July day. The writhing curly morning mists had gone, the plain was tricked out in patterns of green, light and dark brown here and there tinting in sepia and ochre, the far distance in a shimmering blue. The sky was clear but for a few high patches of cirrus cloud. Larks were singing. I looked it over – a beautiful setting, for what? Still waiting . . . The present with its hateful tedium was ticking over . . . Some had been dozing, some smoking, some conversing, passing the time somehow, no matter how. Now all were passive: just waiting . . . How long to zero hour? Officers' watches had been synchronised – time to gird up our loins. We were ready. A last look at rifle, bayonet, equipment, with studied unconcern, but the air had suddenly become tense. 'Half a minute to go, boys', I said, letting wrist and watch drop. 'Wait for it.'

It came with an unbelievable ear-splitting crash merging into a continuous roar. We were off. Within seconds a yawning crater opened up at our feet, and showers of earth, stones and splinters whirled about us. The ground we trod on heaved. My group split automatically, jog-trotted around the gaping hole, joined up and kept going. Already the smoke was thick – we kept our eyes skinned. It was impossible to see how many yards visibility we had – not many. We approached some red-leaded Nissen huts. It was near here that I glimpsed a shell hole with some dead bodies heaped together. Were they tartan clad? I couldn't be sure. I recalled 'Auntie' [the nickname of a fallen fellow officer], and pressed on. It was hard going on rough ground. Like the men, I was carrying rifle, bayonet, equipment and shovel. Additionally, revolver on belt, and a 'Bisley bandolier' of revolver rounds strapped to each wrist for quick reloading.

'D' Company's right flank crossed the Axe Hill road and passed through the remnants of the house where the village thinned out. We found ourselves in an orchard, and as the barrage moved forward I heard the sound of heavy machine gun fire ahead and to the left. Then the smoke cleared sufficiently to disclose a straggling hedge crossing our front obliquely, lined by Jerry gunners. A barrage of H.E. [high-explosive shells] does not creep . . . but lifts and jumps, clearing a space on the ground . . . Here the barrage had obviously come down on one side of the hedge and lifted over it, leaving enemy details intact oblique on this stretch . . . I saw some of my men mown down.

Everybody was prone, myself included, as a stream of bullets whipped past me. Some lads were using their rifles. My first clear view of a Boche was a man getting off at a run from behind the hedge. I had a crack at him and missed, slipping sideways into a crump hole just as I pressed the trigger. Then two more rabbits: I steadied myself and got them both – that was for 'Auntie' for a start. Then I realised, as I should have done straight away without indulging in snap shooting that 'B' Company men were mixed up with mine, and that our front wave had been held up here. Shouting directions was hopeless in this din; I got up, waved a bunch forward, and led them at a rush. This was bayonet work, and we cleared that hedge in a trice . . . It was the only concerted resistance we encountered on our company front till our objective was reached. Meantime, we linked up again and pushed on.

As I passed through a gap in the hedge I threw over a Boche Maxim on its mounting. To have turned it on the Huns now running helter-skelter down the reverse slope of the hill would have been a joy, but many of them were behind our own men who pushed through and forward. Incidentally this particular gun had continued to fire until we were almost on top of it when the man behind it stuck up his arms in the *Kamerad* act. A big man over six-foot, that Jerry, but what could he expect? He got no quarter from a Glaswegian using his bayonet with a will for the first time; he wasn't more than 5ft 3ins. at most, but he had seen his comrades shot down.

Beyond the hedge were cubbies and dug-out used by the gunners, now either scuppered or on their way towards Berlin. Not all of them, though. Mopping up was a dirty job. The men had been warned not to take chances . . . because the enemy so often proved himself treacherous. Despite warnings we lost a number of men done in by Huns who made a show of surrendering and then resisted. I am not likely to forget an individual who emerged from a lair at my feet, his hands high above his head, but he had an egg-bomb in his right fist (the only bomb I saw in the show). I had slung my rifle with its empty magazine, my Webley grasped at the waist until there was time to reload.

Our eyes met, he meant business, and I plugged him, instantly flinging myself flat. The bomb did not explode. I put the revolver away, reloaded the rifle and got to my feet, to be confronted by another Boche carrying an automatic, just three feet away. At that instant a heavy blow struck me full on the pack strapped between my shoulders, flinging me forward involuntarily, bayonet first. Kaput! I had been struck by a fragment from a trench mortar dump which was pooping off in the village. The pack and its contents had saved my back, the bayonet my life.

Crowded moments. I had no notion of how long the rushing of machine guns and the hand-to-hand encounters took. We advanced across the main road to Bailleul, mopping up as we went. No smoke now. The men were well in their stride, if anything pressing forward rather too much. There were lots of Huns breaking cover to be dealt with. The din of the barrage was still deafening, with additional periodic major explosions from the dump in Meteren.

I trotted along what I took to be my own front, signalling to bunches of men to spread out; among them were numbers of lads from 'B' Company who should have been elsewhere. It was quite impossible to issue orders by word of mouth, and nothing but hand signals could be understood. While so engaged, but unknown to me then, it seems that I had a narrow shave from a wounded Boche whom I passed but did not see. He was going through the motions of putting a bullet through my back when a youth called Spalding who was trailing me almost fell over him. He kicked the weapon from his hands and jumped on his face with both feet. Why record so horrible an occurrence? The answer must be that if I have chosen to suppress my qualms in the matter, I must not suppress what was horrible if this record is to be . . . a true and factual story . . .

We had now emerged into open country, with a first vista down the reverse slope of the ridge crowned by the ruined village. We looked downhill over the Meteren Veldt stretching away towards Armentieres, faintly seen behind distant woodlands. I didn't spare any time on the prospect. Only a few Boche were visible in the foreground now, and it seemed to be that too many of our own people were wandering around aimlessly or indulging in stupid chases in attempts to take prisoner fugitives racing in front of us but still to the rear of our front line wave. I was annoyed at the attention given to one lumbering fellow on our left flank who had broken through our moppers-up, dodging and doubling like a hare, out-distancing all pursuit.

What were our chaps thinking about? In a sudden flare of anger I lay down, took quick aim and fired. He bounced into the air and fell over, no one more surprised than myself. I was pulled to my feet by a full private (under-keeper and deer-stalker by occupation) who clapped me vigorously on the shoulder and pronounced in a foghorn voice, 'Eh, man, if you are no' the bonny boy with a service rifle. He was a wheen over a hunner yairds, that yin, I'll say.' I managed to grin at him, though the truth was I had a revulsion in feeling. I shrugged my sore shoulders and told myself 'another one for Auntie'.

We moved into standing corn and I tried to introduce some order into the mopping up. There were still furtive Jerries lying or crawling on hands or knees. A covey of three was flushed from a cleverly concealed cubby and taken prisoner, going to join the ranks of goodish batches now passing back . . . They were a motley crowd. The well set-up soldierly type were in the minority, many of the younger brands were pretty awful specimens, sloppy and bedraggled . . . the majority showed relief or even definite joy at the prospect of being out of the war for keeps . . . Now for the first time shrapnel bursting in the air to our front was giving the prearranged signal: objective reached, dig in. The first headache now was going to be just where to dig, identifying map references on strange ground; the next would be setting down quickly enough. Our position was open and exposed – how [long] would the Boche plastering which was bound to come be deferred?

... I had got a fair proportion of my half company collected when Jones and Fraser appeared ... N.J. radiated satisfaction and determination, and the men took note of the fact that the skipper was well pleased at the way things had gone. He raised a laugh by telling them that they looked like a lot of miners, but there was going to be a long shift of overtime before a bath came along.

We conferred hurriedly ... I [went] forward to the front line to bring back 'D' Company men still with 'B' Company. We had to get cracking, 'Spot' and I, but we were watchful in the corn. Firing was going on in a small basin of ground in the centre of which was an empty, dilapidated hand-cart, and a certain NCO quite on his own was slamming round after round into it. We approached him carefully from behind; the chap was off his rocker, under the impression that he was slaying his thousands. I clapped my revolver to his head and 'Spot' disarmed him ... we pushed him along and handed him over to 'B' Company where he belonged ... His condition was rum-induced. He wasn't the only one in 'B' Company who had gone to pieces. The Company Commander was wild with excitement, dancing about like a marionette, issuing volleys of orders to which no one was paying the slightest attention ... he foamed at the mouth, threatened to place me under arrest and became really obstructive ... I left him muttering, having raked in about a score of men, and pushed them uphill in top gear.

Jones had a pitifully small party at work on the most exposed part of the new line, but by great good luck we were able to make use of a nicely converted slip-trench further along, extending it at both ends. It was a gift indeed, for if the worst came to the worst we could crush in there under something like cover. The men were obviously very tired now. They had stuck to the digging well, but some were showing signs of exhaustion and one or two flopped out. I felt I had been on my feet for hours and glanced at my watch in disbelief when I found it registered precisely thirty-five minutes after zero-hour.

CHAPTER 6

THE SECOND WORLD WAR

The years between the wars weren't particularly good ones for the British army. A distrust of the military, the belief that future wars were now unthinkable, and a lack of funding all contributed to malaise within the armed forces. The Royal Navy was encumbered by international treaties which limited its strength and the air force was starved of the resources it needed to develop. As for the army, it was expected to return to the business of peacetime imperial soldiering, without support from home or government. The 'ten-year rule' was renewed each year until 1932 – a rolling annual political declaration that Britain would not be expected to fight another major war in Europe for a decade. That shaped the government's parsimonious attitude to the army, stifling reform, denying new weapons and equipment, and limiting the size and efficiency of the peacetime army.

During the 1930s growing unrest in Europe led to the abandonment of the 'ten-year rule', but the army still came a poor third behind the other services in the matter of its financing. New warships and aircraft took precedence over the development of tanks, artillery and infantry weapons. Worse, the army was ill-prepared to fight a modern war. It was essentially an imperial police force, whose only experience of the way a modern European war should be fought came from the trenches of Flanders.

During the two decades between 1918 and 1938, all the Scottish regiments took turns serving overseas, mainly in India's

North-West Frontier and Palestine. Like the rest of the army, the Scottish regiments suffered during the lean years of peace, but in Scotland, unlike in most of the rest of Britain, the Territorial Army remained a relatively popular institution. Consequently the Scottish regiments were better placed than many when it came to the rapid wartime expansion of the army. In March 1939 the size of the Territorial Army was doubled, which meant that by the time the Second World War began in September, the bulk of the Scottish regiments were grouped into two divisions – the 51st (Highland) and the 52nd (Lowland) divisions. When the British Expeditionary Force (BEF) arrived in France, additional Scottish regiments were scattered throughout the army.

By May 1940, when the Germans finally invaded France, the British army was perfectly suited to fighting a European war – as long as the Germans fought by the same rules as they had in 1914. The notion of blitzkrieg came as something of a shock to the high command, and soon the BEF found itself in full retreat. The 52nd (Lowland) Division had barely landed in Cherbourg before it was unceremoniously hustled back to its transport ships. The men of the 51st (Highland) Division were less fortunate. As one of these accounts testifies, they were pinned against the coast of the English Channel by the Germans, and had no option but to surrender *en masse*. It was a humiliating introduction to the concept of total war.

However, the division was resurrected, based on the nascent 9th (Scottish) Division, which was renamed, and the regular battalions of the lost regiments fleshed out by conscripts and Territorials. An additional formation, the 15th (Scottish) Division was also created, and like much of the rest of the army, it spent the rest of 1940 guarding the beaches of southern England against an invasion which never came. By then, the Scottish regiments had become formations of conscripts. The loss of the original 51st (Highland) Division meant that there was no longer a large cadre of regular or even experienced Territorial soldiers. Instead, these new conscripts had to learn as they went along, and had to adapt to a new kind of warfare.

The advantage of universal conscription is that the army becomes a cross-section of Scottish society. While this might have created social and educational problems, it did mean that these new units were to develop a sense of belonging, first to their regiment and its regional base, and then to the Scottish divisions in which they served. In other words, the Scottish infantryman managed to retain his identity within the army. The same was not particularly true of the Royal Scots Greys and the Yeomanry. Many of these regiments had recently exchanged their horses for tanks, and while some units such as the Lothian and Border Horse were attached to Scottish infantry divisions as reconnaissance troops, others formed part of British armoured brigades. The rest of the Scottish Yeomanry regiments became artillery or anti-tank units, and the Yeomen were transformed into gunners.

After Dunkirk the 51st (Highland) Division was sent to North Africa, where it won an enviable fighting reputation during the campaign there. Two of the first-hand accounts in this chapter come from men of the Highland Division during its time in the Western Desert. The Division then participated in the landings in Sicily, before landing in Italy. The Highlanders were recalled to Britain in time for the invasion of Normandy in June 1944. By contrast, the 15th (Lowland) Division spent the early years of the war in Britain, but it was fully equipped and trained to take a leading role in the invasion of Nazi-occupied Europe. Similarly, the 52nd (Lowland) Division spent much of the war in Scotland, where it was trained for mountain warfare. The intention was to send it to Norway, by way of a diversion. In the end this never happened, and with the supreme irony the army sometimes excels at, these mountain specialists were eventually sent to the Low Countries.

Inevitably, not all Scottish soldiers served in Scottish divisions. Many regular battalions were already overseas when the war began, and consequently they saw service to the east of Suez. The 2nd Gordons and 2nd Argylls were in Singapore and Malaya when Japan entered the war, while the 2nd Royal Scots were in Hong Kong. All three battalions were captured by the Japanese early in 1942. The 1st Cameronians, the 1st Royal Scots Fusiliers, the 2nd King's Own Scottish Borderers and the re-formed 1st Royal Scots all fought in Burma from 1942 onwards. Additional Scottish regiments joined them during the latter stages of the campaign, including the 2nd Black Watch, which fought in the 'Chindit' operations. An account of an action they participated in is included in this chapter.

In June 1944 the Allies invaded north-west Europe, and two of the three Scottish divisions participated in the subsequent battle for Normandy, and then the pursuit of the Germans through France. Although it isn't listed among these extracts, the 15th (Scottish) Division played an important role in the Epsom offensive, advancing along 'the Scottish Corridor' in the face of elite German panzer formations. The 51st (Highland) Division also fought with distinction, but in this selection of first-hand accounts the Normandy campaign is seen through the eyes of tankers – the men of the 2nd Fife and Forfar Yeomanry, whose regiment was all but destroyed within a matter of minutes during Operation Goodwood. We return to the infantry later in the campaign, with a gripping account of an attack on a German-occupied village in the aftermath of the Battle of the Bulge.

By that time the British 21st Army Group found itself bogged down in Holland. After Operation Market Garden – the doomed attempt to seize the Rhine Bridge at Arnhem by airborne *coup de main* – the campaign ground to a halt. For months men of the three Scottish divisions struggled to root the Germans out of Dutch villages, fighting in miserable, wet, cold, muddy conditions which were vaguely reminiscent of Passchendaele. Spring brought better weather, and a successful Rhine crossing. Then it was on into Germany, and a drive towards Hamburg and the north German plain. After VE Day, few British troops would imagine that their descendants would be garrisoning the same German towns half a century later.

The Scottish soldier emerged from the war with a strong sense of identity. For six years, commanders of Scottish troops had played on the Scottish identity of their 'Jocks', using pipers to lead men into battle, and wearing kilts to strengthen pride. Unlike the slaughter of the Great War, this conflict was one that made sense. These Scottish soldiers were fighting a totalitarian enemy whose bombs had dropped on Scottish soil, and whose racial or political stance was anathema to most Scots. They were fighting a just war – a struggle for democracy and justice. Few conflicts before or since would place the Scottish soldier on such a high moral pedestal.

━━━▶◆◀━━━

1
ST VALERY, 1940

Private Gregor Macdonald
(4th Batallion, Cameron Highlanders)

The son of a Perthshire gamekeeper, Gregor Macdonald was a trainee banker in the Western Isles when the war broke out, and when the Cameronians called for local recruits he decided to volunteer. After training in Inverness and Aldershot he was awarded the regimental 'blue hackle', and in January 1940 he was shipped to France. In May 1940 his regiment tried unsuccessfully to stem the German tide near the River Somme, and by the start of June the 51st Highland Division was being pushed back towards the coast. General Rommel prevented its escape to Le Havre, so instead the Highland Division retreated towards the tiny fishing port of St Valery-en-Caux.

We edged back in a north-westerly direction, taking advantage of any cover in an effort to reach the Channel. We had not seen any Allied aircraft in the past month and were beginning to doubt if we had any left. On the other hand, from dawn the sky was never without enemy planes. At first light close formations of heavy bombers at around four or five thousand feet were heading for the Channel ports and lines of communications in Western France. An hour later we heard the crump as they unloaded their bombs. Escorts of fighters now accompanied them on all raids but, so far as we could see, they were never challenged by Allied planes.

The next three days were very confusing, and it is now very difficult to remember what happened. Each night as darkness fell we retreated in the direction of the Channel until we came to a defensive position where we dug-in to await the enemy advance, which usually came at first light. I doubt if we inflicted many casualties – at best we only delayed them for an hour or two at each position. When night came we repeated the previous night's procedure and on the morning of 10 June we could see the Channel at a distance of about two miles. This greatly cheered us, for we had been told that the Royal Navy would embark us from the small town of St Valery-en-Caux, a few miles down the coast from Dieppe.

The following night, as soon as darkness fell, Sergeant-Major MacDonald, who had rejoined us the previous day, sent me down to the beach to see how the evacuation was proceeding. It was only then that I came to realise the full gravity of the situation. The small town was situated on the only flat ground at the base of cliffs. The main road descended from the escarpment by a very steep hill and running parallel to the road were numerous tracks and paths down the rock face.

Every square foot was occupied by troops, some dead, some wounded, but most sound asleep in the torrential rain which had started at dusk. To make matters worse, fog was rolling in from the sea and there was no sign of any Royal Navy ships. A steady concentration of shellfire was coming from a southwesterly direction and I concluded that the enemy were in possession of the cliff tops between St Valery and Fécamp. All the houses round the harbour were in flames and chimney-pots were rolling about the streets. Stretcher-bearers were carrying bodies to the town square where a huge heap was steadily growing.

There was nothing further to learn and I attempted the return journey through the solid mass of bodies on the narrow tracks. Fortunately they were so tired that they didn't protest when I tramped over them. I finally reached the cliff top but found it very difficult to locate the Camerons in the darkness and confusion. When I stopped to take my bearings a soldier standing in a doorway invited me into the building. 'We're the 1st Black Watch; come in and get a cup of tea, Jock.'

I then discovered I'd landed in a schoolroom which about a dozen men of the Black Watch were defending with two Brens firing from the windows. A wood fire was burning in the grate and an elderly French woman was calmly toasting bread and spreading jam from a large container. The Black Watch had rescued the foodstuffs from a blazing ration truck and a corporal was making tea in a huge pot. He handed me a mug of boiling tea and a piece of bread with jam. That proved to be my last meal for four days.

I finally found B Company sleeping soundly on the eastern outskirts of the town. The rain had continued throughout the night but the island boys did not seem to notice it. I reported to the sergeant-major that no boats were to be seen, but he did not appear to be too concerned and asked me to help him bury the Company box, which contained all the Company funds and records. On second thoughts he distributed all the funds amongst the survivors – the equivalent of twenty-five shillings per man.

The company clerk reported he had spoken to some of the Battalion HQ staff, who informed him that we were surrounded by the enemy; they were giving us one hour to surrender. I refused to believe this and sought out Major Hill, who agreed that the position was critical and asked, 'How are you off for ammunition?' 'Very little left, sir,' I replied, and knew then that the ammunition factor could decide whether the 51st Division would be forced to surrender. Suddenly the shellfire ceased and everything was quiet. Then three German tanks appeared with a high-ranking officer in the first vehicle. At the time we did not recognise him, but later learned that it was Brigadier General Rommel. Following the tanks came battalions of infantry, with many of the officers speaking fluent English. Without fuss they instructed us to place our rifles and bayonets in one pile and the remainder of our equipment on a grassy bank above the road.

To say we were shocked would be an understatement. As infantry soldiers we had at some time imagined ourselves wounded or even killed, but now our only thought was the humiliation of the Highland Division surrendering. Some time after our arrival in France a French Liaison Officer was attached to the Battalion. He held the rank of Lieutenant and was very popular with all ranks because of his ability to obtain almost anything the Battalion requested and to sort out the many problems arising with the French authorities. On the morning of the surrender he calmly walked towards the German tanks and was given a very enthusiastic welcome by the enemy officers. Our troops soon let him know our thoughts and the island boys reverted to Gaelic to express their opinion of him.

⇒◆⇐

2

EL ALAMEIN, 1943

Captain George Green (5th Seaforths)

Since the summer of 1940, a war of thrust and counterthrust had been fought in the desert of North Africa. First the British and their allies had the upper hand, and then the initiative passed to the Axis powers – the Italian army and the highly effective German Afrika Korps, commanded by General Erwin Rommel. By early September 1942 the fate of the Middle East hung in the balance. The German Afrika Korps and their Italian allies had pushed the British 8th Army back to within 50 miles of Alexandria, and Rommel had every reason to expect the advance to continue. However, the 8th Army held the enemy at El Alamein – a prime defensive position. Both sides then dug in, gathering strength for a fresh battle. In the meantime a new commander, General Montgomery, took command of the 8th Army, and began planning a counterattack. The offensive was planned in meticulous detail, and the 51st Highland Division was given the task of piercing the enemy defences near 'Kidney Ridge'. The attack began on the night of 23/24 October, preceded by a 20-minute barrage by more than a thousand guns. George H. Green was the commander of the HQ Company of the 5th Seaforths, and he recounts what happened when the order came to advance. He was later awarded the MC.

I remember a rum bottle. I'd been dishing out the ration on the start line, and then the barrage opened up, and there I was with this bottle in my hand. It was still half full. I couldn't possibly drink it all. I took one good swig out of it, and then laid it down very carefully all by itself in the middle of the desert. I've often wondered what happened to it. Donnie Munro was on my right when we started. The dust was so thick you couldn't see ten yards either side, but up above it wasn't so bad and you could still see the moon. The noise was simply hellish. I kept on going, and after a while Donnie had disappeared and so had everybody else. I must have gone too quickly, because all at once the barrage was coming down on top of me: it seems impossible, but I could actually see big silver slivers of metal flying about. The bursts were all round. I lay down and began to crawl backwards. Then I saw Jack Davidson of 'D' Company lying about three yards away. He heaved his flask over to me, and I was glad of it. It seemed we were on the half-way line. The barrage was to halt in front of us for half an hour, forming a screen while we reorganised; so if I'd gone on I would have had it.

I tried to make my way back to Battalion HQ and landed in the middle of 'C' Company, who were roaming around blazing away with tommy guns into every hole and corner they could find. I decided this was no place for me, and set off again. It was a cold night, but I was sweating like a bull. The sand made walking very tiring. The next one I ran into was Farquhar Macrae, who was in a little scoop of sand working on the casualties. There were a lot of wounded Ities in the background, howling dismally; and I found about twenty of my own chaps near them, unwounded but lost. How Farquhar worked out in the open, with the racket and the dust and the darkness, I don't know. He just had to, I suppose. He was even doing amputations. I gathered my chaps and we set off, leaving him to it, and had another shot at finding Battalion HQ. The barrage was moving again, so we moved with it and went to where we calculated our objective should be. We hadn't worked it out too badly, either because the Verey success signals went up not far away.

This business sounds chaotic; but it wasn't, really. We were nearly all split up into smaller groups than we had planned to move in − it was inevitable with visibility the way it was but the Battalion was still holding direction and we weren't far apart. We just couldn't see each other. Later on, when daylight came, we found that the plan had been carried through to the letter − much to our surprise, I admit, but carried through it was. However, that came later. At that time we imagined we were alone. We began to dig in, but before we had got down any distance a German armoured car appeared and went around and round us, blazing away with a machine gun. I don't think he could have seen us clearly, because most of his shots went wide. Then he belted off at a tangent, still firing, and disappeared into the smoke. It was that kind of battle: things kept popping on and off in a casual sort of way. I heard later that the same car bumped into Farquhar and his medical orderlies next. They were unarmed, of course. They tried to get away, but Private Gallacher was killed and the rest were taken prisoner. They escaped before dawn − trust Farquhar!

Anyway, it was 0430 hours by the time we reached the objective and the whole Battalion was digging in. The dust had subsided, the sun would soon be up, and the German guns were feeling for our range. This was when the real trouble began. The ground was like iron, and it was almost impossible to dig down more than two feet without striking solid limestone.

We couldn't get down at all. For the next five hours my group just lay as the shells came over, heavily and accurately. They were dead on the range. All this time we were trying to dig. It was the worst ever. Stuff was landing continually within twelve yards of us, and some shells were as close as four feet. I never got my head right down: it was just level with the surface. We began to have casualties. One or two went bomb-happy about the second hour and started to scream. There was a chap hit in the mouth, and we couldn't move him. In the afternoon we found some Italian trenches fifty yards behind us − we'd never had our heads up far enough to see them before − and after that it wasn't too bad.

3
WESTERN DESERT, 1943

Sergeant Robert Penman (7th Batallion, Black Watch)

In the months following the British and Commonwealth victory at El Alamein, the Axis forces in North Africa retreated precipitately back through Libya, towards their supply base in Tripoli. By 12 November Tobruk had been recaptured, and eight days layer Benghazi fell to the British. By Christmas Day Sirte had fallen, and by New Year the

8th Army was on the outskirts of Tripoli. For much of the time the 51st (Highland) Division were in the forefront of this thousand-mile pursuit. Transport often had to be improvised, and the advance had to be conducted without proper maps, or even supplies. Therefore, by mid-January 1943, when the leading elements of the division were fighting at Homs on the eastern approaches to Tripoli, Sergeant Penman of the Black Watch was still trying to rejoin his unit.

The three or four months after El Alamein are only half memories – except one – that mix everything up, with no significant dates. Not one of these months could I have known what day of the week or what day of the month it was. I do not think we saw the sea once. All I know is that we used several means of transport. Our own carriers were used several times, and I guess (maybe wrongly) that this was when the Highland Division led the chase after the Germans.

During one of our journeys in our carriers when we stopped for the night we spread our carriers in a huge circle around our Platoon Commanders carrier – not in a tight circle like wagon trains in films. Real warfare is about survival first and last, no other creed is as important as survival.

This particular morning we got the order to move out, it was dark. We were allowed no fires for breakfast, no naked lights at all, no cigarettes, just start your carrier and fall into line behind another carrier. Well, our carrier would not start, Jock could not use lighting of any sort to see what was wrong so we had to wait for daylight. Daylight came, Jock had a look and could see nothing wrong, after an hour or so he looked in the radiator only to find it was dry. We had some 2 gall cans on the outside of the carrier which we used to top up the radiator.

The official ration was two gallons per person per day which seemed generous but then 1½ gallons went to the cookhouse and what was left was for shaving, washing our clothes and replenishing the radiator when needed. With the radiator filled we set off but didn't know which way to go as we'd gone south, then west or north. All we had were tracks in the desert. Remember, we had left in complete darkness. A discussion followed and at last right or wrong we decided to follow the freshest tracks. Jock was getting worried as he thought the radiator was boiling up, we stopped and found he was right, and waited till he thought it safe to move again. We kept on stopping and starting like this for three days without seeing another vehicle.

Almost at the end of the third day we spotted a lorry and waved it down. By now our water was finished. The lorry should have been our salvation as it belonged to our Brigade and it was a Light Aid Detachment (LAD.). These were RÉME who maintained all our Brigade Transport. Instead of being our salvation the CSM who was in charge of the lorry which was like a travelling workshop thought we were deserters. I asked him where he was making for, his answer was 154 Brigade. I said both you and I are following the tracks made by 154 Brigade and that being the case I am trying to catch up with the Brigade, if we were deserting we would be going [in] the opposite direction. If you can't help us please give us some water so we can travel a bit farther on.

His men could have easily seen to our radiator but no help was forthcoming. He gave us two gallons, took all our numbers, ranks and names and told us he would report and check on us when he got to Brigade. He knew our transport number told him we were 7th Battalion, Black Watch. Remember there were 3 battalions of the Black Watch in the Highland Division. He left us and as he went I felt he still didn't believe we were not deserters and that was why we got no radiator repairs.

Next day as we limped along we saw a staff car racing along at the rate of knots. We waved it down and found four newspaper correspondents in it. Now I have seen and read reports of our brave boys at the front where the brave reporters are sharing all the dangers the brave infantry faced and I had actually believed them. Here the truth faced me: these brave reporters were four days behind the chasing troops and goodness knows how far from the Germans, but they did give us two gallons which carried us through to the fifth day.

Once more our radiator was nearly empty. What could we do now? None of us could think of anything we could do. Then it dawned on me. I wouldn't recommend this remedy to the AA or RAC. I climbed on to the carrier and urinated into the radiator and told the others. We waited until each managed to do this two or three times and this special water took us on again.

It was a blessing in more ways than one. Allah was good to us. We came to a wog village with a camel wandering round and round a well bringing up water, can after can came up. Imagine our feelings. We filled all our spare water cans, filled our radiator and our water bottles [and] had a good drink ourselves. I don't remember what Jock bartered with but when we left it seemed all the villagers were waving goodbye.

Jock stopped every so often to look at the radiator but it was bearing up well so he speeded up, and after a few hours we came to a tarmac road which had a Y junction, two tracks met [and] the third went straight on. At one side of the Y there was a large caravan type of vehicle with lots of MPs standing by their jeeps. One MP jumped into our way with his hand up, an order to stop, but Jock went round him as we could see the other MPs weren't interested [as] they were standing to attention. One of my crew looking back exclaimed 'Cor!! See that black beret, no wonder there's so many bleeding MPs'!

Not long after we thankfully rejoined our Platoon, no one asked where we'd been or how we'd managed. Everyone was too busy with their own affairs. We'd arrived and that was all that mattered, but for my crew I'd kept them all together and together we'd stuck and found our way through the desert following tracks which we trusted were our own and Jock who was only 19 proved his worth. (He'd been just 17 in the Shetlands having been a Terrier in Fife pre war.)

It had been a strange five days, no hysterics, no arguing with each other – just a quiet acceptance of 'whatever will be will be' but as we were literally fighting for our lives alone in the desert, our Battalion had been fighting in the battle of Horns, so no wonder we were literally ignored [as] they were all recovering from their own experiences!

⟡

4

TUNISIA, 1943

Private D.G. Antonio
(2nd Lothian and Border Horse)

While Montgomery's 8th Army was busy pursuing the Afrika Korps back towards Tunisia, a second Allied army landed in North Africa, on the coast of Morocco and Algeria. This Anglo-American force overcame the Vichy French garrisons of these two countries, then began advancing westwards towards Tunisia, the last Axis bastion in North Africa. Rommel was cornered, but far from defeated, something the inexperienced troops of the British 1st Army learned to their cost. From January until April these troops pressed the Germans, who by now had been reinforced, and provided with fresh equipment. The 2nd Lothian and Border Horse was an armoured regiment, attached to 26th Armoured Brigade of the 6th Armoured Division. Private Antonio recalls the round of battles and skirmishes fought by his regiment's Sherman tanks in the vicinity of Goubellat and Bou Arada.

Two Messerschmitts, known as Mutt and Jeff (not to be confused with Gert and Daisy who roamed farther north), visited us daily and provided a welcome diversion. At nights, the echelon trucks would arrive in pitch blackness, and usually in pouring rain. Dim, unhappy figures would appear, grasp each a ration box and, stumbling and splashing in the ubiquitous mud, fade away into the gloom, in the general direction of the farmhouse. Mud was everywhere. Great, ponderous clods of it adhered to boots. It caked and dried on trouser-legs and gaiters. In tank turrets it gathered on the floors, smothered the rear ammunition racks and stuck to the seats. Not even our bedding could escape it. And this, we thought bitterly, was 'sunny North Africa'. Give us Glasgow any day!

During this time 'A' Squadron made one uneventful sortie to the south to encourage the French there, and at different times both 'A' and 'B' Squadrons ventured on to the open Goubellat Plain, where stiff opposition was encountered. 'B' Squadron's sortie was made with considerable support from the guns of the Ayrshire Yeomanry. From an artillery observation post on the hills bordering the western side of that notorious plain we could see the preliminary shelling of suspected farmhouses by our 25-pounders. Then, through a gap in the hills, the tanks filed out onto the plain, deployed and advanced. It soon became apparent that the defences were very much stronger than had been expected. Nearly every farmhouse had its garrison of German troops. Anti-tank guns of small calibre were plentiful and were supported by 88mm's farther behind. On the green plain, spread out below our observation post, the tanks seemed to crawl forward with maddening slowness. Now and again a Crusader from Squadron HQ would dart forward among them. Red tracer would float lazily from the tank guns. Everything seemed to be seen in slow motion. Even the smoke of shell-bursts rose unhurriedly.

Occasional sounds of battle drifted up to us. Shells from the 25-pounder batteries behind us continued to swish over the observation post. A haze of dust and smoke from the bursting shells began to obscure the battleground, and after pushing as far forward as possible, the tanks drew back into the shelter of the hills. Their casualties were light, in which respect they were more fortunate than were 'A' Squadron, who had several killed and wounded on their sortie. These apparently profitless expeditions were but a part of the probing and testing of the enemy defence which was taking place all along the line, and if it was not an auspicious beginning for us, we were no less fortunate than any others.

Either by accident or design, our march south to El Aroussa and our arrival there on 18th January coincided with a German armoured thrust from Pont du Fahs to Bou Arada. We arrived in El Aroussa area at 04:00 hours, establishing ourselves, as usual, in and around a farmhouse. At 07:30 hours our fires were lit and we were busily preparing breakfast. At 07:45 the alarm came through. Leaving fires, food, blankets and everything that had been unpacked, we piled aboard our tanks and in a few minutes' time were drumming along the main road to Bou Arada, ahead of which a grey cloud hung low over the battle area. 'That,' remarked our Crew Commander, 'is what is officially known as the smoke of battle.' It arose from a mixture of bursting shells, smoking haystacks, burning tanks and occasional smoke-bombs. 'B' Squadron were engaging the enemy, whose impetus had been checked by artillery fire.

From a hull-down position on a ridge we looked down on them. The German tanks had halted. Shell-bursts blossomed around them. Our Squadrons below, their Troops spread out, would edge forward, trying to close the range with the more heavily gunned Panzers. From their slender 2-pounder guns would come a yellow flash and a tiny red spark would wing its way towards the enemy. Crew Commander tapped Gunner on the shoulder: 'Watch this!' he said, and pointed upwards. Gunner thrust his head out of the hatch, and together they watched a squadron of Stukas circle over the unsuspecting village of Bou Arada, half a mile to the north. Then the leading Stuka peeled off from the 'merry-go-round' and gracefully began its earthward dive. As though playing some new form of 'follow-my-leader', the rest of the bombers dived singly after him. Smoke and dust blossomed up from the debris of shattered buildings as bomb after bomb screamed down on the village. The shattering detonations grew into a long rumble of several seconds' duration and seemed to shake the very air.

It was over quickly. The Stukas were soon winging their way homeward, pursued by desultory anti-aircraft fire and leaving behind them a pillar of smoke to mark the havoc they had wrought on the little township. Towards evening, licking their wounds, the vanquished Panzers, dodging from cover to cover and harried by shell fire, trickled back to Pont du Fahs. The threat had been averted, for the meantime.

There were several casualties in the Regiment, among them one tank of our own Troop. It had been badly hit while on a forward reconnaissance and both the Second-in-Command and the Signals Officer had lost their lives. The gunner and driver had somehow managed to make their escape, though dazed with concussion and subjected to machine-gunning. Of 'B' Squadron, who had borne the brunt of the enemy attack, all but two tanks were out of action. Eleven out of the enemy force of twenty-six had been knocked out, however, and casualties among the 'B' Squadron crews were slight.

With the coming of night the tanks drew back and we made rendezvous with the echelon. We all of us felt still the elation of successful battle. This was the first test of our echelon service in really advanced areas. The echelon men were enthusiastic as they helped carry fuel and water; fitters and electricians were eager to set about repairs. Even unbending quartermasters were in generous mood. By the side of our tank, with the aid of a 'Tommy Cooker' and a mess-tin, we made tea, the whole crew crowding round to conceal the light. At 02:30 hours the tanks moved to forward positions again. In the hurry of our departure the previous morning, we had brought with us neither blankets nor shovels. After scooping for ourselves a long shallow trench (using a steel helmet and bare hands), our crew, clad in greatcoats, huddled together for two hours of fitful and very chilly sleep, less time passed on sentry duty.

Parked on the reverse slope of a hill overlooking the plain, we passed two uneventful days and nights. Burial parties were sent out to the knocked-out tanks on the floor of the valley. The German gunners on the far side of this valley must have watched us closely, for they permitted the burials to take place without interruption, but at once started shelling on our attempting to prepare one of the tanks for recovery. They had evidently given up hope of an armoured break-through at Bou

Arada, and changing their tactics, started infantry operations on the north side of the valley. We then began to move our harbour areas every few days to keep the enemy reconnaissance guessing.

The Squadrons were generally less fortunate than RHQ, being kept on their toes by irregular and unpredictable shelling. The arrival of the unexpected shell, out of the blue, is always disconcerting. One hears the warning whistle that heralds its arrival, but the brain, caught unawares for a moment, refuses to act. Then, to make up for that precious second's delay, one hurls oneself flat, sprawling amongst frying-pan, empty tins and dirty utensils. After the crash and the 'whing!' of flying fragments, one raises his head to see 'who copped that one?' Some fifty yards away perhaps, black smoke, dispersing slowly in the still air, lingers above the shell-hole. If it has landed closer than fifty yards, one 'stays put'; if further, one rises to seek the nearest slit trench. It rapidly becomes a routine.

From this area 'A' Squadron carriers took part in an attack by the 1st Guards Brigade on Djebel Mansour on 4th February and earned high praise for their action. It was here that Virginia Cowles, the American correspondent and authoress, paid us a visit. We had taken a great deal of trouble to try to appear clean and tidy in front of the first 'White Lady' to be seen since leaving Britain. She, however, outdid us completely and arrived looking absolutely immaculate, even down to silk stockings and smart shoes. It was a great boost to our morale to see that someone like that did still exist in the flesh, and not merely as a photograph.

From a hill above our harbour one could look down on the Bou Arada-Pont du Fahs road. In the noonday heat the valley looked faded and grey. The Salt Lake shimmered at the south of Goubellat Plain, just visible. Far to the east, Djebel Zagouan rose, lofty and very blue and craggy. Sometimes it would be girdled with a belt of cloud, and above this the angry rocks would tower, picked out by the sunlight with light and shade in all their forbidding ruggedness. The sunsets, too, had a splendour all their own, the upper clouds in pale pinks and rosy hues, changing into a crescendo of colour to the fierce molten cloud-mass on the horizon, above the departed sun.

These lesser engagements, minor affairs in themselves, were important to us. They gave to the tank crews a final polish to the months and years of training at home. They brought to light defects to be remedied. Above all, they gave us confidence and fostered in each crew a living team-spirit. It was well for us all that it was so. There was in store for us at Kasserine and on the downs south of Thala an unforgettable trial of courage, endurance and skill.

—⊳•◦⊲—

5

GOTHIC LINE, ITALY, 1944

Lieutenant George Martin
(2nd Lothian and Border Horse)

After the Allied landings at Salerno in September 1943 the Allies secured a foothold in Italy, but their advance northwards up the Italian peninsula was halted at Cassino and the Gustav Line. (The latter ran across Italy from the Adriatic to the Tyrrhenian Sea; Cassino formed its central bastion.) For the best part of six months the Allies remained there, despite an ill-fated attempt to bypass the German defences by conducting an amphibious landing at Anzio. However, by June the Allies were on the move again. Rome was captured, and the troops pressed on to the north, towards the next German defensive position – the Gothic Line. By late June the 8th Army were fighting the Germans around Arezzo, where the Sherman tanks of the 2nd Lothian and Border Horse were sent into action against the German rearguard. Lieutenant George Martin recalled what happened as they advanced.

Over to our left we heard a loud bang as a tank on that flank was hit by an AP shot. The crew commander was leaning out talking to an Italian who was killed by the shot. We heard of the incident over the radio and could see some smoke rising from the 'brewed' tank in the vineyard. 'Damn this close country' said my gunner, 'we can't see more than 100 yards in any direction here.'

'Keep a sharp look-out' I said to my turret crew, 'I'm going forward to have a word with the troop sergeant.' Along with his gunner the troop sergeant were replacements [*sic*] in that crew for the day, he was last with me when he slipped a track at Cassino, the rest of the crew, two drivers and wireless operator were the usual crew.

Seconds later I was standing on the back of his tank discussing the danger points to watch out for, especially the house on the corner and our right flank. That done I said 'Cheerio' and jumped down by the side of his tank when I heard what sounded like a bang, a roar and a crack all rolled into one, followed by a hissing sound which blew me to the ground and flung me some yards to the rear of the tank. I came round a few seconds later, I heard voices and getting to my feet, rather drunkenly I suspect, found my right hand and arm quite useless, it hung limply by my side and I recall feeling my fingers with my left hand and thinking 'well they're still there'.

The situation now came sharply into focus, the tank had

been hit and the sergeant was being lifted down from the tank by the driver and co-driver, he had a smashed leg. Quickly he was carried to the corporal's tank while I signalled my tank to request the 'Honey' [MS Stuart Light Tank]. Fortunately the tank was not on fire and the two drivers now helped down the badly wounded wireless operator, he had been pushed out by the gunner. In fact, instead of jumping out himself he had got the wireless operator from his seat, under the gun and then lifted him out where willing hands hauled him out. One of the drivers jumped down and helped me get the wireless operator to a ditch behind the tank; quickly we laid him down while the driver set off to climb back on the tank for the gunner. Before he could rejoin the other driver a second shot crashed through the turret, the driver standing on the tank was blown to the ground, shaken but not bruised, but from the turret we heard a choking cry and a groan – then silence as the tank suddenly burst into flames. If any man died for his friend, that young man did – he knew, as we all did, that any delay in getting out could be fatal.

With the wireless operator some eight yards behind the tank I told the two drivers to make sure the sergeant was well back and to lend a hand when the Honey arrived, I wanted to see what could be done for the wireless operator. Poor lad, he had suffered serious wounds and was barely conscious. He had been sitting with his arm on his knee when the shell came through, severing his leg at the thigh and hand just above the wrist; not only that but he had been badly cut by splinters and shrapnel. By this time the tank was well alight and it was only a matter of time before the ammunition started to explode.

Propped against the side of the ditch the wireless operator was as comfortable as we could make him, with a grimy handkerchief I wiped away some of the blood from his face, but there was little I could do about his other wounds. Suddenly he opened his eyes and looking earnestly at me he said 'Oh hello sir, do me a favour will you.' 'Yes, of course I will – but don't talk, the Honey will be along soon and you'll be off to the Field Dressing Station.' He half smiled and in a weak voice continued 'Thanks, I want you to write to my mother, tell her I've done my best.' He closed his eyes and after a brief pause reopened them, his strength was failing and I very much doubted if he would see the FDS. I simply said 'Don't talk now,' but he continued, 'There's one more thing, I'm sorry I've been rather a trouble to you and the troop – even now . . .', his voice trailed away, mercifully he drifted into unconsciousness as the 'Honey' came to a halt by the rear tanks. Willing hands lifted him on to a stretcher and carried him to the waiting 'Honey'.

Although we were used to losses in battle I felt deeply the loss of these two young men, but there is little time for dreaming, a voice brought me back to reality, 'Sir, I'd get the hell out of here before the tank blows itself to bits.' From inside the burning tank I could hear the ammunition exploding so I got out – and fast!

By now the use was returning to my hand and arm so, climbing into my tank we watched for any further signs of the enemy, but nothing moved and I suspected they had withdrawn. We had been very lucky, and thankful, that we had not been raked with machine gun fire while bailing out, so often crews escaping from a knocked out tank were cut to pieces by machine gun fire. Why, I wondered, could it be that our adversary had a sense of chivalry lacking in many of his compatriots?

Later that night the infantry came up and took over our positions, we pulled back and harboured nearby. Our young wireless operator, who had worked so hard to fit in with the rest of the crew after our chat, died as he reached the FDS.

Next morning we kept in reserve, the other Squadrons taking a turn in front. The Medical Officer paid us a visit and had a look at my arm which was rather swollen and very painful. 'You'll have to go back for dressings, the arm is cut above the elbow, piece of tank or shell I suspect and the cut is septic.' I was inclined to argue that if he dressed it I could stay with the troop. 'No' he said, 'you'll go back, anyway, the Regiment's out of the line just at present so you've a few days to get that arm healed.'

With the Squadron out of action for a spell my objections were overruled. The metal had cut deeply and almost severed the nerve, so, after a dressing I was sent to the A2 echelon and then to a small hospital for an X-ray and treatment. Although I did not like being away from the troop it seemed likely that, because of the close and hilly nature of the country, most actions would be on a troop by troop basis and each regiment would have a spell in reserve; that put my mind at rest.

I was sent to a large house near Lake Trasimeno where I could rest and continue to have the arm dressed at the hospital in Perugia. I was not alone – a number of other officers, all wounded, were having a period of rest and treatment. It all seemed strangely quiet after the noise of the battle area, the noise of tank engines and the whistle of shells. Up the hill beyond the house stood the village of Monte Petriolo, a very old village and a pleasant walk from the house. The inhabitants were poor but friendly and hospitable, it also gave me the opportunity to practise my Italian, limited though it was.

The village carpenter, when he saw me approach would dust off a stool and invite me to sit and talk while he worked. We discussed tools and constructional details and although my knowledge of the language was none too good we managed to make ourselves understood. The workshop seemed to be a meeting place for the 'locals' to drop in for a chat, the pace of life seemed to be slow and easy!

≫•≪

6
TANK LIFE, NORMANDY, 1944

Second Lieutenant William Brownlie
(2nd Fife and Forfar Yeomanry)

Another Scottish armoured unit was the 2nd Fife and Forfar Yeomanry. Like their counterparts in the Lothian and Border Horse they were equipped with Sherman tanks, which were no match for the latest German tanks such as the Panther or Tiger. Worse, they formed part of the 11th Armoured Division, and were sent to Normandy, where the bocage – a latticework of small fields, sunken lanes and high-banked hedgerows – was no place for a tank. This account by a subaltern in the regiment illustrates what life was like for the men who operated these 'bluddy cauld, smelly contraptions' during the Battle of Normandy.

What was it actually like, to be in the Normandy bridgehead? Obviously, for a start, it was extremely dangerous. All sorts of stuff kept flying about, and careful precautions minimised the risks, but did not eliminate them. The country was mostly rolling farmland and, apart from the open plains east of Caen where 'Goodwood' took place, there were tiny fields walled in by high banks thick with trees and bushes. Sunken lanes, created by generations of farm carts and streams of water, wandered between such banks. The hindrance to movement was partly overcome by the 'forks' welded to the front of some Shermans, made from girders that had been part of the German beach defences, so that instead of rearing high over a bank and being shot through the thin belly armour, you forked through the bank and went on carrying a ton or two of earth and a couple of trees. Extra protection!

There was no answer to the problem of visibility. Any half-baked infantryman could lie in wait with a Panzerfaust. A lone PAK gun or tank could camouflage up, and hit any moving target. The only answer was for the leading troop to 'brass up' cover ahead, and hope for the best.

The farms were small and poor, usually ruined. The branches of their orchards were just the right height to prevent a tank commander from seeing anything, and branches with unripe apples cluttered the turret. A bonus was that, in the cellars, there was usually a wooden vat of cider and a few bottles of calvados. This was wicked stuff, not matured, and you either drank it in small quantities or filled your cigarette lighter with it. It gave a clear, blue flame.

Everywhere there were dead bodies – cows, horses or men. They swelled in the summer heat, and if pierced deflated with a hiss and a sweet, sickly smell. The Squadron bulldozer dug holes and buried the cattle. Humans were put in a shallow grave, or a disused slit-trench, with whatever identification was available. The staple diet was Compo ration, which came in 14-man packs. These did a 5-man tank crew for three days, so you felt that you were being diddled. The packs were flung from Echelon trucks in harbour or leaguer, and the trick was for one of the crew to race for a favourite pack (marked A, B, C, etc.), to get Pork & Veg, Meat & Veg, Bully Beef, or what have you. But all the packs had cigarettes, boiled sweets and bum-paper (at the scale of 2½ sheets per man per day), as well as soya sausages, fat bacon, marmalade pudding and the like. You stowed some tins in the hottest parts of the engine each morning, so that there was always something hot to eat that night, if there was no time to cook. There were also hard biscuits and processed cheese, which were kept by the wireless set at the back of the turret, to be munched on a long hard day. It was basic, but nobody went hungry.

Every chance was taken to supplement the rations. In Cully, a Trooper swapped his second pair of boots for a chicken. Eggs were in great demand. 'Oofs?' My tank's cook was the gunner, Buchanan, who could produce hot food very quickly. The hull-gunner, McKenzie, made tea on the move, with a petrol cooker and a canteen of water between his knees. Amazingly, health was never a problem. Could be it was because we were young, and had other things to worry about. 'Naebody but a man could live in a bluddy cauld, smelly contraption lik yin o' thae things,' said someone whose name I forget.

Sleeping arrangements varied. If there was time, a hole was dug big enough to take five men lying side by side, and the tank was parked over it, giving great protection. If things were quiet, the tarpaulin bivvy was used, stretched from the top of tank track to pegs in the ground, and the bed-rolls (army blankets in a waterproof cover) laid out underneath. You took off beret and shoes, and wriggled in. If there was no time, and shit was coming over, we slept in the tank, in various strange positions and with all the hatches shut.

At some ghastly hour, usually before dawn, you were roused by somebody banging on the tank with a hammer. They may have been 'bluddy cauld, smelly contraptions', but unlike the infantry we had at least a bit of space for personal possessions, and were not dependent on soft vehicles lurching up in the dark to provide bedding or hot meals.

The great snag was that the Sherman, mechanically reliable and available in great numbers, was inferior in many ways to the German tanks. The armour was thin, the ammunition was stowed in open bins so that it exploded if there was any penetration. A hit almost inevitably meant a brew-up. Some boffin hit on the idea of welding bits of extra armour to protect the bins, but their only effect, so far as we could see, was to provide an aiming mark. I certainly saw many brewed-up Shermans with a neat hole in the 'extra armour'. Optimistic efforts were made, like fixing spare track plates to the front of the Shermans, but the basic weakness remained. You were in a 'Ronson', and if you were hit it was best to bale out PDQ. The Comets that we had later were different. Their ammunition was in heavy metal bins – awkward to get at, but safer. Then, if hit, it was better to stay in. You just calculated your chances.

Out of all the mish-mash of memories, I have one that is vivid when I walk the dog of an evening. If the wind is blowing quietly through the trees, and everything else is still, I physically feel what it was like to be in a field in Normandy at the end of a day. Not mentally, just physically. It is a strange feeling.

<hr>

7
OPERATION GOODWOOD, NORMANDY, 1944

Trooper John Thorpe (2nd Fife and Forfar Yeomanry)

After six weeks in Normandy, the Allies had still not broken out from their bridgehead, despite several costly attempts, including Operation

Epsom, where the 15th (Scottish) Division suffered so heavily. Field Marshal Montgomery, commanding the British 21st Army Group planned a new offensive – Operation Goodwood – designed to clear the Germans from Caen and the high ground beyond. Three armoured divisions spearheaded the attack, and the Fife and Forfar Yeomanry led the advance of the 11th Armoured Division. Trooper Thorpe, a gunner in one of the regiment's Sherman tanks, recorded the events of 16 July in his diary (a punishable offence at the time), and his frank observations provide us with a stark but evocative account of what happened. The sections written in italics were added by John Thorpe in 1982, by way of explanation, and after the death of the characters involved.

To my Troop Leader, Captain G.G.O. Hutchison, who survived, and after 38 years, I've had the good fortune to meet again in October 1982. Also to my tank commander Sgt Cliff. W. Jones, and all those who fought alongside me in North West Europe.

This is a copy from my small pocket diary written at the time it happened, but now in 1982 when I read it through again, [it] was set out in a series of cryptic, laconic observations, the bare bones, so to speak, necessary to crush them into the small space, with no explanations of some of the happenings, which to anyone reading it who did not experience it, does not convey the feelings, loss, meaning of fear, grief, horror, pain, or pleasure at small things, and excitement experienced. This is not supposed to be an account of the campaign, we did not know how things were going, it is what happened to me. It is not supposed to be a complete story, it is a more detailed account than my poor diary.

These writings are set out in my own way, rough and ready. I say what I think, I'm entitled to my opinion even if it does not agree with other people. I maintain that I am a freeman and so I pull no punches. It was a Court Martial Offence for an enlisted man to keep a diary in case it fell into the hands of the Enemy. This is a factual tale, it is not a happy story and if you are squeamish, don't read it. It was no fault of mine that my Division became known as an Elite Fighting Force, I did not choose it, it happened.

A tank crew is a close knit unit where the men are enclosed in a cell, in close proximity, with no room to stretch out, or stand, with no privacy from one's neighbours. They live together for days and weeks on end perhaps only dismounting at night, and so they rely on each other, each one's life depending on the action of his comrade and so each looking to the other and working as a team. There can be no fighting machine more restricted in space than a tank, hot, or wet and bitterly cold, more uncomfortable, noise of engine or guns plus the constant gyrations of vehicle and turret in motion. Mundane things such as passing an empty shell case round was a necessity and to try to get some rest meant nowhere to stretch out. We lived or we died together!

16th July 1944 Goodwood
A thousand of our planes are bombing a large area in front of us (to soften [the] enemy we are told)! Two hours of bombing.

08:00 hours:
Moved up in line for the charge. We travelled through a minefield taped both sides of us with white tapes to mark the way. Out into country and spread out, being shelled we settle down (you can only be scared to a point, you have to win through, it's like a second wind when you're running). Objective Falaise, no stopping. A creeper barrage keeping pace with us – some Germans coming out with hands on their helmets – up and over a railway embankment, down hill to a second one, over and into a valley.

Tanks are now more or less in line, spread over about 100 yds wide – can almost see the front ones. Severe AP [Armour Piercing] Fire from a coppice on our left front – tanks in front begin to go on fire. My orders are to fire on this wood and keep firing and the Hun is now firing HE [High Explosive] and some AP. My Browning stops and I find the bag for the empty cases is full up, blocking the gun. I've never had to fire so many rounds. I throw the stupid bag away, feed in another belt – belt after belt. My barrel warps, and the tracer leaves the gun in a great circle, I try to change the barrel but it's too hot to handle. No matter – keep firing! My feet are covered with a thick carpet of empties.

Brew up after brew up going on in front – some tank crews are on fire, rolling on the ground but this is a ripe dry cornfield, and soon, what with smoke shells and burning corn, visibility is being shut out. ALL the tanks in front are burning, and immediately in front I see a tank boy climbing out of a turret which is spurting flames, but he does not make it. He falls backwards into the flame. Cliff orders Robby to reverse – right stick, left stick, right stick and we back up over the embankment. We take stock. We've lost contact with the rest of our unit – nobody left to contact! No wireless communication, so we move on again on a different approach and come upon some 23rd Hussar tanks, Cliff goes over and discusses the situation, and we join them and remain with them for the rest of the day. We seem to have lost our whole Regiment.

We are waiting for Cliff, our Tank Commander to return from briefing. Rolly and I were already closed down, with engines warming up. Pat our wireless operator keeps a sharp lookout. Suddenly he shouts into the intercom; 'Hull gunner – target in front – 40 yards – four oh yards – FIRE!' I snatch my periscope and cock my machine gun but I only see a solitary khaki-clad figure passing through my line of fire. It was Captain Leith. I pick up my microphone and yell at Pat; 'What the hell do you mean?' 'Fire' yelled Pat! 'get into the gunner's seat and fire yourself' I yelled back at Pat. 'You're on a charge!' snarls Pat. 'Balls' I replied – 'You couldn't make it stick'! Besides, we are losing too many of our own chaps already without helping the bloody Jerries. So, if you want to knock him off, do your own dirty work, and don't try to catch me out with it!

This illustrates how easy it was to 'accidentally on purpose' bump somebody off if you had a big enough grudge and wanted to seek revenge. I don't think Pat was kidding – it was soonest forgotten, and we remained good comrades. Later, after losing all of our Squadron Leaders, Captain Leith was promoted Major, and became 'C' Squadron Leader, and was awarded the MC. He died in February 1982.

Explosions of ammunition in burning tanks sent up huge smoke rings into the still air of this hot sunny day, rising into a windless sky. This place is Cagny. We move south along the bank and find a new way on a different approach, going for the objective 'Falaise' when we meet and join 23rd Hussars.

We now advance onto some high ground (Bourgebus Ridge). Panthers approach us and we have a shoot. We are hitting – one, two three direct hits but – Oh Christ! His turret is turning towards us – it's time to back off. Our tracer just ricochets up skywards off his armour. As evening comes and the sun goes down we find our Troop Officer – Lieutenant Hutchison – and 16 surviving tanks from the Regiment. From 'C' Squadron there is the whole of our 4th Troop, and the rest are from 'A' Squadron, with Major Powell in command. Some distance off we see some German SPs (Self Propelled Guns) pulling out, and we have a shoot and Bert Long brews one up.

Major Powell says he has an abandoned tank which he

wants to recover, way back in enemy country. He calls for a driver and being 'spare wank' I'm lumbered. I climb up on the engine cover of his tank and we eventually approach the tank. I am told to see if I can get it. He stays well away in case it is now occupied by Germans, to give me covering fire. I go up to it carefully on foot and examine it and find it empty. Alongside it, less than 15 feet away, is a burning Panther – red hot and glowing, with green and blue flames licking out of its turret. A very pretty fire!

I get into the driving seat, and it starts up. I run the engine. It's now completely dark, and I see the Major's tank has turned round so that I can see his exhaust flame. A figure appears in front of me. It is a Sergeant. He climbs up. Good, I think – I've got a tank commander to see me back in the dark! Major Powell moves off, and by this time I've put on a headset, but the funky Sergeant jumps into the turret, slams the lid shut and drops onto the floor of the turret curled up in a ball! I ask him for his assistance, but he pulls rank and bawls out to me to drive, so I'm on my own with my head out, seeking the direction of the Major's tank. The Sergeant was in a blue funk – how do they choose their NCOs?! There is no way of testing a man's metal [sic] except (by) fire. Poor bastard! This tank had seen it twice in a day – once when it was abandoned and once now. My opinion of him can not bear printing. I get back and hand over the 'Jonah' tank. I return to my crew and harbour for the rest of the dark night. Hutchison orders us to eat. We have lost a lot of men and tanks, [and] we don't feel like eating. We are a sorry sight. We've been going for about 30 hours.

We live to see another day, but I shall always see the pathetic, blackened and burnt tank crews who crawled back towards us through the burning corn. We could give them no succour. We were still engaged, and it was against Standing Orders to give assistance to any disabled tank crew during the course of a battle. The sickening thing is we gave them a burst of machine gun fire before we realised they were our own blokes creeping towards us in the corn! We live with that also.

━━━═◆═━━━

8
BURMA, 1944

Major Bernard Fergusson
(2nd Batallion, Black Watch)

In January 1942 the Japanese invaded Burma, and in a gruelling campaign fought in the inhospitable Burmese jungle, the British and their Allies were steadily driven back towards India. By early 1944, the conquest of Burma was virtually complete, and Japanese troops were gathering for a final thrust over the Indian border, towards Kohima and Imphal. In an attempt to disrupt the Japanese offensive, General Wingate proposed a series of raids deep into Japanese territory, aimed at disrupting communications and supply lines. The men of his Long-Range Penetration Force were called 'Chindits', and their ranks included the 'Jocks' of the 2nd Black Watch. Wingate divided his Chindits into several columns, one of which was commanded by Major Fergusson. In late February 1944 these columns crossed the Chindwin River, and entered Japanese-occupied territory.

After a week, two more of the Columns were peeled off from the main body. Mike Calvert's Gurkha Column, No. 3, was sent to attack the main railway line from Mandalay to Myitkyina at a place called Namkhan. Mike was a stocky, cheerful regular sapper, an Army champion at both boxing and swimming, brimming with ideas and brave beyond belief. I rate him as the best fighting man I ever saw. He spoke not a word of Gurkhali, except for a few conventional greetings which I am told he always got wrong; but his Gurkhas adored him, grinned whenever they saw him, and fighting like wildcats under his leadership.

The other Column to be detached was mine: No. 5, all British except for the Burma Riflemen and the muleteers, who were Gurkhas. My task also was to sabotage the railway line by blocking it where it ran through a gorge; but my sapper officer pointed out that this could be quickly cleared, and that it would be much more rewarding to blow the bridge at Bonchaung railway station three miles farther north. I decided to do both. By this time, from talking with the locals, we knew where the enemy posts were and the habits of their patrols. At dusk on the evening of the 5th March, after two very long marches, we settled for the night into a cosy little bivouac 300 yards off a motorable road not shown on the map and with all the appearance of being newly made – three miles short of Bonchaung.

After our evening meal of rice we tuned in to the BBC and heard to our horror our exploit of the morrow being reported as a fait accompli; it even said 'near Indaw,' which was a junction ten miles north of us. I was badly shaken, but Duncan said sleepily; 'Oh, never mind. It'll be all right. And gentlemen in England now abed shall think themselves accursed they were not here.' We rolled up in our blankets and went to sleep, our cooking-fires all out, and no sound except for the familiar bivouac noises: somebody clearing his throat, the calling of a night-bird, the shuffling of the hooves of the mules among the leaves.

At first light I split the Column into four prearranged detachments. I despatched John Fraser and his Burma Riflemen towards the Irrawaddy, thirty miles east of us, to spy out the land. Tommy Roberts, with two other officers and forty men, I sent down the road to the southward, to create a diversion, if they could find a suitable target, while the demolition parties were doing their stuff. The third lot, with a platoon to protect it, was the party to blow up the Gorge, under Jim Harman. The main body, under myself, would go to Bonchaung with David Whitehead and the other demolition party. John Fraser and Tommy Roberts had been gone about ten minutes and the rest of us were just moving off, when the sound of shooting broke out from the south, quite close at hand, light automatics as well as rifles.

I told Jim Harman to get to the Gorge as quick as he could, and Duncan Menzies to take command of the main body and move at once to Bonchaung, where I would join them later. Both were to get on with the demolitions. Then Peter Dorans and I ran out onto the main road as fast as we could with our heavy packs, and down it towards the shooting. In a few hundred yards we came to cultivation on our left, which indicated that we were nearing a village; then to a solitary private soldier, who said: 'Captain Roberts and Mr Kerr are just ahead, but be careful!' and then to a point where a track took off from the road and ran fifty yards down a little slope into a village. At the fork, lying in the road, were two apparently dead Japs, John Ken and three of his NCOs, John with one of his legs in a bloody mess, one of the NCOs dead and the other two wounded. I tried to give John a shot of morphia, but he said: 'Let me tell you what happened first in case it muddles me.'

Apparently they had bumped into a lorry-load of Japanese who were just jumping down over its tailboard, presumably with a view to searching the village; both parties were equally surprised, though Tommy's was naturally the more on the alert. The driver had reversed the lorry quickly, and driven off southwards down the road. Meanwhile a firefight had developed on the ground, and Tommy and John had reckoned that all the Japs who had managed to dismount had been accounted for. To give the Gurkhas a bit of a break from leading mules, which they hated, I had replaced a few of them that morning with temporary British reliefs, and attached them to Tommy's party.

One of them had gone in with the kukri, and killed five Japs with it: John told me of this, indicated where I would find them, and I saw the gruesome evidence. Thinking that all the enemy had been disposed of he had counted sixteen dead – but [since] the lorry driver would soon come back with reinforcements, Tommy had decided to push on and lay an ambush with a roadblock on the road, telling John to collect his men and follow. John had summoned his platoon sergeant and his three section commanders for some rapid orders; and while he was giving them out, a light machine gun which they had not spotted opened up and made casualties of four of them.

While he was speaking, I nearly jumped out of my skin. Peter Dorans, standing beside me, had suddenly fired his rifle twice. I spun round, to see one of the 'dead' Japanese writhing in the road. He had flung himself up on his elbows and pointed his rifle at me. Peter had not been hanging on John's words, as I was, but keeping alert: a lucky break for me.

The enemy machine gun now opened up again from a new position. We stalked and killed the two men manning it. We were now facing in reality the problem that we had decided long before hypothetically: the abandonment of our wounded. In a speech to every column before we ever left base, Wingate had made it clear that there was no question of evacuation. If a wounded man would walk, he could take his chance, but the pace of the march would not be slowed down for him. If he could not walk, he must be left. Anybody who could not face this problem might withdraw now, and no obloquy would attach to him. Not one man chose this option.

Altogether there were two dead men, two dying and six wounded, of whom only one, a subaltern with a hole in his shoulder, could walk. The other five we carried down into the village, from which the inhabitants had run away, and laid them in the shade under one of the houses: houses in Burma are built on stilts. We put earthenware jugs of water beside them, and some bunches of bananas off the trees. John Kerr said: 'Don't you worry about us, Sir, we'll be all right.' Corporal Dale said: 'See and make a good job of that bridge!' Not one of them made it harder to leave them than it already was. Before we left, I had a look at the dying; but they were already dead.

I hoped the villagers would succour my wounded when they came back, but the hope was vain. After the war, John Kerr, the only survivor of the five, told me that one of the men, a stout-hearted chap I well remember, said he reckoned he had a chance of being able to walk if he could lie up in hiding for a few days, and then perhaps make his way back to the Chindwin. John gave him permission to try, and wished him luck. He punted his way painfully with a stick out of the village and into the trees, but he was hardly out of sight when there were sounds of a scuffle, and the man's voice cried out: 'Mr Kerr, Mr Kerr, they're murdering me!' When the Japs arrived in force later on, John told them what had happened; they went to look, and found the man with his head battered in by the villagers. They then turned on John and treated him to a brutal interrogation, running a stick of bamboo to and fro through the hole in his leg to make him answer, but he managed to hold his tongue until it mattered no longer.

We blew the Bonchaung Bridge without interruption at nine o'clock that night, a most stimulating performance. David Whitehead warned us when it was about to happen, and I passed the word to get a good grip of their Beasts. There was a glorious bang which echoed round the hills, a tremendous flash which showed the jungle a dazzling green, and the plunging mules chocolate smudges against it. David Whitehead inspected the damage and pronounced himself satisfied. A little later we heard the explosions from the Gorge, as we marched on towards where we had planned to bivouac. We had done what we had come so far to do, but John Kerr and his men hung heavily on my mind.

9

THE ATTACK ON HUBERMONT, ARDENNES, 1945

Private Tom Renouf (5th Black Watch)

Tom Renouf was born in Musselburgh in 1925, and joined the 5th Black Watch when he was 17. As a member of the battalion's 7th Platoon (A Company) he participated in the Normandy campaign, and the subsequent breakout through France and into Belgium. In December 1944 the Germans launched an offensive in the Ardennes

region of Belgium – a campaign which was subsequently named
the Battle of the Bulge. In early January the British launched a series
of attacks designed to 'collapse' the northern flank of the bulge,
and to drive the Germans back into Germany. The 51st Highland
Division were at the forefront of this counter-offensive. One of its
attacks involved a battalion assault on the hamlet of Hubermont, a
few miles south-east of La Roche-en-Ardennes. The 5th Black Watch
were given the job of clearing the Germans from the village.

We were transported by troop carriers along the main approach
road to La Roche. I remember disembarking from the carriers
and setting off on a march of a few miles. It was mid-morning,
there was snow on the ground but the skies were clear-blue
and the sun was shining at this time. As we were approaching
La Roche there was the sound of distant gunfire but we did
not suffer any shelling. Our platoon sergeant was Sgt Bob
Fowler, DCM, an outstanding soldier and a great leader. There
was no platoon officer, because our officers were ambushed
when out on recce in Opheusden (Holland) on 28th November
1944. Bob ordered us to march in staggered sections – he
always did things the correct way.

As we approached La Roche the skies began to fill with
clouds and soon it began to snow. The snowflakes were very
very large. One of my section, Milligan, carrying the PIAT
bombs, kept falling behind and I had to tell him to keep up.
We entered La Roche from the high ground, the road bounded
on our right by cliffs. I will never forget the sight of the town.
It was completely demolished. All the buildings it seemed were
razed to the ground, with a few chimneystacks sticking out of
the rubble. It was worse than most of the towns in Normandy
– rather of the devastation like Caen. The Royal Engineers
were working in the town centre, trying to clear the rubble

and open the road. As we moved through the centre of town it was snowing quite hard (with big flakes) and the snow on the ground was getting visibly thicker.

Another sight I will never forget was three Derbyshire Yeoman walking towards us, the one in the centre with his head covered by blood-stained bandages and being led by the others. This might have been the crew of the reconnaissance car, which was blown up by a mine, but there were more Derbyshire Yeomanry casualties to be seen. Our march towards the Start Line was punctuated with stops and starts. We moved out of La Roche uphill into the forests. It was about 1400 hours, the sky was heavy with clouds, it was now a dark day, with snow still falling. We travelled up this road for about one and a half miles, 'A' Company now in the lead, but not our platoon. There were many stops and starts and there were a few shells coming into our direction. By this time we were beginning to feel the cold.

The leading section reached the open ground and was making to the Farme du Vivier when they were fired upon by an enemy tank. One man, Alexander Close, was killed, others were wounded but the section was able to withdraw. The Company was deployed in defensive positions and told to 'dig in'. The ground, however, was too hard to dig slit trenches. So we had to lay [*sic*] down in the snow among the trees, seeking what cover we could find. By now it was beginning to darken. Our platoon was deployed on the left-hand side of the road, where we were mortar-bombed. Since we had no adequate protection from slit trenches, several of the platoon were hit (Stan Suskins for the third time). The farm building was shelled by our artillery. An attack was mounted, but the odds were uneven – it was 'A' Company against enemy armour – and the attack was unsuccessful. Later that night a further attack on the farm was made, but it was found abandoned by the enemy. We heard the enemy tanks pulling out.

The temperature had dropped well below zero, in fact it was one of the coldest nights during the coldest winter for 40 years. We did not wear our great coats in the attack, but had only our oil-skin gas capes, which kept us dry but not warm. Additionally we had had no rest for over 20 hours, and our exhaustion made us feel colder. Our bodies were chilled right through and our limbs were beginning to lose all feeling. Only by moving and stamping our feet could we fight the cold. Our hands were completely numb and our rifles were like solid ice, and beginning to be seized up with frozen bolts. When the cold seemed to be at its worst and we seemed to have reached a limit of endurance, we were rescued once again by our wonderful Platoon sergeant, Bob Fowler, who – like a big St Bernard – appeared with a large mug of rum, and dished out two large spoonfuls to everyone in the section. After this I began to feel my body again, although I still did not feel my limbs.

The forward platoons had reached the crossroads, where there was a row of cottages, one of them a café/bar. There had been a skirmish and an exchange of fire. The Germans had been driven out but none of them had been injured or taken prisoner. By this time it was nearly dawn, we were still crouched in the ditch and I remember being so tired that as I lay back against the wall I fell asleep. I slept for 20 minutes until we moved on. When I awoke I was numb with the cold, but much revived. 'A' Company occupied the crossroads and Major Mathew, MC, the Company commander, deployed the three platoons in defensive positions. My platoon fortunately occupied the cottages, but the other platoons were out in the open. Day came with clear skies and the sun shining brightly. It had been one of the worst nights during the campaign, mainly because of the extreme cold and the utter exhaustion. Inside the cottages we relaxed our vigilance and lay down to rest.

Suddenly we heard the sound of what seemed to be tanks heading from the village toward us. When we checked our rifles we found that the bolts still were frozen solid, the Bren gun also would not cock. We were at a low morale and not knowing what was heading toward us, our section panicked. Fortunately Major Mathew rushed us into the cottage and ordered us in harsh terms to get into our defensive positions. We recovered our arms and manned our positions by the windows. The German vehicle was not a tank but a large half-track loaded with troops. They approached the crossroads with all guns firing. They had to pass a platoon which was able to get some cover from their positions. Private Reeves lay at the side of the road with the platoon PIAT ready for action.

As they got near he fired at the half-track and although he hit the vehicle, it did not damage the traction and the vehicle continued at speed, heading south. It passed No. 8 Platoon, which was out in open ground, devoid of any cover. The machine guns on the half-track raked the platoon, which returned fire as best it could. Several of our comrades were hit, one of them died on the way back to the Aid Post. Although one of the Germans fell off the half-track and was killed, the vehicle sped off into the distance and back to the German lines. Next day 'A' Company moved into the village of Hubermont, where we finally were able to thaw out.

CHAPTER 7

THE WORLD'S POLICEMAN

When the Second World War ended, Britain still had almost three million people under arms. Most were demobilised within a year, but while this was unavoidable, it left the army with a serious problem. Britain still had an empire, albeit one in the process of being dismantled. The army still had extensive overseas commitments, and still needed to maintain a force larger than the size of the prewar army. This manpower shortage was solved in 1947 by the introduction of National Service. For the next thirteen years, all able-bodied British males with no previous military experience were conscripted into the forces. Initially this compulsory service lasted a year, but in 1950 the term was doubled. At a stroke the army had the manpower it needed to supervise the dismemberment of an empire, and Britain could still maintain the illusion of being a world power.

Of course, national conscription was widely unpopular. The conscripts resented having to give up two years of their lives, while the army itself felt shortchanged. After all, recruits represented a cross-section of British youth – from the brightest young things to the dregs of humanity. The army had two years to turn these youths into soldiers – a process that could often take as long as eighteen months. Another restriction was that no conscript under 19 could serve in a war zone. While this was a necessary expedient for politicians, anxious to avoid unsavoury headlines being read over the breakfast table, it also tied the hands of the army, forcing them to concentrate the raw recruits into only some regiments, while filling the ranks of others with professional soldiers. The effect was to create two tiers of units – those capable of active service, and those merely fit for garrison duties. However, National Service put thousands of men into uniform when the army needed them. For instance, during the Suez Crisis in 1956, over 370,000 British troops were under arms, of which more than half were National Servicemen.

The last National Servicemen were demobilised in 1963, by which time the role of the army had changed. During the period spanned by National Service, Britain had lost much of her empire. While this transition to independence was achieved peacefully in many countries, in others – most notably in India and Palestine – the process was marred by violence. Increasingly, British troops found themselves having to maintain law and order in places where the local population was bitterly divided. This thankless task meant that these same soldiers often found themselves caught up in these conflicts. A generation of commanders who learned their business fighting the Germans or Japanese now had to learn a whole new set of skills. In effect, those who were once seen as liberators were now viewed as oppressors – the lackeys and running dogs of capitalism, imperialism or simply Western arrogance. Half a century later these accusations are still made, but in the process the commanders and their men learned the skills they needed to become the world's policemen. Meanwhile these young men from Dunfermline, Forfar or Maryhill still had to face the mob, armed with obsolete equipment and their bare wits.

In the midst of colonial dismemberment came the Cold War. By 1949, not only had an 'Iron Curtain' descended across Europe, but this ideological division was exported around the world. First, Britain became involved in the war in Korea

(1950–53), and four Scottish regiments played their part alongside other UN forces. In the process they fought in some of the bloodiest battles of a generation. Next came a series of policing actions, where Scottish soldiers found themselves fighting politically inspired insurgents in Malaya, Indonesia, Kenya, the Arabian Peninsula, Cyprus and the Middle East. Then came the débâcle of Suez, where Britain and France attempted to intimidate the Egyptians into relinquishing state control of the Suez Canal by using military force. Britain and France acted in opposition to the wishes of the UN, and – more importantly – to those of the USA. They were forced to back down, and in the process they were found to lack the military power and political will needed to maintain their position in the world. In effect, Suez revealed that for the best part of a decade, the British army had been punching above its weight.

After Suez it became clear that Britain was no longer a global power. With fewer overseas commitments, the army was scaled down. Many regiments had been reduced to single battalions after the war. Now they were amalgamated or disbanded. Given that the army revolves around the integrity of the regiment, this was an unpopular move, but a necessary one. In Scotland the Seaforths and Camerons merged into the Queen's Own Highlanders, the Royal Scots Fusiliers and the Highland Light Infantry became the Royal Highland Fusiliers, and in 1968 the Cameronians were disbanded. Other regiments such as the Argyll and Sutherland Highlanders and even the Scots Guards were reduced to the size of companies, before being expanded again when circumstances changed.

Another feature of postwar life was service in Germany. From 1949 onwards, the British army of the Rhine (BAOR) existed to thwart any Soviet-inspired attack on NATO, and during the decades of the Cold War some 55,000 British servicemen were stationed across North Germany. Germany was never a popular posting, mainly because language problems meant that most soldiers spent their time in their barracks.

Then came Northern Ireland. In 1969 sectarian divisions in the province flared into violence, and the army was sent in to keep the peace. Skills learned in the jungles of Malaya or the alleys of Aden were now applied to the streets of Belfast. The only difference was that the soldiers were now policing British streets. It took time for the army to settle into this new role, but for two decades Scottish troops patrolled the region, and tried to keep the two factions from killing each other. In the process many of these soldiers lost their lives, particularly after the conflict developed into a battle for control of Ulster, fought against the Irish Republican Army (IRA).

While Prime Minister Tony Blair may have supervised the Good Friday Agreement, which brought peace to Northern Ireland, he also committed the army to a series of fresh overseas conflicts. Of course, he was able to use the army more freely after 1991, when the Cold War came to an end. That year British troops fought alongside an American-led coalition in the Middle East, an operation designed to drive the Iraqi army out of Kuwait. Political necessities forced President Bush Sr from following this up with an invasion of Iraq. Just over a decade later, his son would be less reticent. Meanwhile Scottish troops found themselves performing their old world-policeman role in the Balkans, and once again had to keep two warring factions apart. At least by now they had plenty of training.

The next challenge was the 'War on Terror', launched after '9/11' (the attack on the twin towers of the World Trade Center in New York on 11 September 2001). Britain became a willing supporter of American foreign policy, and in 2001 British troops participated in an invasion of Afghanistan. While this move probably did make a significant contribution to the global war against Al Qaeda, a few recalled that previous British incursions into the region had been as spectacularly unsuccessful as had the more recent Russian involvement in Afghanistan. Scottish troops are still fighting and dying there, in a conflict that lacks clear political and military goals. A far more controversial operation was the invasion of Iraq in 2003. Egged on by spurious claims that Iraq harboured dangerous 'weapons of mass destruction', Prime Minister Blair agreed to support President Bush Jr's ill-planned invasion, and consequently the British army found itself fighting a new and particularly vicious kind of war – one that was wholly unnecessary. While some benefits might come from the conflict, the cost in Scottish lives has been high.

One consequence of these recent conflicts is that a career in the army has lost much of its former lustre. As recruiting numbers declined, so too did the ability of the army to resist another round of amalgamations. The Royal Regiment of Scotland is the most recent manifestation of this, creating a hybrid formation which – according to the Ministry of Defence – draws on Scotland's fine military heritage, and the traditions of its regiments to forge a stronger, more efficient, fighting force. Unfortunately, over the years Scots have developed a strong affinity for 'their' regiments. People remember that their fathers or grandfathers served in the Black Watch or the Royal Scots, or know that their local war memorial honours the dead of their local regiment. This popular association with Scottish regiments effectively dates back to the mass conscription of the First and Second World Wars. In all likelihood this affinity will also outlast this latest byproduct of amalgamation. However, regardless of regiment, uniform, or 'manufactured' traditions, the men of the Royal Regiment are Scottish soldiers, and that, after all, is the strongest bond of them all.

━━━➤◆☚━━━

1

THE HOOK, KOREA, 1953

Corporal Derek Halley (1st Battalion, Black Watch)

The Korean War is a largely forgotten conflict, despite being the first major clash of the new postwar age – a struggle between East and West. In June 1950, when South Korea was invaded by the Communist North, United Nations contingents from over twenty countries were sent to support the South Koreans. These UN troops included a sizeable British contingent, which formed the bulk of the Commonwealth Division.

Four Scottish regiments saw action in Korea, the first being the Argyll and Sutherland Highlanders who served there as part of the 1st Commonwealth Division. They saw some heavy action, including a particularly brutal fight where Major Muir of the battalion won a posthumous VC. In April 1951 they were replaced by the King's Own Scottish Borderers, and this battalion had their own VC winner, when Private Speakman drove off waves of Chinese attackers by using hand grenades. When the Black Watch replaced them in August 1951 it was felt that the worst of the fighting was over. However, as peace negotiations were underway, the Chinese launched one last offensive. The men of the Black Watch, holding a hilltop position called 'The Hook', found themselves in harm's way. This account of the action which followed comes from a young and inexperienced conscript, barely out of his teens. For a few terrifying moments, he fought for his life in one of the most brutal struggles of the war.

May took up where April left off, and by the 18th the Chinks were massing as never before. From deep dugouts in a semi-circle of hills around us like 'Betty Grable', 'Rome', 'Goose' and 'Pheasant', 122mm guns launched a barrage on us. The patrol on 'Warsaw', next to us, was drawn in after reconnaissance planes noted movement in caves below. Then the standing patrol reported the places were filling up with Chinese infantry. The US Corps '8-inch Persuaders' were put on overtime, their shells designed to penetrate the ground before exploding, but even with the earth erupting all around them the ants just kept coming, oblivious to the shrapnel and splinters of rock.

They advanced along 'Ronson Ridge', where the standing patrol were waiting, and with 60mm mortar flares and searchlights on them, they were soon caught in the crossfire from 'A' Company on 'The Hook' and 'B Company' on '121' – but they swarmed on. The artillery sent fused high explosives over the ridge, and the Black Watch lobbed their mortars, but still the ants kept coming.

Having just survived one disaster with the Americans, the Turks were desperate to avoid another one with us, and in the command post Lieutenant-Colonel David Rose received a telephone call. In his best English the Turkish commander inquired if we had sustained many casualties. 'A few.' And we would be withdrawing . . . ? 'The Black Watch don't withdraw.' Phone down.

By then the ants were within 20 yards of our own trenches and grappling with the Dannert [wire entanglements]. Private Cash fired 6,000 rounds into 50 of them through his Browning, only to earn himself a verrah stern reproof later from Regimental Sergeant Major Scott; 'Wi' that many roonds ye should've taken oot the whole bloody Chinese Brigade!' Private Cash he may have been, but these were public resources he had spent.

On they came, cutting their way into our ground, all ghoulish screams and empty eyes, each little ant doped up on the worthlessness of its own life and dazzled by the price put on mine. I watched a young private tackle the first arrival by scrambling onto its back and smashing its face with a rifle butt. It died instantly. The second one got the same, but as three more broke through he pulled back. Another private had his Bren snatched, so tore off his helmet and crashed the rim into the ant's head, splitting it open and leaving it to die under his boot.

It was a blur. Panoramic panic. Bugles blaring, rifles and brens and stens and burp-guns blasting, shells screaming, mortars thundering, ants screeching. The trip-flares soared over it all to display the awesome density of the ant hordes, which multiplied as they died – each ant that fell seemed to give spontaneous birth to twins, which emerged through the showers of bone and blood to take up the remorseless advance. Our own umbilical cord of communication had been cut, and the ammunition was running perilously low. The Browning was so hot it was reddening, and the trenches were collapsing under the weight of numberless shells as more and more of us resorted to bayonets, knives, shovels, fists, fingernails . . .

Desperate for back-up, I made it to the command post. Dick had had the same idea, but it was just as pointless – the carnage had beaten us to it. The wireless operator sat behind his crocked equipment, tending his own wounds with the others unable to assist. Lieutenant Haugh and Sergeant Wilson were already dead.

The cruellest irony. Sergeant 'Tug' Wilson had once tugged me back to earth for posing as an old soldier, when I was nothing more than a nyaff in a dirty nappy. He had me marched up and down the platform at Inverness station, and hauled me off to Fort George to give me the benefit of his boot, and there he lay, lifeless at mine, his unseeing eyes staring at a real old soldier at last.

We were on our own. 1 Platoon, 'A' Company had lost their officer and sergeant. It was think-on-your-feet time, every-man-for-himself − old soldier time. We left the command post and headed for the Browning pit in the hope of finding more firepower. Our light automatic Patchets were something to hold onto in the night, but even full their magazines held just 32 rounds − not too handy when red ants were swarming into the house.

The evil bastards were even upstairs, within ten feet of me . . . I heard them clicking as I passed a darkened hootchie, little hidden Red ants, mumbling and clicking in the blackness. Red pinpricks pierced it as I stood transfixed. When they flared at me I clenched my fingers and the Patchet flared back, and spat its last rounds at them. Sparks of metal cascaded into them, put them out, extinguished them. With my trigger finger still locked I stood there, on my black watch . . .

Dick urged me away, yelling about pits. We found ours soon enough, despairing at the sight of nothing but grenades, everything else long gone. After stuffing them anywhere they would go, loading pockets and arms and fists with them, we clambered to what was left of the trenches and started lobbing the things into the horde. The Black Watch did not withdraw. That was for the ants . . .

And suddenly the buglers were playing a sweeter tune through their mouthpieces, and the shells were melting into smoke bombs.

The spray of shrapnel became just a misty shroud, a soft fog enveloping us so densely it muzzled the screaming mouths and muffled the madness. After half an hour we were finally swathed in silence. It came as suddenly as the ants had, out of the red, and when the fog finally cleared the ants had gone. All of them. We were left with dead and dying communists, scattered around our tattered trenches and into the distance.

2
BRUNEI, 1962

Lieutenant-Colonel McHardy MBE MC
(Queen's Own Highlanders)

During the decades following the end of the Second World War, the British army found itself faced with a new role – policing countries within Britain's shrinking but still extensive sphere of influence, and helping to protect friendly states when faced with insurrection. By 1961 a long-running conflict in Malaya was drawing to a close, and a political solution was proposed – a new Federation of Malaya. The new state would include British Borneo, which divided into the three smaller states of Brunei, Sarawak and Sahab. This frustrated the territorial ambitions of President Sukarno of Indonesia, who trained armed supporters of the Brunei People's Party and encouraged them to rebel. In December 1962 these armed insurgents seized the important oil-producing town of Seria.

The 1st Battalion of the Queen's Own Highlanders were on garrison duty in Hong Kong at the time, and they were ordered to deal with the insurgents, to protect British oil interests in the area, and to rescue any European hostages. On 10 December, the first wave of Highlanders disembarked from Beverley transport planes at a nearby airfield. A second, smaller, group landed on the western outskirts of Seria, where they captured the police headquarters, freeing the policemen inside. Blocking positions (codenamed 'Aberdeen', 'Angus', 'Inverness' and 'Perth') were established around the town, and the following morning the battalion began the task of clearing it of insurgents. Although the following account is written in military style, and uses the third person, it remains a remarkable account, a rare chance to follow one of these counter-insurgency operations as it unfolded.

At 09:30 hours the CO ordered Major Cameron of 'A' Company to establish a firm roadblock in the area of the Brunei Police Mobile Reserve Unit Barracks, at the extreme west end of Seria. As the Police were reluctant to operate alone, Major Cameron decided to move 2 Platoon from their roadblock about ½ mile east of Panaga Police Station, and to command the mixed force personally until it was established.

At 11:00 hours 2 Platoon and two sections of the Brunei Police, under the command of Major Cameron left Panaga Police Station in transport. Shortly after moving off, a jeep or Land Rover appeared in the far distance, turned round and disappeared. Taking no chances, Major Cameron gave the order to debus. 2 Platoon took up the lead with Corporal McGovern's section in front, moving in broken arrowhead formation on either side of road. There was a halt after the first ½ mile as the Company Commander realised that the Police had not followed. They were quickly brought to heel, and followed on. Moving quickly, 2 Platoon reached the roundabout without incident. The leading section doubled across the roundabout and started off down the Kuala Belait road, but when they were 100 yards short of the Istana Kota Menggalela (the Sultan's Palace) a car suddenly appeared from the Palace grounds.

The Company Commander ordered Corporal McGovern's section to open fire. The car was hit several times and rolled into the ditch. The driver, obviously seriously wounded, fell out of the door but got away during the ensuing battle. As the leading section fired at the car, heavy fire came from the Palace – there was obviously an LMG there, and a number of rifles. Fortunately no one was hit, and Corporal McGovern quickly got his section lying down and returned the fire. The Company Commander ordered the two rear sections of 2 Platoon to fan out on the right flank with Corporal Hoddinott's section on the left and L/Corporal Turner's section on the right. The Police were given the task of watching the beach.

Corporal Hoddinott and L/Corporal Turner got their sections leapfrogging towards the Palace until they were in a position at the forward edge of the jungle strip, in fire positions. This movement was made under fire of the rebels' LMG, which was then covering that approach along a track which divided L/Corporal Turner's section, and it was very lucky that no one was hit. The order was given to watch and shoot, and Corporal McGovern's section was ordered to leapfrog into a better position, which they did quickly. Fire control was bad to start with, but after a short time it became very good and the shooting in many cases was excellent. Under covering fire from L/Corporal Turner's section, Major Cameron, Lieutenant McCall, and Privates Cowie and Firmstone, all armed with teargas grenades, doubled forward to the edge of the building. Major Cameron and Lieutenant McCall threw their grenades through ground-floor windows. Lieutenant McCall, moving round the corner, saw a rebel who was holding a No. 4 rifle and shot him in the centre of his body.

After this brief action, the party returned to the jungle strip as it was hoped that the teargas would persuade the rebels to surrender. After about five minutes, it was obvious that they were determined to stay, and they increased their fire. Corporal Hoddinott's section, under covering fire from L/Corporal Turner's section, then moved out parallel to the sea along a line of trees. From there they doubled forward to the bay windows and threw in one teargas grenade and one irritant grenade, and then returned to their original position.

Still the rebels continued firing. Major Cameron, Lieutenant McCall and L/Corporal Turner's section approached the house from the jungle strip and took up firing positions along the balcony outside the bay windows, covering all the windows on their side. Lieutenant McCall and Major Cameron entered the large room, which was empty. They then cleared the other two rooms on the ground floor, finding one wounded rebel (the one Lieutenant McCall shot), who surrendered. Major Cameron followed by L/Corporal Turner and his section moved upstairs. Suddenly a rebel appeared with his hands up. Major Cameron doubled up the stairs and handed him over to L/Corporal Turner. He then entered the first room on the first floor to be confronted by five armed rebels. He fired a shot over their heads and they dropped their weapons and put their hands up. The rest of the house was then cleared room by room. A dead rebel sniper was found on the roof. Corporal Hoddinott was ordered to search the rear building and one more rebel surrendered. A total of nine rebels were taken, one of whom was killed and one wounded. During the attack, five had escaped – two of whom were fired at and hit by Sergeant McLeman, and three of whom were seen, but not fired at, by the Police. Eight No. 4 rifles, one LMG, one Sten gun, teargas, a lot of ammunition and police uniforms were taken.

2 Platoon, having reorganised, then advanced to clear the Brunei Police Mobile Reserve Unit (MRU) Barracks approximately ½ mile due west of Istana. Lieutenant McCall and a small group moved through the scrub and jungle while Sergeant McLeman commanded the rest of the platoon as it moved astride the road. Two rebels got up in the jungle and ran towards the road, and although both were fired at and hit, both escaped. Two LMGs had failed to work during the attack on the Istana. On reaching the MRU, Sergeant McLeman began repairing them, and had finished the second one when a car approached. He tested the LMG, and stopped the car with one shot through the windscreen grazing the side of the passenger's head. The driver leaped out of the car carrying a shotgun and ammunition, and ran towards the platoon. He had taken only a few steps when he was shot dead. 2 Platoon then cleared the MRU Barracks, which had been ransacked, as had the surrounding houses. Having completed their task and pulled down the rebel flag, the platoon moved back down the road to the roundabout, and took up defensive positions covering all three roads leading to it.

The battalion went on to clear the insurgents from the town, and the neighbouring settlement of Kuala Belait. In the process they rounded up substantial quantities of weapons and ammunition, and captured numerous prisoners. They also managed to free all the hostages (mainly oil workers), who were shaken by their ordeal but unharmed. All this was achieved without any serious casualties – a testimony to the professionalism of the Highlanders and Gurkhas who took part in the three-day operation.

3
THE CRATER, ADEN, 1967

Lieutenant-Colonel Colin Mitchell
(Argyll and Sutherland Highlanders)

In 1962 Yemen was plunged into civil war as forces loyal to the deposed Imam (backed by Saudi Arabia) fought those of a new regime (backed by Egypt). In 1964 a self-governing federation was proposed by Britain, who also sent troops to police the southern Yemeni port of Aden during the transition to full independence. At the time Aden was seen as an important strategic base, and Britain wanted to ensure its safe transfer to federal control. In 1967 the Argyll and Sutherland Highlanders were sent to police the city, where federal authority was challenged by three rebel groups, most notable of which was the National Liberation Front (NLF).

The Crater district of Aden was regarded as a hotbed of NLF activity, and as British casualties mounted, troops were withdrawn from Crater. However, after further attacks, Lieutenant-Colonel Mitchell ('Mad Mitch') decided to reoccupy the district, and so deny the rebels their secure base. This was a bold decision, as excessive casualties would be politically and militarily disastrous. In the end it proved a complete success. This account of the action is supplied by 'Mad Mitch' himself.

The Argylls were ready at the start-line, awaiting my order to advance. As we waited on the start-line nobody on the British side knew how much opposition we would have to face. Remembering the killing of our friends on 20th June [when 12 British soldiers died], many were perhaps hoping for strong opposition so that they could avenge their murders and defeat the enemy once and for all. But I was determined to avoid any recriminations of that nature. None of us needed reminding about these lost friends; but Ian Mackay carried into action the cromach – shepherd's crook – that had belonged to Bryan Malcolm, and every armoured car of the Queen's Dragoon Guards had, tied to the top of its wireless aerial, the red and white feather hackle of the Royal Northumberland Fusiliers.

It used to be traditional in Highland regiments to be piped into battle, and the custom survives if and when the tactical situation allows. The younger generation of officers and soldiers had never seen it happen, so, when training at Stanford the previous February, I had purposely staged a dawn attack with the Pipe playing along the axis of advance beside me. It is the most thrilling sound in the world to go into action with the pipes playing, it stirs the blood, reminds one of the great heritage of Scotland and the Regiment. Best of all, it frightens the enemy to death! In an Internal Security operation against a lot of third-rate, flyblown terrorists and mutineers in Crater on 3rd July 1967, it seemed utterly appropriate. I ordered Pipe Major Kenneth Robson to sound the Regimental Charge – 'Monymusk'. As he began the Jocks started to move down the road leading from the start-line into Crater.

In addition to my own Battalion I had under command 'A' Squadron of the Queen's Dragoon Guards in their armoured cars; a troop of 60th Squadron Royal Engineers; a helicopter from 47th Light Regiment Royal Artillery; a rear link wireless set from 15th Signal Regiment Royal Corps of Signals and additional transport from 60th Squadron Royal Corps of Transport. All of these soldiers did magnificent work; it is this co-operation of various types of unit which brings success.

Hardly had we started than we were machine-gunned from the edge of the town. Everyone bit the dust – with a few notable exceptions! The Pipe Major, oblivious to the noise of shooting, played and marched on. Our forward section in the

Supreme Court began to return the fire. I climbed up on the side of the forward armoured car and spoke to the commander to see if he could identify where the fire was coming from. Paddy Palmer, a few yards ahead, came up on the wireless saying, 'They're firing from either side of the Sultan of Lahej's Palace.'

I told the armoured car commander to brass them up and ordered the advance to continue. Despite the weight of fire we put back at them, and although the terrorist machine gunners eventually stopped, a single sniper on the roof of the Sultan's Palace continued to fire. His bullets pinged above our heads, well above I thought, so I ordered no retaliation as it was too dark to return accurate fire at that range. I walked back to my Land Rover a few yards away, took up the radio microphone and said to all stations, 'Play it cool.' I was quite determined that our fire control should be absolute until we met the main enemy positions which I believed to be in the centre of Crater.

Captain Robin Buchanan and the rest of 'B' Company, advancing to join up with us from Ras Marshag, had had to kill the only man to die that night. Near a cinema on the outskirts of Crater, they called on a group of Arab men to halt. They did so, but one armed man made a dash to escape. He was shot dead. That, indeed, was the extent of the 'bloodbath' so gloomily forecast.

'B' Company carried on and I walked along beside my Land Rover. The newspaper correspondents and Terry Fincher came too. They were utterly co-operative and friendly and shared the experience – in every sense. This is why the Press were more reliable guides to the activities of the Argylls in Crater than many people in authority.

Within an hour we had established an observation post on the Chartered Bank and in the shell of the burnt-out Legislative

Council Building. I sent Ian Robertson across our rear with a mixed force of armoured cars and infantry to take Sira Island. He dashed off like an express train. The Jocks climbed its steep sides in the dark and clambered up over the walls of the old Turkish forts. The terrorists had flown, leaving their banners and flags limply hanging in the hot darkness of a South Arabian night. These were hauled down from the topmost flagpole and an Argyll flag put up.

My next problem was to take over the Treasury Building. This contained the whole of the treasury reserve currency for South Arabia and was occupied by the Armed Police. There was no way of knowing how they would react to our appearance so I decided to send Nigel Crowe with the assault platoon to see if he could charm them into submission. It was a dramatic performance. In the circumstances we would have been justified in shooting it out had the Armed Police sentries offered any resistance. But I continually stressed the need to avoid unnecessary bloodshed and, rather whimsically at that moment of danger and tension, my mind went back to my schooldays and to Plutarch's account of the life of Marcus Cato:

Accustomed as he was to hard exercise, temperate living and frequent campaigning so that his body was healthy and strong, he also practised the power of speech, thinking it a necessary instrument for a man who does not intend to live an obscure and inactive life. In battle he was prompt, steadfast and undismayed and was wont to address the enemy with threats and rough language, rightly pointing out that this often cows their spirit as effectively as blows.

Nigel, with his usual courage, stood out in the open street and negotiated in Arabic, pointing out that we were not going to kill them but intended to occupy the building. It was a tense moment but he gradually won their confidence, they opened the steel doors of the Treasury and, although showing signs of extreme nervousness, accepted our occupation of the building. It was a brilliant bit of work by Nigel and the NCOs and Jocks who were with him. While it was going on Ian Mackay was exploiting quickly and with a feeling of exhilaration I realized that we were well into the second phase of my original plan and it was not yet 11 o'clock – four hours from the start of the operation.

It was now obvious that we were over-reaching the limits of exploitation agreed by Charles Dunbar, so I spoke to the acting Brigade Commander on the wireless and said that the initiative was so completely ours that to pause might lose it, and he should ask permission to let us go on and exploit up to the civil Police Station, where I planned to repeat Nigel Crowe's successful tactics at the Treasury. The one thing I was determined to do was retain the initiative and not stop.

This was the rewarding moment for any commander, when you know that your own chaps have got their tails up and will cut through opposition like a knife through butter. You can feel it in the air, and breathe in the aggressive confidence. It is the battle-winning factor that only experience can gauge. To me, that single moment in Crater was worth all my quarter of a century of soldiering. I felt, as we all did, thrilled to be an Argyll and to be writing another chapter of regimental history in the tradition of our forebears.

We were in luck. Charles Dunbar gave us the 'green light' to go ahead as far as the Civil Police Station. I ordered Ian Robertson to take another mixed infantry and armoured car group to escort Nigel's Arabic-speaking party, and off they set. It went without a hitch, except that during the complicated regrouping of his company and the armoured cars Ian Robertson and his Company Headquarters were fired on from an armoured car which mistook them for a group of terrorists. It was typical of the tremendous spirit of co-operation which existed between ourselves and HA Squadron of the Queen's Dragoon Guards that the situation was very quickly restored and the regrouping of the Jocks and the cars completed, without imposing any delay or halting operations because of the risk of further mistakes of identity, which in the circumstances were almost inevitable. This incident confirmed my earlier contention that the re-occupation was best carried out by a single battalion because of the difficulties of controlling fire in the dark.

By the early hours of 4th July I was fully confident that our aggressive and spirited behaviour had frightened the life out of any potential enemy. What was more important, the feel of the Battalion was good and I knew we were capable of exploiting our initiative to the full. Opposition had been slight, but we had to remember that the most dangerous areas – those surrounding the Armed Police Barracks and the Aidrus mosque, which was a terrorist stronghold – were still an unknown quantity. But we were well satisfied with the night's work. Our 'little probe' had given us half of the enemy's territory and he now knew that he was up against British soldiers who had come to stay.

Some of them must have recognized that we wore on our heads the same red and white glengarries as had three of the British soldiers they had seen so treacherously killed on 20th June. I expected that they were frightened. I hoped that they were. The snap and whine of bullets and the armoured cars prowling through the narrow streets had kept the citizens of Crater behind locked doors. When dawn broke on 4th

July they heard a new sound, one that was to remind them that, until the British finally left South Arabia, here in Crater the rule of law would be enforced. They heard the Pipes and Drums. On the roof of the Educational Institution, overlooking the flat roofs and minarets towards the horseshoe of mountains and the Arabian Sea, our pipers played. We had riflemen guarding them but they played as well and with as much composure as if they had been back at Stirling Castle.

⟫⟪

4

WARRENPOINT, CO. DOWN, NORTHERN IRELAND, 1979

Major Nicholas Ridley (Queen's Own Highlanders)

The 'Troubles' is a convenient historical shorthand for more than three decades of violence which plagued Northern Ireland from 1966 until the Good Friday Agreement of 1998. The British army were sent to the province to maintain order, and to keep the rival republican and loyalist paramilitary groups from plunging the province into chaos. In the process they found themselves the target of extremist groups, the most notable of which was the Provisional wing of the Irish Republican Army. The Troubles in Northern Ireland presented the British army with a new problem – the fighting of a policing action on home soil, and maintaining order in a bitterly divided province. Every Scottish battalion saw service in Northern Ireland, and a new generation of Scottish soldiers learned their trade in the mean streets of Belfast, or while patrolling the country lanes of Ulster. For almost two decades, the troubles facing Northern

Ireland remained a running sore in British politics, but they also provided a challenging training ground for the soldiers who served there. During this time, one of the worst 'incidents' took place on 27 August 1979 – a Bank Holiday Monday. First, the IRA killed Lord Mountbatten, a war hero and member of the royal family. Then came Warrenpoint, a brutal display of the effectiveness of this new type of warfare. When his Commanding Officer was killed in the explosion, Major Ridley of the Queen's Own Highlanders was given command of the battalion. This is his account of what happened that day.

Bank Holiday Monday the 27th August 1979 will be recorded as a particularly black day in the history of the Northern Ireland troubles, and in the annals of the IRA it will be remembered as the day of their greatest triumph. The month was hot and sunny and the day began peacefully as people set off to enjoy a day's holiday in the sun. Just before lunch, at 11.55 a.m., an air-rending explosion, which could be heard for miles around, shook the sleepy little fishing village of Mullaghmore in County Sligo. Within minutes the world news was broadcasting that Lord Mountbatten and other members of his family had been blown to pieces when his boat was destroyed by a 50lb IRA bomb. Those killed with him were his grandson, Nicholas Knatchbull, the boy's paternal grandmother, the Dowager Lady Brabourne, and a local boy, Paul Maxwell, who was acting as boatman. Another atrocity was about to follow at Warrenpoint.

Whilst studying the British army's procedures, the IRA had noticed that their reaction to bombing incidents was invariably to establish an incident control point near the scene of an explosion from which they would mount their follow-up, collect forensic evidence and evacuate casualties. They also observed that the army tended to place a cordon around the incident area sufficiently far back to prevent the engagement of soldiers following up after the incident. The IRA, therefore, with imagination and great precision planned to exploit these procedures. They found an ideal piece of ground at Narrow Water Castle near Warrenpoint. Here the border between Northern and Southern Ireland ran along a stretch of water only 200 metres wide. A dual-carriageway ran along the northern shore, a mile stretch of which was clearly visible from the Republic. Consequently, from a vantage point in the South, a bomb could be detonated remotely. The British army would not only be unable to follow up the attack but could be overlooked whilst it evacuated its wounded and carried out its follow-up action.

On the southern side of the dual-carriageway there was a lay-by, an ideal place to put a bomb. This lay-by was just south of the old Narrow Water Castle which, by jutting into the lough, was only some 50 metres from the border. The castle was one of a series of stone tower houses, built in Elizabethan times, to defend the east coast of Ulster. Situated opposite the castle, on the northern side of the road, was an imposing gateway set back from the road with a gate-lodge built into the eastern side of the entrance. Both the castle and the gate-lodge would make convenient incident control points for the army, but which one would they use? The IRA must have thought long and hard before correctly assessing the gate-lodge, although the castle, being on the same side of the road as the lay-by, was probably the more obvious site.

There were only two drawbacks. Firstly, the ambush would only be effective against traffic travelling north-west up the road to Newry. Secondly, they could not predict when an army patrol might use the road. The army, having realised the vulnerability of this stretch of road, frequently put it out of bounds. However, as it was one of very few routes into Newry from County Down and into Warrenpoint docks, where the Royal Marines regularly checked the container port, they had to relax this rule from time to time if they were to carry out their tasks and not become predictable targets on other routes. It was, therefore, only a matter of time before the army used the road, and time was something the IRA had in abundance.

The trap was laid, the first bomb, hidden in a trailer camouflaged with bales of barley straw, was parked the previous night in the lay-by, and the second and larger bomb was hidden in the gate-lodge. Two members of the IRA settled into their vantage point amongst the ferns next to a disused railway on the other side of the water, about 400 yards from the ambush and were ready, relaxed in the knowledge that they were safe from capture. It is thought that their aim was to ambush the Royal Marine detachment that patrolled the lough as they frequently used this road. In the event the plan exceeded all their expectations as, instead of a small detachment of marines, a convoy of Paratroopers drove into the killing area.

At 4:40 p.m., when most of the members of the security forces were already in a sombre mood as a result of the Mountbatten murder, a Landrover and two 4-ton lorries, carrying about 26 members of 2 Para on a routine changeover, drove into the ambush. They were driving north on a circuitous route from Ballykinler to Newry, where 2 Para, the resident battalion at Ballykinler, provided a company which was under the command of the South Armagh battalion, then the 1st Battalion Queen's Own Highlanders. The IRA must have been delighted as they could not have expected these vehicles for this convoy route, being one of three, had only been chosen minutes before departure. It was, in fact, the longest and most unlikely of the possible routes that the Paras could have chosen.

As the rear 4-tonner passed the trailer, the bomb was detonated by remote control. 700lb of explosives, packed into milk churns and surrounded by petrol cans concealed in the straw, exploded and a ball of fire enveloped the trailer. This truck, which contained 9 soldiers, took the full force of the explosion and of these only 2 survived. The Landrover driver immediately drove across the central reservation about 100 metres ahead, turned round and faced the direction from which it had come and it was here that the platoon commander set up an initial Incident Control Point. The front 4-ton vehicle also crossed the reservation but did not turn round and parked under some trees. The occupants of the Landrover then left their vehicle to render what assistance they could to the dead and 2 injured soldiers from the now destroyed truck. The explosion was so great that it had been heard over two miles away by the Royal Marines who immediately radioed a contact report to the Para's Company base in Newry and initiated a reaction force. The marines' initial report said that there had been an explosion on the Warrenpoint–Newry road in the area of the golf course some 500 metres further south than the actual site of the ambush.

Meanwhile, the troops on the ground were also sending a contact report and the Royal Marines sent a further report to the Queen's Own Highlanders' headquarters in Bessbrook. The crew of a Wessex helicopter on a routine trip to Crossmaglen heard one of these radio reports. The helicopter was flown by Flight-Lieutenant Nick Grose with Flight-Lieutenant Dick Holmes as co-pilot and Sergeant Muir as crewman. The call was repeated several times before the crew of the helicopter realised that no one at Bessbrook could hear. Dick Holmes tried to reply but came to the conclusion that his calls were not getting through. It was obvious to all the crew that there was distress and desperation in his voice. The crewman Sergeant Muir posed the question: 'Maybe the unit could not receive our call as they were deafened by something.' The helicopter contacted Bessbrook and told them they thought there might have been an incident somewhere and they were returning ASAP.

For some reason, radio communications between the battalion headquarters at Bessbrook and the company at Newry had broken down and they had to rely on the telephone. This and the inability to talk to the troops on the ground greatly complicated Bessbrook's ability to control this incident and provide support. Lieutenant-Colonel David Blair, commanding officer of the Queen's Own Highlanders, quickly realised that his presence was needed on the ground and set off in a small Gazelle helicopter.

After receiving the contact report from the marines, 2 Para's Newry Company Commander, Major Barry Rogan, commanding Support Company, immediately despatched his machine gun platoon to the scene in two Landrovers. A few minutes later he and his relief, Major Peter Fursman, commanding A Company, set off in two further Landrovers and drove to the incident. Upon arrival the machine gun platoon Landrovers were positioned both north and south of the incident in order to prevent civilian vehicles entering the area. Meanwhile at Bessbrook, the Queen's Own Highlanders' Operations room had tasked their airborne quick reaction force, commanded by Lieutenant Archie Gibson, to the scene, and they circled the area as a deterrent to further terrorist activity but they were not asked to land as there were by now sufficient troops on the ground.

For some time this airborne reaction force was Bessbrook and Newry's only reliable communications link with those on the ground. Almost simultaneously Colonel Blair landed with his signaller Lance-Corporal Victor MacLeod in a field on the eastern side of the nearby lodge. They alighted from the helicopter and ran down the road to the front of the lodge where a new Incident Control Point had been set up and where they could see Major Peter Fursman's group of Landrovers.

Meanwhile, the Wessex helicopter, having returned to Bessbrook, collected the medical team and the Quick Reaction Force and was despatched to Warrenpoint. Flying at its normal operating height, about 50ft above ground level, the helicopter flew in the direction of the incident. As they did not know the exact location of the incident, they flew down the eastern shore line, which gave them a good view of the main road and allowed them to stay low level. Nick Grose soon saw the area of carnage and, having made a quick recce, decided to land 30–40 metres away from the nearest debris on the northbound carriageway near the lay-by. He remembers thinking that he must land as close as possible but not so close that the downwash might affect the casualties and it needed to be somewhere that would allow good access.

The doctor, Captain Barry Barber, and his medic, were immediately despatched, closely followed by the Quick Reaction Force. As the Wessex had no direct communications with any of the ground troops, the pilot decided the best course of action was to remain on the ground. Shortly afterwards a soldier came and spoke to the crewman telling him that they should expect only 2 casualties as all the others were dead. About 5 minutes later the first stretcher arrived and was loaded into the cabin. A couple of minutes later the second casualty was brought to the starboard side to be loaded.

It was now nearly 5 o'clock. At this point the vehicles were in the following positions: two Landrovers parked outside the lodge, a four-tonner (the first one) parked further down the road to the north, the two machine gun Landrovers acting as road-blocks at either end of the first incident site, and the convoy Landrover parked ahead of the explosion area. The Wessex helicopter was still on the northern carriageway 30 metres north of the first bomb and the Gazelle helicopter that had brought Colonel Blair and his signaller Lance-Corporal Macleod had just departed. Further away was the Royal Marine detachment.

At 16:59 the second casualty was being loaded into the helicopter and Lt-Col. David Blair was approaching Major Peter Fursman's group. At that moment the second explosion occurred. This was a 1,000lb bomb also initiated by radio control, but this time the initiation signal had been sent 20 minutes earlier and had been used to start a clockwork timing device. It was this delayed timing device which actually detonated the bomb. The bomb was concealed inside the gate-lodge and on exploding, completely demolished the building and killed a further 12 men, seriously wounded two more and damaged the helicopter. In Nick Grose's words:

As the second casualty was part way through the door, we experienced a huge explosion of air. There was no sound at that moment. I remember saying 'What the f— . . . ?' I did not finish the statement, as I looked and saw the helicopter enveloped in debris and smoke and only then heard the sounds of the bomb. The aircraft shifted slightly across the ground, throwing the second stretcher into the rear cabin. I sat mesmerised for what appeared to be several seconds, hearing debris hitting the aircraft. I looked up at the rotor and saw what looked like pebbles coming towards me. It turned out to be a boulder about

18 inches cubed and it came down through the rotor blades, making an awful clatter and bounced off the nose of the aircraft, some 2 feet in front of me. Many large pieces of stone followed making an enormous din, even over the sound of the engine and rotor. I shouted to the crewman asking 'Are we all clear in the rear'? I was told the stretcher was on board, so I called 'Lifting'.

I could not see very much, so remembering that there were trees ahead of me I brought the tail around so I would depart to the South. All the instruments appeared to be reading as I expected, so I pulled in power and set off southwards very low towards Bessbrook. The FM radio received a call from the remaining ground troops, wanting us to return as they had many casualties. Dick Holmes replied that we were going, with casualties, to Bessbrook and would return ASAP but that we had sustained damage.

As Newry hospital was at this stage not secure and Musgrave Park too far, the helicopter returned to Bessbrook and landed 10 minutes after leaving the scene. The helicopter had suffered serious damage to all four rotor blades and the nose and port side had sustained further damage. The port windows had disappeared and there was a bullet hole in the rear pylon – the bullet having miraculously gone between the rotating tail rotor blades without touching them. The helicopter was not able to fly again until new rotor blades had been fitted.

Amongst those killed in this second explosion were Lt-Col. David Blair and Major Peter Fursman. The loss of Colonel Blair was a particularly serious blow to the army as he was destined for high command. He was an exceptionally talented officer and inspirational leader who in a very short space of time had trained his battalion to the very highest standard of professionalism and it says much for his leadership that these standards never wavered despite his death.

There was one other casualty at Warrenpoint. After the second explosion the surviving soldiers were convinced that they were under attack from automatic fire. They consequently returned fire, killing Michael Hudson, a young English tourist on the Eire side of the lough. It later transpired that he was killed close to where the bombs had been remotely detonated. It is possible, as no expended ammunition cases were found on the far side of the lough, that the ammunition exploding in the blazing vehicles had created the impression that the troops were under fire. The soldiers involved, however, maintained that the firing came from across the border and asserted that the IRA must have collected up their empty cases to ensure that no evidence was left behind. The bullet hole in the helicopter and the traces of firearms residue subsequently found on the clothing of suspects support the soldiers' assertions, as do the views of Peter Molloy, a freelance photographer, and Billy McKinley, a fireman, who were both on the scene before the second bomb exploded. On the other hand, the IRA say that there was no shooting and the RUC are also of this view and it does seem strange, in an incident so carefully planned and in which the second bomb was initiated by a 20-minute-delay timing device, presumably to give the bombers plenty of time to make good their escape, that the bombers should have remained at the scene in order to fire at the British army thereby increasing their chance of being caught. In any event no soldier was hit.

The devastation was terrible and the carnage horrendous. There were two large scorch marks, one on the road and the other a few hundred yards away in the driveway to a castle. The castle's gate-lodge had been completely destroyed and granite blocks were strewn over an area of a hundred yards or more and bodies blown twice that distance. Worse was the horrifying human debris – mostly unidentifiable lumps of raw red flesh interspersed with legs, arms, ears, hands or heads. The area was red with blood and flesh. There was no clothing, just human flesh. That the death toll was not greater is surprising particularly when it transpired that one soldier was blown 30 feet through the air and escaped with only shock and another remained unscathed although he was sheltering behind a bush right by the lodge gates when the second bomb exploded.

At the time of the first explosion, Johnny Hudson, a 19-year-old Castle estate worker, was working only 200 yards away when it went off. He described the explosion 'as being like a large mushroom cloud about a hundred metres high'. He was blown to the ground and remembers 'debris floating down and the soldiers acting in a panicky way'. When he got up he ran towards the explosion. The next thing he remembered was a soldier pointing a rifle at him. He thought the soldier suspected him of being the bomber. He eventually stood behind the gate lodge with one of the soldiers, but was told to make his way back to the castle. He had gone only about 40 yards when the second bomb went off killing the soldier he had been talking to. He remembered huge boulders from the lodge going over his head, trucks on fire and ammunition going off very loudly. He also saw lumps of bodies in trees on his way to the castle, where all the windows had been blown in. Three weeks later while working in a field he felt his tractor hit something. It was a soldier's leg.

The police and ambulance services were on the scene very quickly before the second bomb detonated and before the shooting had started, and were there for several days carrying out the gruesome task of picking up the human remains and collecting forensic evidence. Shortly afterwards, about 30 minutes after the second blast, B Company of 2 Para who were providing short-term support for the Bessbrook battalion and were commanded by Major Mike Jackson – later to become a full General and Chief of the General Staff – arrived from Bessbrook to relieve the troops on the ground, and they established a cordon around the area and set up a new incident control point.

Brigadier David Thorne, the 39 Brigade Commander, was also quickly on the scene. On discovering that Colonel Blair had been killed and that two different units were involved, he realised that a new overall commander was required. As the second-in-command of the Queen's Own Highlanders was in Hong Kong, he immediately flew to Crossmaglen, where Major Nick Ridley, now their senior officer was commanding D Company. He told him:

There has been a terrible explosion at Warrenpoint and a large number of soldiers have been killed, mostly Paras but the dead include David Blair, your commanding officer. I am promoting you Lieutenant-Colonel with immediate effect and you are now in command of your battalion. You are to go with the RSM to Warrenpoint, take charge of the situation and, if you feel it necessary, relieve the Paras who are still there and a little bit shaken. You must also go round your companies and tell them what has happened. Go now, take my helicopter and you may use the brigade reserve if you need them.

He then produced a pair of lieutenant-colonel's shoulder badges and slipped them on Nick Ridley's shoulders.

At about 6 p.m. Nick Ridley, accompanied by RSM Duffus,

arrived at the scene and met up with Major Mike Jackson. As those soldiers who were originally on the ground were in the process of being relieved by Mike Jackson's men there was no need to use the brigade reserve. Consequently, within an hour of the second explosion there were fresh troops on the ground cordoning off and protecting the area, the Garda were alerted and securing the far side on the lough, and a new line of command had been established which allowed the follow-up to take place in as secure and calm a way as was possible.

The devastation was such that B Company of 2 Para had to man the cordon for 5 days while the police, ambulance services and other agencies carried out their painstaking work clearing up the debris and gathering forensic evidence. This task was particularly distasteful. Major Fursman had been almost entirely vaporised and was initially declared missing believed killed, Colonel Blair was only identified through an epaulette. Two paratroopers were decapitated with one of the heads being recovered from the lough by a police diver, three others could only be identified by their shoe sizes and blood groups because the top half of their bodies had disintegrated. One of the Constables who was detailed to clear the area said:

> You're talking about three to four hundred yards . . . bits of leg, bits of arm. It got to the stage that the fourth day, you had to have a handkerchief on your mouth. We were picking up bits with sticks. People wonder why people always blow up that way. It's because when a bomb goes off, the air inside the body has to get out somewhere and the easiest way out is the joints. We found a hand embedded in a tree about 50 yards away.

In the immediate follow-up to the incident [two suspects

were detained, but despite being linked to the incident they were released due to lack of evidence] it was concluded in a report, 'The Garda can connect the motorcycle and the two suspects to what is thought to be the alleged detonation point on the Southern side.' But proving it is another matter.

No arrests were ever made regarding this incident.

⟫⟪

5
TUMBLEDOWN HILL, FALKLANDS, 1982

Lieutenant Robert Lawrence (Scots Guards)

The Falklands War came as a surprise to most British servicemen, who never imagined they could be pitched into a fight to win back control of British territory from an invader, especially on such a far-flung corner of the globe. The Scots Guards formed part of the British force which sailed to the Falklands, and which landed on a beachhead at San Carlos, despite the sickening loss of several Royal Naval warships. After 2 Para secured Goose Green, the British began their advance on the island's capital, Port Stanley. By the evening of 11 June, they were less than ten miles west of the town, facing the Argentinians' main defensive line. It ran along a series of craggy ridges. One of these was Tumbledown Hill, a position which the 2nd Battalion Scots Guards was ordered to capture in a night assault. The position was divided into three sections, and one each was allocated as the objective for G Company, Left Flank and Right Flank detachments. Lieutenant Lawrence and his platoon were ordered to follow up the first wave, in support of G Company.

I was extremely excited. And I made up my mind then that I would never, later, be saying to myself, 'If only I'd done this or that at the time.' I was really going to go for it. Yes, I told myself, what the fuck? I am really going to go for it now.

Myself, my company commander Simon Price, plus the two other platoon commanders, Mark Matthewson and James Dalrymple, were all briefed by Major Kiszely on the Argentinian machine-gun post which lay ahead. And we decided on a right-flanking attack.

I led off to a gully on the right with my platoon in front, and Mark's followed behind. One of the big problems, of course, in doing a right-hand attack was that, not knowing where the enemy were, we could end up, when we finally turned in left, either too far in front of them or too far behind. It was essential to turn precisely where they were, and hit them from the side.

Not far down the gully, I collected a rifle with an IWS [Individual Weapon Scope] on it, saw some Argentinians moving position across the back of Tumbledown, and picked off about four of them. I then radioed to James Dalrymple's platoon, who were joining Left Flank to add fire protection, and asked them to put some fire down on the Argentinian machine gun post, so that we could see where it was. I also hoped their fire would keep the Argentinians' heads down while we came in on the attack.

The minute we started leading our assault in, however, the machine gun post saw us coming, and switched its fire on to us. We hit the ground at about the time Mark's platoon were coming up level with us, and then tried to return fire. I began crawling forward on my own for about forty or fifty feet, and remember feeling desperately scared. There were bullets flying everywhere – from James's platoon on my left, from the

Argentinians ahead, from my own guys behind – and they were all ricocheting off the rocks. This is it, I thought. This is the end. And, as I continued to crawl along, I tried to make myself disappear into the ground, face right down in the dirt.

Eventually I got behind a rock and attempted to pull the pin out of a white phosphorus grenade. I had never used such a grenade before, and discovered that they have very heavy-duty pins. I should have ensured that they had been pre-prepared with a pair of pliers so I could get the bloody things out. Instead I had to crawl back again, under all this fire, to Corporal Simpson. He held the pin, I held the grenade, and together we got the thing out. Holding the safety lever of the grenade down, I then had to crawl all the way back to my original position and screamed at my men to reduce their fire. Then I hurled the thing into the air, and the grenade went straight into the machine gun post and blew up.

I took off, and screamed at my men to follow me. In that instant, my one sudden thought was, are they going to follow me, or will I be left to run off on my own? But when I glanced round, there was this unbelievably fantastic sight of every man getting up and running in. I remember thinking at that moment that this was life on a knife edge. Amazing. Fantastic. Nothing would ever bother me again from then on. If I got back to London and found that my flat had burned down, it would be a totally insignificant event in comparison to this experience.

The other thing that occurred to me was that people just don't die in real life the way they do on television. If a man is shot, a bit of him might come off, but he doesn't drop imme-diately. He just carries on coming. It takes an enormous amount to kill a man. Usually he has to be shot three or four times before he dies.

As well as being told that the Argentinians were ill-equipped, we had also been led to believe that they were starving. This was another myth. In the first Argentinian trench I came across, cans and cans of food had been poured into the bottom, just to keep the occupiers' feet out of the water. And the other thing these Argentinians didn't do, as we'd been informed they did, was run away.

There were numerous Argentinians in the machine gun post. They were wearing American-style uniforms: big green parkas with webbing over the top. I remember searching my first prisoner frantically for a Colt 45 pistol, because I desperately wanted one as a souvenir to take back to England.

The horrible thing about having your first prisoner is that it's rather like being a man with a snake. Snakes are quite probably more terrified of humans than humans can ever believe they are. The same applies to prisoners. I was terrified that the prisoner might suddenly do something fast and clever and kill me, or that he would do something that meant I would have to kill him. There's an appalling tension, a feeling that at any minute the horror could all suddenly erupt again.

There were panics when we asked the Argentinians to put their hands up and they went on clutching their rifles in the pandemonium. We'd scream, 'Drop your fucking rifle!' But they didn't understand us.

Just as the assault appeared to have come to a grinding halt, and we were dealing with the wounded and the prisoners, we suddenly came under sniper fire from the crags above us. There was a danger we'd all get picked off there and then, so we moved away. I grabbed two of my Guardsmen, and we set off to go round the Stanley end of Tumbledown. We stepped round a craggy rock – and then the whole bloody world seemed to explode.

Gunfire, grenades, explosions, booby traps maybe, everything erupted on the other side of this rock, so we quickly jumped back again. Guardsman Pengelly, who was with me, started climbing up the rocks to try to reach the top and get at one of the sniper positions. As he was climbing, he was hit and fell back down again, wounded but not killed. I felt I had to keep the momentum going. I grabbed two or three people, including Corporal Rennie and Sergeant McDermot, and went round the other end of the rock, and we started skirmishing down – one guy moving on while the other covered him. Again, I remember thinking that this was just like the movies.

By now it was becoming daylight and, among the grass and rocks, I saw an Argentinian lying face down, with his arms back. I thought to myself, is he dead or alive? But instead of just kicking or prodding him, I stuck my bayonet into the back of his arm, dug it right in because I had run out of ammunition. He spun wildly on the ground, and my bayonet snapped. And as he spun, he was trying to get a Colt 45 out of an army holster on his waist. So I had to stab him to death. I stabbed him and I stabbed him, again and again, in the mouth, in the face, in the guts, with a snapped bayonet.

It was absolutely horrific. Stabbing a man to death is not a clean way to kill somebody, and what made it doubly horrific was that at one point he started screaming 'Please…' in English to me. But had I left him he could have ended up shooting me in the back.

When I did finally leave him, I took his FN [Fabrique Nationale] rifle, moved on, shot a sniper, picked up his FN and moved on again. I was moving on with other men when suddenly Guardsman McEntaggart turned to me and said, 'Excuse me, Sir, I think I've been shot.' I thought, don't be stupid, if you've been shot you'd know all about it. He had in fact been grazed by a bullet in the upper arm.

I still desperately wanted to push on at this stage and get

to an Argentinian administration and supply area, at the very end of Tumbledown. Once we had taken that, we would have taken the whole mountain. It was also in the direction of Stanley – the goal we were all heading for.

Men from the different platoons behind me were dealing with the wounded and prisoners, but I was aware, as I moved along, of other people coming up behind me, taking various routes. Ian Bryden, our company second-in-command, was dashing along the top of the mountain doing all sorts of heroics. Sergeant Jackson handed his rifle and webbing to a Guardsman and went off on his own, with two grenades, to take some Argentinians out. It was all incredible stuff.

I remember seeing the lights of Stanley below us and thinking how strange that it hadn't been blacked out. This was supposed to be a war. I turned to Guardsman McEntaggart as we went along and, for some inexplicable reason, suddenly cried out, 'Isn't this fun?'

Seconds later, it happened. I felt a blast in the back of my head that seemed more as if I'd been hit by a train than by a bullet. It was a high-velocity bullet, travelling at a speed of around 3,800 feet per second, but the air turbulence and shock wave travelling with it was what caused so much damage. I found this out later. At the time, all I knew was that my knees had gone and that I had collapsed, totally paralysed, on to the ground.

The pain in my head was quite indescribable. The wound was so hot and burning that I wanted to rub it into the mud and snow. But I couldn't move. Only after a little while did any feeling return to my right side. And I remember thinking, oh my God, everybody's going to think I'm dead because I'm not moving, and they're not going to come and help me.

I think Sergeant McDermot was the first to arrive.

He took my beret off – headgear the British wore to distinguish themselves from the Argentinians in their steel helmets – and my head just kept gushing blood. I think Mark Matthewson arrived soon after, and suggested packing snow into the wound, which seemed a pretty good idea. Then I was struck by the awful thought that I had led all my men into a trap, and that most of them would now be dead owing to my stupid foolishness in being too gung-ho.

Then I started worrying about my family back home, and Mitty, my girlfriend at the time. And I started getting very, very panicky about dying. By this stage, I'd lost about five pints of blood, the temperature was sub-zero, the wind-chill factor brought it even lower, and there was a fierce blizzard. I was wondering, where are the sleeping bags the platoon were meant to be carrying for casualties, and where the hell was the helicopter that was meant to come and pick me up?

I was getting really irate, and remember looking at Sergeant McDermot and saying, 'Get on your bloody radio and find out where that helicopter is. I'm dying.' He looked at me, sort of lost, and said, 'My radio isn't working, Sir.'

It was all quite ghastly and incredible, but I knew at that point that there was no point in yelling at him. Then, with the fear and frustration, I suddenly began to cry.

Sergeant McDermot came up to me and said, 'Go on, Sir, you have a good cry.'

And I thought, you bastard, I'm *not* going to cry. I had been all for crying up to the minute he said that and then I just thought stuff it, I won't.

Lieutenant Lawrence was eventually airlifted to safety; amazingly he survived his near-mortal head wound and made a full recovery. His modesty in recounting these events all but concealed the true nature of his actions that night. For his outstanding performance in destroying the Argentinian machine gun position, and for the leadership he showed to his men, Lieutenant Lawrence was awarded the Military Cross.

⎯⎯⎯⋙⋗⋘⎯⎯⎯

6
KUWAIT, 1991

Private Mark Morrice (Royal Scots)

The Gulf War of 1990–1 (or the First Gulf War) was a conflict that took the world largely by surprise – an unprovoked invasion of an oil-rich state by its more powerful neighbour. When Iraq attacked neighbouring Kuwait in 1990, President Saddam Hussein found he had seriously miscalculated the world's response. A powerful coalition was formed, charged with liberating Kuwait, and defeating the Iraqi army. The 1st Battalion of the Royal Scots formed part of this army, and were attached to the 1st British Armoured Division. When the push came, the Iraqi defences crumbled, in the face of overwhelming Allied airpower and ground forces who outclassed them in training, morale and technology. Soon the Royal Scots found themselves 'mopping up', clearing bypassed Iraqi strongpoints of troops, rounding up prisoners, and driving the remainder of Saddam Hussein's army from Kuwaiti territory. Private Morrice's account captures the confusion and uncertainty caused by the speed of the Allied victory.

I remember one occasion we were all lined up in formation. We were always unloading and loading our vehicle, anything that couldnae fit anywhere went in the back of ours, you could guarantee it. We had to completely unload the vehicle and go and collect this mail. This was about five o'clock. I used to have this wee tape recorder that I bought from one of the garages and I had the Royal Scots' Pipes and Drums and a few other [tapes], and wherever we would go, I had this little Scotland flag where the windshield should have been, and we'd always turn up the music full blast to 'Flower of Scotland' as we drove past everyone, just so they'd know we'd be the Jocks.

Off we went, we were told [to] go about sixty Ks that way, it was just like a point. We were told there might be a Chinook coming in dropping off mail and that we'd meet up with other people, but we were the only ones there and there was no sign of nothing!

On the way back I noticed, it must have just caught my eye, it was like a figure, and I was telling Jimmy this, 'I'm sure I've seen someone over there', because there was a lot of trenches and it must have been an Iraqi position. There were the two of us, and I'm a bit worried about this. He was saying, 'Och, there's nothing there!' I said, 'I'm telling you I'm sure there's someone there.' So he slowed down where I said to him; it was on the right-hand side. I jumped out, and I thought, 'My rifle, I'm no going without my rifle.' So I picked up my rifle. It was like trenches in a square, and as I was walking towards it I just seen this figure pop up and he had a pistol! Oh, I was in bits!

I cocked my weapon, and it wouldnae cock properly. I just [thought]; 'What'll I do now?' I just took no notice of the guy at this time. I ran round the back of the truck. Jimmy was in the front. He used to put his rifle into a bag to keep all the sand out and it was always behind him while he was driving and of course he was still sitting there. I'm at the back of this wagon banging my rifle to cock it and [the Iraqi] must have thought, 'Oh this is the best Britain's got to offer!'

Anyway eventually it did cock, so I went around, well peeked my head round. I'd seen something in his hands and actually he was showing me that it was pointing towards the ground and he put up his hands, but I didn't stay in one place, trying to move about all the time, making sure I was covering him. I said, 'Come on, Jimmy, get your rifle out. Come on. What do I do?' He got up to walk towards me and another one popped up and 'Oh God', I thought, 'I'd better get myself under control', and so I just aimed my rifle at them, told them to come a wee bit closer to me. Those two came close. By that time Jimmy had his rifle and he was covering them, and I actually took a step over towards the trench, which I was very careful about because I had ideas of me going towards this trench to see if there was anyone else in it and, as I was looking over, something happening to me. I tried it as sneaky as possible, and there was someone in there still. I don't know if he was too frightened to come out or not, but he came out, so we told them to take off their jackets, gave them the search.

We put them in the back and I went in the back with them. On the way there, we passed a POW camp. They were in the back and I thought, 'Right, we'll take them to the POW camp.' So off we went. We got lost for a while so we had to backtrack and eventually we got there and while in the back I had my wee cassette with me. While I was covering them, my cassette [was] hanging on the mirror. I took it off and it was playing 'Flower of Scotland' to them as they were getting searched, [to] which Jimmy said, 'Put that off you nutter!' I think I just put it on to relax me.

So we took them to the POW camp and as I was in the back playing my tapes, they were getting quite into it, these Iraqis, and of course being a cheap cassette, I mangled up my tape. I was furious; 'My Pipes!' One of them [motioned] to me and I didnae ken what he's wanting, and one of them started pointing to one of the Iraquis beside him. He was about 16, this one and he sort of pointed, and what I thought he was telling me was he's got a weapon there or something. I was banging on (the wagon), 'Jimmy, stop, stop! I think one of these has got a weapon!'

Obviously I did search them before, but I thought I might have forgot something. What it was, I'm sure, was a bit of hash or something; it was a cube, and what I think he was trying to do was maybe trying to give us it as a sort of present or something. That's when my tape got mangled up. One of them came quite close to me picked it up, and wound up my tape for me. Fixed it all and put it back in and sort of pointed to see if it was OK if he played it. So he pressed the play button and I was quite surprised that they liked the Pipes. Anyway, we dropped them off at this POW camp. There was some Captain and we says, 'Next time we catch anyone we'll come back; make sure you've got the kettle on!' He says, 'Right, I will do.'

That afternoon there was another mail collection. On the way back there were about three trucks [from] English regiments and they wanted to stop to pick up souvenirs from these trenches. Myself and Jimmy, after our experience that morning, said, 'If you go, take your weapon and make sure it can cock!' They said, 'No, no, this place has been cleared.' So out they went and one of them went into this trench and he came running back out. Of course I had my weapon with me because from then on it was [with me] everywhere. He says, 'I'm sure there's someone in there', so here we go again!

I went down there and it was like an armoury. There were hundreds of Kalashnikovs on the floor and five Iraqis in that place. Some of them didn't have any trousers on. One of them must have been 60 at least. I think they'd been missed or run away or something and they'd just took shelter. These English guys would not have them: 'They're not going in the back of my truck!' So we took them in ours again. Since that morning incident, we met up with the chefs and they started giving us their oatmeal biscuits. We had a big cornflakes box full of oatmeal biscuits and wee sucky sweeties. So we started giving them it and they were loving it. The way they were putting it down was like they hadn't been fed. We stopped off at this POW camp. 'Yous a-bloody-gain!'

⫸◆⫷

7

BASRA, IRAQ, 2003

Warrant Officer Tam Henderson (Black Watch)

In 2002, President George W. Bush claimed that Iraq possessed 'Weapons of Mass Destruction' which posed a serious risk to regional stability. It was decided to neutralise this perceived threat by invading Iraq, and plans were prepared. Despite attempts by the United States to create a multi-national force similar to the coalition force which participated in the First Gulf War, most of the international community refused to sanction military intervention. Britain was an exception, and Prime Minister Blair readily agreed to provide British troops. In March 2003 the Black Watch Battle Group took part in the Allied invasion of Iraq, and were charged with the seizure of Az Zubayr, on the outskirts of Basra. On 22 March C Company were involved in a bitterly contested engagement in the grounds of an Iraqi army barracks, a battle where both Company Commander Major James Ord and Company Sergeant Major WO Tam Henderson distinguished themselves. The Scots relied on the Warrior Infantry Fighting Vehicle, which served both as an armoured troop carrier and as a weapons platform, armed with a 30mm Rarden cannon and a 7.63mm chain gun. In the Warrior used by Ord and Henderson (which they named Christine), neither the vehicle nor its weaponry were wholly reliable, the chain gun in particular failing several times during the day. Then, two days later, they were called into action again. Riding with them were the rest of the vehicle's crew – Captain Tim Petransky, Corporal Mark Calder and Lance-Corporal Lee Kirby.

The Company radio crackled. 'Hello Zero. This is 24 Alpha. Contact. Ambush. Wait. Out.' Ambush! It was like an electric shock. 'Mount up!' I shouted to the crew, and we jumped into the Warrior. Tim Petransky sat in the back, peering at maps and maintaining radio contact with 24 Alpha. It was a Scimitar [a light reconnaissance vehicle], part of a small convoy, with another Scimitar and a 432 personnel carrier, sent to reinforce beleaguered men from 'D' Company at Bridge 4, a position at the Shat-el-Arab river. But the ambush was at the mosque. What on earth were they doing there? We had been told to stay well clear of it after John Rose's showdown on 22nd, as it was taboo to storm a Muslim place of worship, even when the enemy used it as sanctuary to shoot at us. Our convoy must have taken a wrong turning, and ran into some raging hornets.

24 Alpha came on the radio again. 'Contact. We have bugged out. One man left behind.' James came back and I quickly briefed him. 'Let's go now,' he said. One of Charlie Company's men is missing. I visualised him surrounded by a howling mob. There had been no more news on the kidnapped Royal Engineers. We had to go immediately to bring our boy back. We raced south towards Az Zubayr. Tim was hassling 24 Alpha on the radio. 'Send report of one man down,' he kept saying. 'Wait. Out,' was the repeated reply. Then we got a report from the other Scimitar. 'Hello, Zero, this is 24. Contact with RPG and small arms, One man left behind and we have lost contact with the 432.'

They gave us the zap [personal identification] number of

the missing man, and we worked out that he was Lance-Corporal Barry Stephen. Then news came that the 432 had been located again. They had lost Barry after he had bravely climbed onto their roof to fire at the enemy. At first, the others in the 432 didn't realise it, but Barry must have been swept off the vehicle by an RPG that had been targeted just above them. We agreed to rendezvous at VCP2, a checkpoint manned by the Royal Engineers and military police, at a junction where several roads merged into a single drag into town.

One of the Scimitars had taken a turret strike and was out of action. Corporal Leathley commanded the other. I called him over. 'Do you know where Barry is?' 'I think so,' he answered. 'We came under fire from a shack in front of the mosque.' 'OK. Get back in your vehicle and let's go there.' He paused, still in battle shock, and I needed to urge him on and back into action: 'Get in your fucking vehicle and let's go!' 'Yes Sir,' he replied, without further hesitation.

We were driving and firing: one vehicle lid down covering fire as another advanced, and then we swapped roles. It was a pitch-dark night, with no ambient light except the flicker of oil wells burning in the distance. We could just make out the outline of the mosque. In daylight, it was an imposing white building with a blue minaret. There was no movement as we approached: no cars, no dogs, nothing. James stood up in the turret, using his night-sight to look for Barry.

Then we heard machine gun fire to our rear right. I traversed the turret and raked the ground with a burst from the chain gun before focusing on the muzzle flashes with my Raven sight and firing again. The flashes vanished. 'Target stop,' said James. He had summoned help on the battalion network, and we were joined by two Warriors, including Zero Alpha, our CO's vehicle, and a couple of Challenger 2 tanks. We spotted a shape on the ground, and James guided a Warrior towards it. Two men ran to pick it up. A pair of arms and legs flopped down. 'He's dead, isn't he, Sir?' 'I very much think so,' replied James.

Barry Stephen was in the mortar platoon. A good guy. He had been disappointed when an injury had stopped him from finishing his Junior Brecon training and promoting to corporal. He wasn't one of the bevvy monsters and I never had any disciplinary issues with him. He was always keen to get home, when he could, to his wife and kids. I had lost another man from Charlie Company. I felt like vomiting.

James radioed the CO. 'You should head back now Sir,' he said. 'We'll provide protective cover.' Lee reversed our Warrior as the other vehicles began to withdraw. While traversing the turret to stay facing the mosque, I spotted a two-man RPG team. One knelt down with the launcher on his shoulder and the other stood beside him to load the rounds. The shooter was facing towards Zero Alpha. I put the armed selector switch on, pressed down on the foot-firing switch, and destroyed him. The other guy ran away, and I traversed the turret slightly to catch him.

'Target destroyed. Target stop,' said James. I cursed quietly. I wanted to kill the other RPG guy. However, I pushed the armed selector switch back to off, and the green light on the chain-gun control panel lit up. Zero Alpha had gone and we were the only ones left. 'Sir, they're all over the place. We've got to get the fuck out of here.' 'Calm down,' I urged him, traversing the turret away from the mosque. 'Move out but keep a steady pace. Don't overtake anyone, and make sure we stay at the back.'

We stopped at VCP2 to check that everyone was OK, and then pressed on to the 'Crown Jewels'. James stood up in the turret and surveyed the road, using the weapon sight detached from his SA80 rifle. We were the last back, and a dark confusion of vehicles blocked our path to our hastily abandoned gear.

James jumped out to get an update on Barry Stephen. He gave me his weapon sight, and I stood on the gunner's seat with my torso in full view above the turret. I loosened my chinstrap to shout down to the men below. Could we go around the inner perimeter? Someone said that we could, but we would have to go through a berm – a defensive ditch. 'Can anyone guide us through?' Sergeant Albert Thomson – 'Tommo' – stepped forward. 'Sure,' he said, 'I've got a cylume' [night vision helmet]. 'Sergeant Thomson is the ground commander,' I told Lee on the intercom.

Slowly we moved forward, following the blue light from Tommo's cylume as he walked backwards a few steps ahead of us. The light wobbled and vanished as he stepped into the berm. 'What the fuck's he doing?' I asked Lee, who had halted the Warrior. 'Must have fallen over.' Then we saw the light again, and inched forward. With my left hand, I removed my goggles, dropping them into the exterior plastic bin, while with my right hand I gripped the rim of the turret.

Suddenly, with unexpected force, we dipped into the ditch. I felt the nose-cone hit the earth, and was knocked forwards and backwards against the edge of the turret. The force jolted my loosened helmet and detached my earpiece. I heard a noise and saw that Lee had switched on the Warrior's headlights. Jesus! Had we crushed Tommo? My helmet came off as I pitched myself out of the turret and jumped down to the ground. *Christine* dipped into the sand at a 45° angle and Tommo lay face down on the opposite slope. Blood seeped from the back of his left thigh.

'Medic!' I heard shouts. Someone was kneeling over Tommo. I was stunned. What had happened? It must have been the chain gun. Leee confirmed that he had heard the gun fire and seen the tracer. But how? I couldn't have fired it standing up in the turret. And I'd switched it off earlier. Knowing too well the ferocity of the gun, I feared the worst for Tommo. Then James knelt beside me. 'What happened?' he asked. 'The gun must have fired. The vehicle must be isolated and inspected. No one can use it,' I said robotically. James climbed inside the turret to check that the gun was switched off.

Tommo was stretchered away. The commanding officer, Lieutenant-Colonel Mike Riddell-Webster appeared. 'What have you done?' he asked. I said nothing. It wasn't even in my mind to protest my innocence. What do you mean, what have *I* done? I thought. With Mark Calder acting as ground commander, Lee drove the Warrior out of the berm and back to our original position. I followed them on foot and sat on an exposed sand dune, looking down on *Christine*. She had just killed one of my men. I didn't expect Tommo to survive the chain gun's terrible assault. Two men lost in one day. It was unthinkable.

Sergeant Thomson survived, but only after the amputation of his left leg. In an effort to cover up technical inadequacies, WO Henderson was ordered to take responsibility for the 'negligent discharge' of the chain gun. When he refused he was summarily transferred from the regiment which he had served with distinction for two decades. However, Henderson was determined to fight back, and in 2004 his case was heard at a military appeal court. He was fully exonerated, and the blame was placed firmly where it belonged – with the faulty equipment and its manufacturers. The army treatment of Sergeant Thomson was equally shoddy. He was denied the compensation he was due, a decision which was finally overturned in the wake of WO Henderson's victory in court.

NOTES

The numbers on the left correspond to the account numbers in the relevant chapters.

Chapter 2

1   Oudenarde, 1708: John Blackader, *Diary and Letter of John Blackader Esq., Formerly Lt. Col. Of the XXVI Cameronian Regiment of Foot, and afterwards Deputy Governor of Stirling Castle* (Edinburgh, 1806).
2   Sheriffmuir, 1715: ibid.
3   Culloden, 1746: James, Chevalier de Johnstone, *Memoirs of the Rebellion in 1745 and 1746* (London, 1822).
4   Captured by Indians, 1758: Robert Kirk, *The Memoirs and Adventures of Robert Kirk, Late of the Royal Highland Regiment* (London, 1775). Repr. as Peter Way, *Through so Many Dangers* (New York: Purple Mountain Press, 2004).
5   The Landing at Louisbourg, 1758: *The Memoirs of Volunteer Sergeant James Thompson, of the 78th – Fraser's Highlanders* (National Museum of Scotland).
6   Skirmish at Bushy Run, 1763: Kirk, *Memoirs and Adventures*, op. cit.
7   New York, 1776: Captain James Murray, *Letters from America, 1773 to 1780* (London, 1842).
8   Battle of Savannah, 1778: Lieutenant-Colonel Archibald Campbell, *Journal of an Expedition against the Rebels of Georgia* (National Museum of Scotland).

Chapter 3

1   Battle of Alexandria, 1801: Lieutenant George Sutherland, *A Journal of the Expedition to Egypt in 1801* (Edinburgh, 1818).
2   Buenos Aires, 1806: Balfour Kennach, *The Campaigns of Corporal Balfour Kennach, 71st Regiment, 1806–14* (Edinburgh, 1832).

3   Battle of Vimeiro, 1808: *Diary of William Gavin, Ensign and Quartermaster, 71st Highlanders, 1806–16* (National Museum of Scotland).

4   Retreat to Corunna, 1809: *Diary of John Maclerlan, Private of the 91st* (National Museum of Scotland).

5   Battle of Talavera, 1809: Sergeant Daniel Nicol, *With Napoleon at Waterloo and other Unpublished Documents of the Waterloo and Peninsula Campaign* (London: Francis Griffiths, 1911).

6   Storming of Badajoz, 1812: Robert Eadie, *Recollections of Robert Eadie, Private of the 79th* (Kincardine, 1829).

7   The Field Hospital, 1812: Private Joseph Donaldson, *Recollections of the Eventful Life of a Soldier* (London, 1825).

8   Battle of Salamanca, 1812: Private James Anton, *Retrospect of a Military Life* (London, 1841).

9   Battle of Waterloo, 1815: Private Thomas Howell, in Anon., *The Personal Narrative of a Private Soldier* (Glasgow, 1821). Repr. as *A Soldier of the Seventy-First* (London: Purnell, 1975).

Chapter 4

1   Garrison Duty, Goa, 1824: John Williamson, *The Diary of a Commuted Pensioner of the 78th Rgt.* (Montreal, 1838).

2   Battle of the Alma, Crimea, 1854: Alexander Robb, *Reminiscences of a Veteran* (Edinburgh, 1888).

3   Battle of Balaclava, 1854: *Diary of Donald Cameron, 79th (Cameron) Highlanders and 93rd (Sutherland) Highlanders, 1847–56* (National Museum of Scotland).

4   Lucknow, the Indian Mutiny, 1857: *Reminiscences of Sergeant Forbes Mitchell, 93rd Highlanders* (National Museum of Scotland).

5   The Egyptian Campaign, 1882: *Diary of Lieut. H.H.L. Malcolm, 79th Q.O. Cameron Highrs., during the Egyptian War, 1882* (National Museum of Scotland).

6   Dargai, 1897: *Diary of the Late Lieutenant George Douglas Mackenzie DSO* (Gordon Highlanders Museum).

7   The Boer War, 1900: Thomas F. Dewar, *With the Scottish Yeomanry* (Edinburgh: T. Bunck, 1903).

8   The Boer War, 1900: *Letter from Simon, Lord Lovat to Sir Francis Linley, 21st May 1900* (National Museum of Scotland).

Chapter 5

1 Joining Kitchener's Army, 1914: *Memoirs of Sergeant Charles Forman* (Black Watch Regimental Archives).

2 The Battle of Ypres, 1914: *Diary of Capt. A.D.C. Krook* (Black Watch Regimental Archives).

3 The Battle of Loos, 1915: *Memoirs of Sergeant Charles Forman*, loc. cit.

4 The Battle of Loos, 1915: *Diary of Lt. Col. J. Stewart* (Black Watch Regimental Archives).

5 Captured, Ypres, 1915: *Diary of Lance-Corporal William Anderson* (Black Watch Regimental Archives).

6 Letters Home, 1915: *Letters of Sergeant Jack Barbour* (Black Watch Regimental Archives).

7 Loos, 1915: *Letters of Alexander Douglas Gillespie, 4th Argylls, 1915* (National Museum of Scotland).

8 Field Dressing Station, Ypres, 1915: Revd A.M. Maclean, *With the Gordons at Ypres* (Aberdeen, 1917).

9 Gallipoli, 1915: P.M. Campbell, *Letters from Gallipoli* (Edinburgh: self-published by T&A Constable, 1916).

10 The Drill Sergeant, 1916: Thomas M. Lyon, *In Kilt and Khaki* (Kilmarnock: The Standard Press, 1916).

11 Istabulat, Mesopotamia, 1917: *Diary of Lt. Col. J. Stewart*, loc. cit.

12 Passchendaele, 1917: *Memoirs of Private John Jackson MM, Queen's Own Cameron Highlanders* (National Museum of Scotland). Repr. as *John Jackson, Private 12768: Memoirs of a Tommy* (London: The History Press, 2004). Reprinted with permission from The History Press.

13 The Advance, Meteren, 1918: Lieutenant Douglas Wilson, *Reminiscences of a Queen's Own Cameron Highlander* (Stirling: E. Mackays, 1926).

Chapter 6

1 St Valery, 1940: Private Gregor Macdonald (courtesy of 51st Highland Division Online Museum).

2 El Alamein, 1943: Captain George Green, in Alastair Borthwick, *Battalion* (London: Baton Wicks, 1994). Reprinted with permission from Baton Wicks Publications.

3 Western Desert, 1943: *One Man's War: Memoirs of Sergeant Robert Penman, 7th Black Watch* (Black Watch Regimental Archives).

4   Tunisia, 1943: in D.G. Antonio, *Driver Advance: A Short History of the 2nd Lothian and Border Horse, 1939–46* (unpublished, National Museum of Scotland).

5   Gothic Line, Italy, 1944: George Martin, *Cassino to the River Po* (Chesterfield: self-published by Intaprint, 1995). Reprinted with permission of the author.

6   Tank Life, Normandy, 1944: in *Memoirs of Wm. Stel Brownlie, 2/Lt, 2nd Fife and Forfar Yeomanry* (unpublished, National Museum of Scotland).

7   Operation Goodwood, Normandy, *Diary of Gunner Thorpe, Fife and Forfar Yeomanry* (unpublished, National Museum of Scotland).

8   Burma, 1944: Bernard Fergusson, *The Trumpet in the Hall* (London: Collins, 1970). Reprinted with permission from HarperCollins Publishers.

9   The attack on Hubermont, Ardennes, 1945: *Memoirs of Private Tom Renouf* (courtesy of 51st Highland Division Online Museum).

Chapter 7

1   The Hook, Korea, 1953: Derek Halley, *Iron Claw: A Conscript's Tale* (Finavon: self-published by Finavon Print and Design, 1998). Reprinted with permission of the author.

2   Brunei, 1962: Lieutenant-Colonel McHardy, published in *The Queen's Own Highlander Magazine* (Inverness, 1996).

3   The Crater, Aden, 1967: Lieutenant-Colonel Colin Mitchell, *Having Been a Soldier* (London: Hamish Hamilton, 1969). Reprinted with permission from the Penguin Group.

4   Warrenpoint, Co. Down, Northern Ireland, 1979: Nicholas Ridley, *Warrenpoint* (unpublished, courtesy of Brigadier-General N. Ridley).

5   Tumbledown Hill, Falklands, 1982: John Lawrence and Robert Lawrence, *When the Fighting Is Over* (London: Bloomsbury, 1988). Reprinted with permission from Bloomsbury Publishing Ltd.

6   Kuwait, 1991: Private Mark Morrice, Royal Scots, in Laurie Milner, *Royal Scots in the Gulf* (Barnsley: Pen & Sword, 1994). Reprinted with permission from Pen & Sword Books Ltd.

7   Basra, Iraq, 2003: Captain Tam Henderson, *Warrior: A True Story of Bravery and Betrayal in the Iraq War* (Edinburgh: Mainstream, 2008). Reprinted with permission from Mainstream Publishing Ltd.

FURTHER READING

Chapter 1

Leask, Anthony, *The Sword of Scotland: Jocks at War* (Barnsley: Pen & Sword, 2006).

Mileham, Patrick, *The Scottish Regiments, 1633–1996* (Staplehurst: Spellmount, 1996).

Wood, Stephen, *The Scottish Soldier* (Manchester: Archive Publications, 1987).

Chapter 2

Devine, T.M., *Scotland's Empire, 1600–1815* (London: Penguin, 2003).

Duffy, Christopher, *The Military Experience in the Age of Reason* (New York: Barnes & Noble, 1987).

Duffy, Christopher, *The '45* (London: Cassell, 2003).

Falkner, James, *Great and Glorious Days: Marlborough's Battles, 1704–09* (Staplehurst: Spellmount, 2002).

Fowler, William A., *Empires at War: The French and Indian War and the Struggle for North America, 1754–63* (New York: Walker, 2005).

MacKillop, Andrew, *More Fruitful than the Soil: Army, Empire and the Scottish Highlands, 1715–1815* (East Linton: Tuckwell, 2001).

Reid, Stuart, *The Last Scots Army, 1661–1714* (Leigh-on-Sea: Partizan Press, 2003).

Roberts, John L., *The Jacobite Wars* (Edinburgh: Polygon, 2002).

Szechi, Daniel, *1715: The Great Jacobite Rebellion* (New Haven, CT: Yale University Press, 2006).

Chapter 3

Glover, Michael, *The Peninsular War, 1807–1814: A Concise History* (London: David & Charles, 1974).

Grant, C.S., *The Road to Corunna, 1808–09* (Leigh-on-Sea: Partizan Press, 2008).

Grant, C.S., *Wellington's First Campaign, 1808* (Leigh-on-Sea: Partizan Press, 2008).

Oman, Sir Charles, *A History of the Peninsular War*, 7 vols (London: 1908; repr. Greenhill Books, 2004).

Chapter 4

David, Saul, *The Indian Mutiny, 1857* (London: Penguin, 2002).

David, Saul, *Victoria's Wars: The Rise of Empire* (London: Penguin, 2007).

Pakenham, Thomas, *The Boer War* (London: Weidenfeld & Nicolson, 1979).

Ponting, Clive, *The Crimean War: The Truth behind the Myth* (London: Pimlico, 2005).

Spiers, Edward, *The Scottish Soldier and Empire, 1854–1902* (Edinburgh: Edinburgh University Press, 2006).

Chapter 5

Corrigan, Gordon, *Mud, Blood and Poppycock* (London: Cassell, 2003).

Royle, Trevor, *The Flowers of the Forest: Scotland and the Great War* (Edinburgh: Birlinn, 2007).

Weir, Alec, *Come on Highlanders! Glasgow Territorials in the Great War* (London: Sutton, 2005).

Wilson, Trevor, *The Myriad Faces of War: Britain and the Great War, 1914–18* (Oxford: Polity Press, 1986).

Winter, J.M., *The Great War and the British People* (New York: Palgrave Macmillan, 2003).

Young, Derek, *Scottish Voices from the Great War* (Stroud: Tempus, 2006).

Chapter 6

Borthwick, Alastair, *Batallion* (London: Baton Wicks, 1994).

Dargie, Richard, *Lest We Forget: Scotland in the Second World War, 1939–45* (London: Hodder Wayland, 1997).

David, Saul, *Churchill's Sacrifice of the Highland Division, France, 1940* (London: Brasseys, 2004).

Delaforce, Patrick, *Monty's Highlanders: The 51st Highland Division in the Second World War* (Barnsley: Pen & Sword, 2007).

Doherty, Richard, *None Bolder: The History of the 51st Highland Division in the Second World War* (Staplehurst: Spellmount, 2006).

Wollcombe, Robert, *Lion Rampant* (London: Chatto & Windus, 1955).

Chapter 7

Dewar, Michael, *Brush Fire Wars: Minor Campaigns of the British Army since 1945* (London: Robert Hale, 1985).

Dewar, Michael, *The British Army in Northern Ireland* (London: Arms & Armour Press, 1985).

Henderson, Tam, *Warrior: A True Story of Bravery and Betrayal in the Iraq War* (Edinburgh: Mainstream, 2006).

Royle, Trevor, *The Best Years of their Lives: The National Service Experience, 1945–63* (London: Michael Joseph, 1886).

INDEX

Note: Regimental and other numbers are filed alphabetically (in decades) as main headings, but numerically as subheadings.